Civilisation Hijacked

and

Rescuing Jesus from Christianity and the human spirit From Bondage

A book in two parts by
Al Morris

iUniverse, Inc.
New York   Bloomington

Civilisation Hijacked
Rescuing Jesus from Christianity and the human spirit From Bondage

iUniverse books may be ordered through booksellers or by contacting:

iUniverse
1663 Liberty Drive
Bloomington, IN 47403
www.iuniverse.com
1-800-Authors (1-800-288-4677)

ISBN: 978-1-4401-8242-6 (pbk)
ISBN: 978-1-4401-8241-9 (ebook)

Printed in the United States of America

iUniverse rev. date: 3/2/10

TABLE OF CONTENTS

PART TWO

TABLE OF CONTENTS

ACKNOWLEDGEMENTS

I wish to thank my brother Ron for his grammatical corrections, encouragement and help in tireless philosophical discussions.
John England: For proof reading.
Lionel Robson. MA, MEA, GDBM and BT. For editing.

Dedicated to my wife Jean, but for whose understanding and patience this book would never have been written.

Also to Doctors Without Borders, who risk life and limb to treat thousands of hapless victims of wars, famine and natural disasters.

FOREWARD

Harold Pinter, the Nobel prize winner for literature in 2005, ended his acceptance speech, which was a scathing criticism of American and British foreign policy, with the words: "It is the duty of the writer to present an image for scrutiny, and the duty of (the reader) to determine the real truth of our lives and our societies. If such a determination is not embodied in our political vision, we have no hope of restoring the dignity of man; that which we have come so very close to losing." Pinter's words well describe the reason for producing this book. I feel compelled to present an image for the reader's scrutiny of particular organizations as enemies of humanity that have hijacked the whole of the "civilised" world without its citizens even being conscious of it.

INTRODUCTION

I invite you to join me in a journey: it may be a journey of discovery to a place that you will recognize: it may also be a journey leading to the confirmation of ideas that have occurred to you but have not been previously articulated. We don't have to travel far, as our area of discovery is within our brain. Our mind!

With me, the journey started one day way back in 1967 when I read a headlined editorial in a Sydney (Australia) newspaper. It bitterly condemned the growing numbers of young trouble makers in our society, suggesting that we, quote: "kick out these foul little hoodlums". This prompted me to write to the editor and ask: "Where does he suggest that we kick them out to"? I suggested that these young people were the product of our making. We made them, we have them, and if we want something better we had better make our future ones better. So there I was, hopping mad wanting to convince society that we should embark on an educative program from infancy to produce a better crop of young people. I was "gob smacked" by the degree of utter hopelessness and apathy found amongst the many people that I approached on the subject.

In my efforts to find a solution to that problem, I have written what I believe to be the causes of the problems that confront society as a whole, and also suggest practical solutions to these problems. IF you think my thoughts have merit, and are practicable, I ask you to join me on the path of what is for me, an exciting voyage of discovery.

CHAPTER 1

Theology: The Mother of Politics

It is impossible for any of us to have 20:20 vision in a political sense. The vision or worldview held by the majority of the world's population has been distorted and manipulated to suit the aims and ambitions of a small number of powerful groups. We all fit into the sphere of influence of one or the other of these groups. And it's us, in our numbers that lends them power. For instance, is it natural for a person to kill someone because they do not believe in your concept of God, or their social and cultural habits are different to yours? Who are the ones that incite and encourage such behaviour, how is it managed and what is the purpose behind the influence and persuasion that recruits millions of people to kill millions of others?

For clarity and complete understanding of how power and politics are used internationally, socially, politically, theologically and commercially, the following definitions of the words politics and power[1] are important. Politics is the process by which groups of people make decisions. It is the allocation of values by an authority. Although the term is generally applied to behaviour within governments, politics is observed in all human group interactions, including corporate, academic and religious institutions. In its most basic form, politics consists of *social relations involving authority or power.* In practice,

[1] I.C. MacMillan (1978) Strategy Formulation: political concepts, St Paul, MN, West Publishing

1

the term refers to the regulation and government of a nation-state or other political unit and to the methods and tactics used to formulate and apply government policy. In a broader sense, any situation involving power or any **strategy** to enhance one's power or status within a group may be described as politics, as in the expression **office politics**. This form of politics is mostly associated with a struggle for ascendancy among groups having different priorities and power relations.

Power may be held by a person or by a group in a society. There are many ways to hold such power. Traditionally, political power equated to sovereign power but it is not limited to heads of states. However, the extent to which a person or group holds such power is related to the amount of social influence they can wield formally, or informally. This influence is not contained within a single state, as it can also be exerted internationally. Political scientists have frequently defined power as the ability to influence the behaviour of others, with or without resistance. Power its acquisition and application, is an objective study within the arena of political science. For easier understanding, MacMillan separates the concepts of power and influence. He defines power as: "**the capacity to alter actual situations**" whereas Influence is: "**the capacity to control and change the perceptions of other's.**" Power and influence however, although theoretically separated, are both universally exercised by a hierarchy established within any group, be it a close or extended family, a tribe or a group of related tribes or ethnic groups. It is the recognised and accepted leaders of a group who determine the actions, moral and social codes which then become the norm for their particular group of people.

The earliest form of control recorded by one of these groups is in the sphere of religious belief or theology. It is in this context that I explore today's effects of the social and political theological manipulation by past religious leaders. Very early example of this manipulation is demonstrated in what I believe to be a mythical story, the story of Abraham's covenant with God and also, in the story of Moses when presented the tribes of Israel with the stone tablets containing the Ten Commandments and the subsequent actions by their leaders. The first story tells us that God spoke to Abraham and made a covenant or contract whereby Abraham and all his progeny were given the land bordered by the Egyptian border and the Euphrates River. In the

Moses story we are told that when Moses, as a descendent of Abraham, returned from the mountain with his list of commandments, he and his brother Aaron organized the immediate and brutal killing of 3,000 of their own people for daring to worship a statue of a golden calf. Following this mass slaying, his progeny, the twelve tribes of Israel, became the beneficiaries referred to prophetically in the covenant story of Abraham. They are the people who committed cruel and savage genocide on the peoples inhabiting the lands they claim had been given to them through this alleged covenant made with Abraham, by God.

This example and many others that follow will clearly show how mass acceptance was induced through fear. The sole intended purpose of these religious stories was to show explicitly what happens to disbelievers. They are, I believe, purely mythical stories that are the foundations of the lessons and values that have been handed down to us, generation by generation, through our various exclusive belief systems. It is by these means that the religious hierarchies have influenced political systems, resulting in the dangerous and powerful cultural conditioning that created the various distorted economic and social value systems that we have today. This is especially so for the Jewish, Judeo/Christian and Islamic religions, which are the three major belief systems seriously affecting the present state of world affairs.

Any objective view of the evolutionary, historical path of the so-called civilized world will show that there is a far better and more desirable method of human development than this competitive, dog-eat-dog, survival of the fittest, social system. The human cost of this political behaviour is incalculable.

I am not an academic. Nor am I a theologian. However, I have observed and studied the development of world affairs to the present time and the following chapters represent my understanding of the present situation. It will not meet with anyone's complete satisfaction, including my own. My understanding is from my particular perspective and draws on experiences and knowledge gained over eighty-odd years and through a long working life engaged in a wide area and variety of activities.

I was born in Shanghai in January 1925 of Jewish parents, who after moving from Mesopotamia lived in Shanghai for three years before migrating to Sydney Australia in September of 1925. After a public school education, I entered the workforce at fourteen, worked in thirty different areas of activity before being apprenticed and qualifying as a marine engineer at twenty-one. I then left home and spent the next four years working and travelling around Australia gathering life experience and eventually, resumed marine engineering in Port Moresby New Guinea as engineer on a government fishing and pearling survey vessel and spent the next two years diving and fishing around New Guinea and the adjacent South Pacific Islands. I married at twenty-five, built my own home, started and managed a successful engineering, building construction and equipment hire business in Sydney Australia for thirty-five years. A further three years managing an American multinational garment company's production office based in Hong Kong. Travelling to Europe, the US and factories in China, Thailand, Indonesia, the Philippines and Taiwan. Having raised a family, travelled extensively and read widely and now retired, I feel qualified and duty bound to analyse this society of ours, confidant to expose its faults and the people and organizations responsible for them. I also present a practical and rational structural solution that is capable of eliminating the socially destructive nature of some of these organizations and creating strong foundations on which to build a better world. This solution is designed to produce and inspire future generations to create world wide social consciousness as a monument to global human intellectual progress.

The world must move away from group and individual greed, reject the cut and thrust for power and wealth. We must follow the path towards desperately needed worldwide collective social justice and peace. Instead of trying to gain a competitive edge, we must strive to establish a co-operative centre, serving the common good through the sacrifice of selfishness. This does not mean that some may not have more than others, but what they have will not be gained at the expense of others. Only that which is good for all is good for each one. Nothing less is acceptable. The very survival of humanity and our planet as a viable, life-sustaining habitat is at stake.

CHAPTER 2

A Theology beyond its use by Date

This and the following chapters explore the nature of theology in general and describe how the origins and continued use of various belief systems have affected the evolutionary intellectual development of humanity. In order to address this, it is necessary to understand the language and context in which theology has been and is still being used. What do we understand by the term secular as opposed to mystical? Why is it important to know the difference?

Mysticism includes a wide range of controversial phenomena believed by many people to exist beyond the physical world. This belief requires faith, which is, to put it simply, belief without verifiable proof. In mysticism, there are two contrasting and separate traditions within the area of religious belief. One refers to unsubstantiated sources of knowledge and unity with the Ultimate, the Divine or God commonly interpreted as the God who is love. The other is the occult (which literally means hidden) and extends to a belief in extra sensory perception, including telepathy, clairvoyance, pre and retro-cognition, medium-ship and the practice of psycho-kinesis (beyond the usually recognised fields of human activity). It is also know as psychical research and more recently, para-psychology. Both the mystical and the occult involve: (a) The thought (theory) and b) Action on the thought (practice).

The distinction is the same as the division between science and technology: One describes the idea or theory, The other applies it by putting the knowledge to work. Secularity, on the other hand, is a non-mystical or purely rational worldview. In my experience in searching for truth, I am of the opinion that there exists a middle ground between the purely scientific, rational approach and the mystical/occult approach. To explore this path, I use the term secular in the sense of being of this world. To put it simply, a secular person might say "only with proof can there be conviction", whereas a mystical person with blind faith believes without proof. Historically, religion's social influence is to give a transcendental basis to the origins of life, the way life should be lived and the journey beyond death. Religions have a system of belief about spiritual origins and goals. For believers, these beliefs give a structure and meaning to their lives, and a hope of reward after death. It is for this reason that, for many people, their religious beliefs are an adult version of a comfort blanket. Their beliefs are not based on scientific evidence but on faith and hope.

At the fundamentalist end of belief, religions have a strong sense of authority. This authority may be a rigidly held code, such as a literalist view of the Bible, or obedience to a hierarchical authority, such as bishops and the Pope. These are Christian terms, but the principle applies to other religions to a greater or lesser degree. For those who consider themselves members of a religious group, there are varying degrees of commitment to the principles which are held so rigidly by fundamentalists. At the liberal end of the spectrum, faith may mean a commitment to a group through a need to belong, without necessarily having a clear understanding of the dogma of their faith. In this fundamentalist or mystical concept, members experience an intimate connection to the figures of their faith. This connection is a state of mind in which the believer is absorbed into the divine figure. Alternatively, the believer experiences a psychological surrender to the ideals of a theologically based organization or to humanity in general as [their] god's creation. This mystical approach, in its extreme form, overlaps with the occult and new age movements. These movements look to experience immediate results rather than existing in an overall belief system.

On the other hand, there is a branch of science that has also developed an attitude that accommodates religion and does not require an outright rejection of faith. Some see science and religion as representing humanity's major intellectual streams and in this sense can be compared to opposing political parties. However, some scientists see their study of nature as a respectful investigation of God's creation. In recent years, developments in relativity and **quantum physics**, have led to new ideas in the study of the cosmos and of consciousness. These have led to a potential link between science and religion where consciousness is seen as going beyond the mere physical construction of the brain. (This concept also requires a blind leap of faith; as it cannot be replicated, produced, or proven.)[2] It should be noted that the more hierarchical forms of religion resemble the existing social structure. It is this form of religion, which has led to the most extreme acts of human oppression. It is also favoured by people who like continuity and certainty in their lives and who, by following rigid beliefs, are able to excuse, or totally ignore repression, cruelty and injustice perpetrated in the name of their faith Conventional science can bring rationality and systematic investigation to bear in the way the world is constructed, the formation of societies, and the development of human behaviour. Rational investigation shows that decisions in high places such as governments and the church leadership are based upon arbitrary authority.[3] Arbitrary authority, whether religious or secular, is the enemy of, and actually retards, the full development of human life and ecology in the world. Up to the present time, all human knowledge and advancement has been achieved through secular thoughts, ideas and actions. Many beliefs, ideas and mystical understanding have been utterly and totally discredited by modern science.

Adherence to religious ideas based on mystical beliefs has resulted in a great deal of pain and suffering being inflicted on a large number of great thinkers and scientists of the past. Torture and execution were encouraged by various religious leaders purely because these ideas contradicted mystical beliefs that were stubbornly held by the religious hierarchy and their followers of the time. Such savage treatment of dissenters serves a twofold purpose: it demonstrates the power of the theological hierarchy and instils fear, discouraging people from ever challenging the authority of the religious teachings. However, in the

---

[2] **Space/Time Foam**. Quantum physicist **John Hagelin**, Ph.D.,

[3] Decisions based solely on personal wishes, feelings, or perceptions, rather than on objective facts, reasons, or principles (Encarta English dictionary).

spirit of learning from history, all claims of mystical knowledge and authority should be vigorously challenged.

This brings us back to the two distinct levels of knowledge and knowledge gathering: Namely the mystical or occult level, which is derived by non-physical or unscientific means and sustained only by faith; and the secular or physical level which is derived through rational thought and can be verified by means of science and technology. Whenever the unverifiable mystical takes precedence over the verifiable rational secular, there is the danger of unknown and unforeseeable consequences.

The Salem Witch Hunt is one example from history of the application of extreme mystical understanding. In Salem, USA, in the year 1692, twenty women were deemed to be possessed by demons or other satanic forces and were executed as witches. Dr. Linnda Caporael a scientist, in the USA, exploring the background and symptoms shown by the Salem victims, was not satisfied that satanic forces accounted for this isolated outbreak in just one small area of the country. She began an investigation to find some other explanation for this phenomenon and searched for affected areas with a common denominator. What was it that caused some people to be affected so that their behaviour was deemed to be witch-like? Caporael finally isolated a particular grain used in that area for the baking of bread: rye. Rye is particularly susceptible to a fungal growth called ergot. However, not all rye crops are affected, only the crops grown in low lying areas where damp and marshy conditions prevail. By going through old records and diaries, she discovered that 1692, the year of the outbreak, had a particularly wet growing season. Working on this evidence, she then investigated similar outbreaks and witch executions in Europe and England from the time of the Middle Ages and found that similar environmental conditions had prevailed. All these so called witches had been victims of ergot poisoning. Caporael's research found strong, scientifically based circumstantial evidence that shows beyond any reasonable doubt that the common and widespread religious belief in mysticism and the occult had been guilty of the murder of these people in Salem, as well as thousands of innocent people throughout history. The tragic Salem Witch Hunt clearly demonstrates the inherent danger of all faith based reliance on mystical knowledge and its assumption of truth rather than on practical investigation and the application of scientific understanding.

CHAPTER 3

Doubt and Scepticism

For many years, I have been of the opinion that the power of prayer and extra-sensory perception were tools used by the misguided and/ or charlatans; and they derive from the same area; the rational mind. My scepticism was modified by a particular episode as follows In the above context, I began to explore the connection between the power of prayer, positive thinking and E.S.P (Extra Sensory Perception) sometimes called Clairvoyance by some, who classify it as being a Satanic power. I formed the opinion, based on personal experience and observation, that these three phenomena are, in some as yet obscure way, a manifestation of the same physically, (brain) based, psychic ability or (gift). It stretches the point a little to link prayer to positive thinking; but to include E.S.P in the same category, will be beyond the pale to most people.

Firstly, I will relate my conversion from extreme sceptic, to convinced believer in 'limited' E.S.P. (The limit of my belief being within the present or past events. Events stored in the minds of us all. Against future events, which are innumerable, incalculable and un-fore-see-able.

My wife Jean, who in most ways is just an ordinary person with the normal insecurities and more than normal fears regarding perceived life threatening situations, (due, I must add to certain traumatic experiences in her life from birth to maturity). Has, from about the age of forty-five, developed the ability to sense experiences in peoples past life with amazing chronological and physical accuracy.

The following describes some of the instances and circumstances that convinced me of her ability in this area: all the examples given are verifiable. To the best of my knowledge, the people to whom the information was given are, at the time of writing, still alive and I feel sure that they would testify to the truth of the conversations described. The time-frame is from 1987 when we went to live in Hong Kong up to the present.

Prior to this, Jean was only mildly interested in Palmistry. However, the KCC, our club in H.K, planned a charity fete at which someone suggested that Jean should dress as a Gipsy fortune teller, set up in a small tent and read palms for a small fee. Among the Chinese and Indian population many are superstitious and believe all that claptrap. It proved to be a very successful and popular sideshow. And that is all it started out to be.

While she was given a time limit of 5 minutes per person, (which is a long time to hold someone's attention and talk about something you know little about) she found that the information that came into her mind was largely unrelated to reading one's palm. Both she and the client were surprised at the results. She then decided to ask, not just for the agreed payment, but also a mark for accuracy on a scale from 1 to 10. There were none below eight; and mostly nine's and ten's. From that time on, her reputation, not only in our bowling club, but at all the other clubs at which she competed became well known, (if not legendary). None of the "readings" were for profit, but either for charity, or towards the H.K Women's Bowling Association funds. For which she raised H.K.$6,000.00 in that the year. My personal experiences were only a very few of the many "readings," and I relate some of them only because they can be verified.

1). A particular person at the club, a very astute woman in the legal profession in H.K. expressed doubts as to Jean's ability to apparently, tune in to a person's mind. Jean held her hand and promptly told her that she was one of twin girls, and the other twin died at birth. That alone convinced her, as she knew that no other person in H.K. was aware of this fact.

2). Closer to home, Jean and I were sitting with a small group of women at our social club. The conversation got around to E.S.P. and palmistry. The husband of one of the group arrived just as the topic started, he emphatically stated his total disbelief in all that stuff . Jean asked to see if she could convince him to the contrary. She held and looked at his hand for a moment, and told him that at about the age of thirty-three, a great tragedy occurred in his life. He seemed mildly interested and asked her to continue. When she told him that his first wife had been an epileptic, and she experienced a seizure while in the bath and drowned, he was converted. It was true in every particular. Prior to this, none of us knew that he had been married before, let alone those vivid details.

3). This third example shows that this ability or power transcends language and cultural barriers: Our firm in H.K was asked to officially open a new factory that one of our manufacturers had built in a town near the city of Zaimin in Southern China. Seated at the official table were all the important local provincial representatives, it so happened, that Jean was seated next to a very high government official. The prospective manageress of the factory, Mary was Chinese and spoke fluent English and Mandarin. Knowing of Jean's ability, she suggested that Jean read his palm. He could not speak a word of English, but Mary would interpret. Jean agreed, and started to tell him that he had two children. Mary tried to correct her telling her that he in fact only had one child, a boy. Jean's reply to this was "Just tell him what I say, not what you think." she then carried on with the fact that he had a boy and a girl, they were both adopted by him and his wife, and that at the age of fifteen, the girl had fought with them and ran away. By this time his eyes were moist. Jean went on to tell him that his wife was not from around this part of China, but is Cambodian. She also told him that she saw a wheelchair. Not clearly; just an impression. It transpired that his wife had Multiple Sclerosis, and although had not at that time been completely immobile, the next time Jean went to the factory, Mary was under strict instructions to bring her to visit him at his home. His wife could not walk and was in a wheelchair.

These and many other examples convinced me that, although there are still many areas of our existence that are yet to be discovered, there is no reason to believe that the answers will come from any other place than from where the thousands of previous answers have come. From Secular science!

CHAPTER 4

Learning from history

There is a lesson here for humanity:
For the moment, let's postpone the battle between the theological mystics and the secular scientists about how we as a specie developed or arrived on this planet. With the state of the world politically, philosophically, economically and ecologically, whether we were created or evolved becomes irrelevant. It is a fact that we are here; and we had better devise a way of peaceful co-existence, or perish.

The picture of human development over the last 5,000 years, painted with a very broad brush, is that we as individuals, (in many ways are very diverse), but collectively we are one. Tribal, national, racial identity, colour, creed or culture, are man made psychological divisions; biologically and genetically we are the same specie. From observation and my reading of reported evidence derived through archaeology, anthropology, mythology, and written records, we have experienced changing relationships between different ethnic, tribal and national groups throughout our history due to wars, political groupings, and alliances. Also within these various groups, the relationships between sub groups also changes dramatically. It appears that, as our knowledge of our immediate environment and other communal cultural ideas and activities develop, a corresponding change in social attitude and behaviour patterns occur. This is understandable as everything is then seen from a new perspective. This constitutes collective intellectual growth. The rate of this human development process in the various geographical areas, are very different. This also applies to smaller groups within each major geographical group and so it is, down to the most important part of humanity, the individual. With the individual, there are observable "specific periods" of intellectual growth within the lifespan from birth to maturity. In today's environment, we are exposed to subconscious assimilation of the available forms of knowledge that leads to the fulfilment of life up to age five or six. After which, we are encouraged to learn a particular educational curriculum, up to about age sixteen. (frequently modified to suit the needs of industry, commerce and the community of the time). This is both a conscious and subconscious absorption of the prevailing community values. It is the political, commercial and religious environmental material in which we are all immersed. I suggest that this material absorbed by our young, is a pollutant. It has the effect of turning vast numbers of people, potential human resources, from useful contributors, into the material of:

a) The marketplace, (producers, and consumers).Or,
b) Those of us that are paid to fight, protect and further the agenda of a particular controlling group. Or,
c) The uneducated, disabled, disadvantaged and the small percentage of shirkers that are just a social liability and a drain on the economy

In past history over the last two to three thousand years, our rulers (controlling groups) were royalty, nobility and the priesthood, who assumed, from their inherited, or politically contrived positions of privilege and power, that only the privileged minority of the population was worthy or capable of reaching particular intellectual and social standards. This assumption of intellectual and social superiority, brought with it differentiation –and in some cases polarization of social groups in various (advanced) early societies. This privileged group, the so-called intelligentsia, although themselves socially segregated, had a distinct economic and social advantage over the peasants and others who they considered to be of an inferior social order in society.

Environmental conditions play a significant part in determining the psychological and intellectual growth of a nation, society or community. This fact was completely ignored by the rulers of so-called more advanced nations. The controlling elite in these more advanced and powerful nations considered the people who lived in an environment of tropical and temperate climates, that provided them with food, very little need for shelter or clothing, as unintelligent savages (backward) people.

It is recorded, chapter and verse, in the pages of human history that the more "advanced" nations inflicted a horrific toll on the lives, freedoms, resources and land of people such as these. The alternative, could and should have been, to offer mutually beneficial opportunities for natural development, and improved facilities for change. I think that we are all now aware that in those days pure unadulterated greed was the sole motivating force behind the drive for discovery of new worlds. Sovereigns, princes, pirates, plunderers and priests would not allow a few (ignorant) local inhabitants to get in the way of boundless wealth or souls.

With the advent of the industrial age, pillage, piracy, slavery, conquest and genocide continued at top national levels worldwide at an even more rapid rate. The social system in the early industrial societies was geared up and the people educated to believe that these activities were a source of national pride. Crimes against the rest of humanity was the "God given right" of the bright and more intelligent people. To either seduce them with their God of love, and if that failed, defeat them in battle with all the power and might at their disposal. Then subjugate and treat the various people or nations (some, that had developed a different culture that was in many aspects more civilized than their own) as "dull" or ignorant people who could and should be guided (manipulated) and exploited by them. History books are full of the legendary exploits of the British East India Company. British conquests also included Africa, North America, Burma and sections of China. The Dutch in Indo-China and Indonesia, the Belgians in Biafra and the Congo, the Germans in New Guinea, the French in North Africa, the Arab slave trade to America, The Spanish genocide in South America, the Turkish conquest of the Middle East, including the near complete genocide of the Armenians and Kurds by the Turks.

The British conquest of Turkey and the Ottoman Empire led to the final act of British bastardry; "The Balfour Declaration of 1917" promising the Mandated territory of Palestine captured in World War 1, as a homeland for the Zionist Jews[3]..Subsequently, in 1948 the UN voted to grant Israel sovereign rights to a large portion of the Palestinian territory. This was done in such an arbitrary fashion that would guarantee prolonged and bitter internecine conflict. (A Peace to end all peace) And so it goes on. . and on. . .

We have not yet learned The Lesson!

---

[3]   Balfour declaration of 1917. (Google)

CHAPTER 5

A journey towards a rational religion.

The Hebrew, Judeo-Christian and Moslem religions of today are founded on mysticism, ancient rituals and superstitious beliefs. These religious structures are based on over a five thousand year old perception and people's misconception of the nature of the universe, planet earth and humanity.

If we were to take the mysticism, superstitious rituals and pagan sacrificial practices out of religion, what would be left would be a much clearer path and a far more efficient tool for the achievement of peace and tranquillity for the whole of humanity.

The following is an introduction to how the origins of misguided practices of early priesthood developed into fraudulent behaviour designed to deceive and control a simple and primitive tribal people. These practices, used for the sole purpose of acquiring and retaining power, have become a major encumbrance to human social advancement. How the ancient belief in Jewish biblical mythology, starting with the big lie of Abraham, finally lead to disastrous consequences. Also, how the continued belief in those primitive stories, hides the truth, beauty and fulfilling ideals contained in the philosophical message of Jesus as a prophet The scriptures of the Christian Bible are clouded, and at times completely misleading and contradictory because they are a combination of translations of prior translations of both oral and literary works from the pre-Jesus era, the Torah, the Talmud and the comparatively new books of the Christian era, the New Testament. Let's consider the type of life led by our early ancestors in the times that the early religious beliefs were formulated and practiced.

Before the time of Abraham (man or myth), the various roving tribes and ethnic groups that slowly developed from a hunter gatherer existence, evolved into agricultural tribal groups. In the need for protection from marauding tribes, gradually, City/State structures developed. These thrived under the various leaders (Priest/Kings).Such as: Melchisadek, Sargon, Gilgamesh, Hammurabi, Nebuchadnezzar and many others; Too numerous to mention.

They were rulers of simple, primitive and superstitious people, who created and worshiped their various Gods. For instance, in ancient Egypt, there were over twenty-two districts each with their own god. The gods were represented by tangible idols, made by man. They were attributed super-natural powers. These powers were associated directly to the God/idols by the people. In Mesopotamia, (the biblical Garden of Eden?) the Babylonians, Sumerians, Hittites, Assyrians also had their own separate gods. The Babylonian God was Marduk; and Abraham's father, Terah, - we are told - was a craftsman fashioning images of idols in Babylon.

Both secular and biblical history records many wars waged between the various states and tribes, with the victor destroying not only the enemy but, more importantly their God. Gods such as Ishtar, Marduk, Asarluhi, Ea, Baal, Ptah, Isis, Osiris or whatever. All destroyed and long forgotten. Except for the God ascribed to Abraham, (man, or myth personified,) who is invulnerable by the virtue of his invisibility. As a consequence, this God has endured until now and may endure into eternity (or as long as the mind of mankind persists, whichever is the shorter).

Abraham's father is supposed to have been a maker of the idols in Babylon. It is my belief that early leaders of the tribes of Israel, developed the mythical story of Abraham showing a God that could not be dealt with as easy as those in the past. They observed that when an enemy was defeated in battle and their idols destroyed, the people were then completely demoralized and became subservient to a stronger god[4]. So the Israelites invented their own God; a God that was beyond the

---

[4]   Districts and Gods of ancient Egypt. (Google)

reach of any enemy either in victory or defeat. They also, through this myth, claimed exclusive rights of inheritance for themselves and their progeny. This claim was much more than patent rights on their god's benevolence. Modern patent rights expire after a nominal period, but the "Abrahamic" claim was, that the covenant made between Abraham and this God was in perpetuity, and for whom, His descendants only. (detailed in chapter 13).

The idea that there is a universal power which controls our lives, and over which we have no control, has been with us from before recorded history. However, throughout recorded history, there have been small numbers of people who had above average abilities. (referred to by Paul in Corinthians 1 CH. 12: as *gifts*). In ancient civilizations, small groups developed the study of astronomy and mathematics, and could forecast the positions of the stars and planets in relation to the Earth, Sun and Moon. This knowledge, handed down to family or only a select few, gave them an elevated status within their relatively primitive societies. This ability placed them in the position of a priest-hood with what appeared to be supernatural abilities. Being able to forecast astronomical movements and events must have appeared as though they actually controlled the movements of the planets; or at least, were in communication with the power behind them. The gullible masses would naturally look to them for guidance and advice in matters of natural phenomena that they themselves could not understand. Over time, as the priesthood's understanding and knowledge of the laws of nature increased and expanded, they became a very powerful group within the community. In the exercise of their power, they introduced a variety of ritual practices and superstitions. Among which were blood sacrifices, prayers and seasonal offerings to various Gods. This suggested that they, through their priests, could in some mysterious way influence their god. Who better to lead the people in these activities than they who understood and had the ability to communicate with their gods?

In this way, over some thousands of years, because of early humanity's fears and proclivity to superstitious beliefs, priests became more powerful than kings. In those times, ignorance and superstition were the norm. Different physical skills also developed in the community, through various activities required for the maintenance and survival of the community.

Priests were the inner circle, the top of the pecking order. Outside of this, others would have developed various ways to treat illnesses and to cure ailments by physical means. Normal ailments and conditions that would arise in communities involved in hard manual labour, such as agriculture, hunting, erecting and maintaining dwellings etc. A body of knowledge slowly developed in the use of herbs, drugs and physical manipulation. Knowledge we now know as chiropractics, naturopathy and pharmaceutics, applied by the folk healer, medicine man or witch doctor. Still others developed the skill of mental psychological manipulation. So there we were historically, with the kneelers, the healers and the stealers. The modern stealers are the persuaders, the opportunistic psychic predators who are evident today in the guise of, diplomats, lawyers, politicians, media moguls, social engineering P.R spin doctors and other greed driven secular groups seeking power and/ or wealth.

In time, through their seemingly miraculous and simulated godlike knowledge, religious leaders, the High Priests, slowly gained positions of power and control in society. Not much different from today but without the miracles. Today's miracles are called "spectacular discoveries", performed in large numbers by medical and technological research men and women.

Over time, through wars, travel, trade and commerce between neighbouring states, basic knowledge of a wider world became widespread among the general populations of the area we now know as the Middle East. The need for a more sophisticated means of control became necessary. An early indication of this is observed in ancient Mesopotamia with the Jewish biblical stories of Abraham's alleged covenant with God and the Jewish tribes. A great number of legends and myths, referring to mystical incidents and events were introduced into the Jewish religious stories. The stories of God appearing to Moses as a burning bush, exile and enslavement in Egypt, the Exodus (deliverance from Egypt). Add to this, the many supplications of Moses to the Egyptian Pharaoh to release the Jews, his refusal and how Moses in collusion with God, brought about so many catastrophes that concession was forced. The forty years in the wilderness and God's Ten Commandments. All this makes for a powerful cultural bonding as long as faith and belief are maintained. (Incidentally, there is no Egyptian historic or any archaeological evidence of Jewish slaves in Egypt, or for that matter, no reference to the Jewish biblical account of the exodus.) And so began the long list of mystical acts. (So called miracles) to show that certain powerful people had a direct line of communication with God. This persists until we come to the stories of Jesus, of whom it was said, not only communicated with God, but in fact was claimed by some to **BE GOD** in the flesh. This is where our journey back to reality must start. It is a journey of faith. A search for nothing less than the practical reality of a GOD that I believe is revealed through Jesus' Message.

CHAPTER 6

How it came about

In the following chapters we see how the use of myth and the continued cultural conditioning of humanity by particular controlling groups, generation after generation, (traditions) led to the serious imbalance between our "collective technical" and "individual intellectual" growth. An important segment of this manufactured cultural mindset of humanity (the-man-in-the-street), are the ideas fostered and encouraged by all theological diehards. These true believers are still stuck in ancient literal interpretation of belief systems which are mutually exclusive, politically motivated and if not seriously modified, will prove to be mutually destructive.

In the process of this work, I recognized two main streams of evolutionary growth. The first, deals with the theological aspect, of our misguided and shackled evolutionary spiritual growth. This has had the affect of blinding us from both the enormous power and strength of our collective consciousness and stunting the growth of our mass world-view and human condition.

The second part of this book deals with the purely secular aspect and the result of the failure of our present theological belief systems to deliver our hopes and expectations. We now find that the whole of western society is in a position where the unbridled greed of the controllers of secular commercial and political world affairs (the second stream of evolutionary growth), is bringing humanity to the very brink of extinction. This is in the midst of technological intellectual advancement beyond the dreams of humanity only a mere two hundred years ago. There are strong tribal, ethnic, national and religious barriers that have been built and are used to separate, keep us fighting and killing each other. But these barriers will prove to be not strong enough to withstand the strength of our unshackled collective consciousness. Here is a story, fable (or parable if you like), that illustrates my point:

"There was a wise father that had many children who were always fighting and squabbling for individual supremacy. One day, when the fighting reached a dangerous level, he gathered them all together to try to teach them that there is a better, more fruitful and comfortable way to live than hurting and maiming each other. He asked them each to go and bring him back two dry sticks. When they all returned, he asked them in turn to select one of their sticks and break it which they all did. He then collected the other stick from each, bound them together as one and asked them to individually or collectively to try to break it. They learnt the lesson and lived harmoniously together to achieve collectively what they could not get individually." This is the lesson that the human family is yet to grasp. We continue to kill, maim, torture, and exploit each other to achieve selfish goals set by example of the commercial, theological and political leaders of the world.

There is however, a life line available and offered in the form of an effective means of education that I believe is capable of reversing the current trend of degenerating morality and ethics. A description of which is presented in a later chapter. In the meantime, however, there has been in our recent past, many attempts by enlightened theologians to come to grips with the dichotomy presented by the interpretation and understanding of a God as represented in the Torah, the Old Testament, the New Testament and that of the Qur'an. On the one hand, the ancient biblical and modern history of the Jewish, Judeo-Christian and Islamic beliefs have displayed an interfering, cruel, vengeful and condemning God while on the other hand, attempting to describing him as a loving caring and kind God. These attempts have been born from a growing conviction by sincere and thoughtful religious leaders, that this separate and interfering God out there somewhere, is an erroneous God-view. Most of the people that have expressed this comparatively new concept have been branded heretics by the hierarchy of their particular denomination. But the fact is, that here (in Australia), wherever they have preached in this vein, they have found large numbers in church congregations in agreement. It is my fervent hope that this movement will ultimately grow to the extent that the structure of the old established religious belief system will be changed. I contend that God exists in the form of the human spirit within humankind and we need to find a way of interpreting and expressing this understanding of just what God is and not who God is.

We have recently had the opportunity to read other gospels that have become available, supposedly written within 100 years after the execution of Jesus. They include the gospel of Jesus according to Judas, also the gospel according to Thomas and others. These are part of a large number of theological works that were written and available at the time when the sixty-six books that comprise the present day New Testament were selected as material suitable for political purposes of the Roman Emperor Constantine. On reading only some of the verses from this gospel, the reason for rejection becomes obvious.

For instance, in the gospel of Thomas, the prologue says: "These are the secret sayings that the living Jesus spoke and Didymus Judas Thomas recorded"[5]

1). Jesus said, "Whoever discovers the interpretation of these sayings will not taste death."

2). Jesus said, "Those who seek should not stop seeking until they find. When they find, they will be disturbed. When they are disturbed, they will marvel, and will reign over all. [And after they have reigned they will rest.]"

3). Jesus said, "If your leaders say to you, 'Look, the (Father's) kingdom is in the sky,' then the birds of the sky will precede you. If they say to you, 'It is in the sea,' then the fish will precede you. Rather, the kingdom is within you and it is outside you. When you know yourselves, then you will be known, and you will understand that you are children of

---

[5]

[6] Reference: Sacred-texts Christianity Apocrypha THE GOSPEL OF THOMAS Translations by: |Thomas O. Lambdin |(Coptic version) B.P Grenfell & A.S. Hunt. (Greek fragments) Bentley Layton (Greek Fragments)

[7] Wikipedia

the living Father. But if you do not know yourselves, then you live in poverty, and you are the poverty."

5). Jesus said, "Know what is in front of your face, and what is hidden from you will be disclosed to you. For there is nothing hidden that will not be revealed. [And there is nothing buried that will not be raised."

35). Jesus said: "One cannot to go into a strong man's house (and) take it by force, unless he binds his hands; then he will plunder his house."

70). Jesus said, "If you bring forth what is within you, what you have will save you. If you do not have that within you, what you do not have within you [will] kill you."

77). Jesus said, "I am the light that is over all things. I am all: from me all came forth, and through me, all attained. Split a piece of wood;

I am there. Lift up the stone, and you will find me there." The above are just a few excerpts that lead to the following conclusions:

a). That **God is not** an outside and separate entity who exercises control, judgment and punishment.

b). **God is** the collective consciousness of humanity; and human life is the manifestation, the embodiment of the spirit within us. It is this spirit that works and does all that must be done, in order to exist evolve and grow. This intellectual growth, I believe, will take us out of the state of ignorance and confused blind adherence to these mystical belief systems. Only then will we be enlightened, free and strong enough to overcome the forces of greed and self interest in our society.. When this state of awareness is widely present in the world, will we have the knowledge, understanding and ability to achieve the necessary intellectual and social change, A transformation *from the instinct driven primitive savage, to intelligent living gods.*

In order to achieve this stage, we first should consider just what it is that permeates every living creature, that force of nature, these functions we have in common that must be performed for us to exist, reproduce and grow; **Our Genetic Imperative**[6] Genetic imperatives are the biological needs that follow a progression of instinctive qualities necessary for all living organisms (from microbes in a Petri dish, to the most advanced form of life). These are: Survival, territory, competition, reproduction, security seeking, and group forming. Let's consider these in sequence;

---

6   Wikipedia.

1. Survival: The primary innate genetic predisposition of self preservation.

2. Competition: The individual competes for territory, food, a mating partner.

3. Territory: Need of land area to gather food and necessities to secure the growth of off spring. This leads to possession and protection of sufficient area; territorial sovereignty.

4. Reproduction: With mating, the need for a group becomes evident. Territorial rights are so much easier for a group to secure. In this competitive area, there are two distinct natural evolutionary paths.

a). The Individual path in which the specie is involved in the process of natural selection. A very slow and almost imperceptible change in the individual compared with that of the group. And

b.) The group; the threats against persons and property of the group creates stressful situations that must be addressed. The effect of the general wellbeing of the individual is dependent on the degree of stress applied.

5. Security: The groups that seek to maintain and improve the physical health, security and wellbeing of its members improve the group's chances of survival. We can observe this in the international political scene today, where national groups upon whom the stress of economic and resource sanctions are applied by other more powerful groups, succumb very easily to an invading group. 6. Group forming: In today's society group forming involves notions of territory, collective identity and culture. It is the product of family, clan, tribe and the nation. It is also the result of our biological structure. The comparatively large size of the human brain determines the period of time that our children are dependent on their parents. This being much longer than in most animals, the biological mating and infant survival period requires an extended time frame to suit this parenting function. These factors coupled with our ability to communicate, brings about the formation of the family group. Over a few generations, many more families are formed into extended groupings or clans. A few more generations and we have many clans forming a tribe. These then become too large for the available resources; necessitating geographical migration. Over time, the speech dialects and languages also change. In time the tribes enlarge to the stage of city states; and systems of managing a large

social group become necessary. In primitive societies animistic religion filled this role Competition for resources and territory produced the need for further knowledge. This leads to an evolutionary process of both physical and intellectual growth. All knowledge seeking life forms enhance their chances of survival by learning how to best utilize their natural environment and pass on this knowledge to their progeny. This genetic transfer becomes an instinctive behaviour pattern. Humans are not the only specie to do this, ants, birds, bees, and all other mammals do the same in their own particular way. Humans formed and used communication and religions as a traditional way of managing the growing tribal social groups.

It is at this stage where civilizations begin to emerge and we see the start of Theistic religions. The earliest religious practices have been uncovered as far back as 70,000 years in Botswana in Africa, and 30,000 yrs. in Central Europe. In the very early civilizations in China, Egypt, Babylon, Canaan and Mexico, where urbanized communities developed, religious influence spread. It is these religious systems that effectively perpetuated the tribal hierarchical political systems of monarchy and oligarchy.

Unfortunately, religions by their very nature are fundamentally prescriptive and work against expanded knowledge seeking. Therein lays their failings and the ultimate demise of the current theological concepts.

CHAPTER 7

Tackling the root cause

During times of universal deceit, telling the truth becomes a revolutionary act. (George Orwell)

As far back as Abraham, of the Old Testament, we read of rampant greed for territory, resources, power and wealth. Allegedly, at the behest and blessing of their God, the Hebrew tribes raped and pillaged and enslaved all the tribes in the land that that Abraham said God had so generously given him. This consisted of all the land between the border of Egypt and the Euphrates River. The covenant (read contract), as recorded in the Old Testament, Gen.15: 7 -21, in all respects, was wrong, immoral, obscene, genocidal and criminal. On an elevated level, this conflict is still going on today - after 5000 years - for the same piece of land. ***Why Is It So?***

The fault lies directly at the feet of the religious leaders of our ancestors with their misconceived ancient mystical ideas of their environment, accompanied by the mythical stories, which science now knows was an entirely erroneous analysis of our origins. The mystical explanations were believed by ignorant tribal people that gradually developed into history's infant "civilized" societies. These same people carried their beliefs, stories, myths, rituals and traditions with them in the form of the Jewish, Judeo-Christian and Moslem religions of today - and have been the primary and major drawback to the advancement of their own followers and humanity as a whole.

The great lie:

Populations "En Masse'" have been deliberately and grossly misled into believing that their various leaders, both religious and political, are people of honesty and integrity. Under their guidance, leadership and social policies, the world will thrive and achieve the ideals and aspirations of the vast majority of humanity. They will lead us to a state of world peace, harmony and prosperity (it sounds like heaven). Even if this is not achieved on a global scale, at least our own particular nation or religious group will be the beneficiaries of their wise counsel and leadership. What a joke! This is so far from the truth as to make it comical if it were not for the fact that, as the result of the agendas of these Psycho-maniacal oligarchs, that created heart wrenching misery in the Balkans, Africa, Sudan, Afghanistan, Palestine, and Iraq in particular and for all practical purposes, "worldwide". With one hand playing power politics with the world's population as their pawns and with the other – precipitating the dismantling, destruction and devouring the earth's resources.

In the area of social-political awareness, the vast majority of people in the Western World, fall broadly into two main categories. Those that are aware of the lies and duplicity but feel powerless to change the situation, and those that are not aware, hopelessly or willingly accepting their condition and carry on doing their best to enjoy whatever creature comforts and happiness that are available within their immediate environment.

However, there is a smaller third category of people, who do not fit into the first two. As the present, too few to make an appreciable impact on curing the human destruction, despair and misery suffered by a large proportion of the world's population. In this third category, are the people that are inspired to devote a great deal of time, eff ort and money in areas of extreme need such as: Refugee programs, aid for the destitute and homeless, indigenous reconciliation, gender discrimination, women's rights and a vast number of worthy causes. In every case in which caring people have been involved, be it individual, community and up to the level of state, national and international charitable organizations, there has been a conscientious effort to try to cure the symptoms of the condition. The majority of which were brought about by large-scale human action. Religious groups have been in the forefront of service in all these areas. Helping to ease the pain and suffering of the more unfortunate. However, their main activity is contained within their own religious or cultural group. In exceptional circumstances on humanitarian grounds, the aid is extended to all and sundry. If the truth be known, a few of the contributors to the welfare of the hungry, homeless and helpless are in fact among the forces that caused the problem in the first place; our various religions being at the top of the list. To be more effective, we could afford to ignore the attempts to cure the great number and persistent symptoms of a terminally flawed culture and concentrate on a method of prevention. Until the thousands of do-gooders of the world who, incidentally deserve our greatest respect and admiration, wake up to the fact that the world is controlled by a comparatively small number of psychic–predators and no matter where a patch is applied, more and more areas of need will arise. It is a bottomless pit. It is a well known fact that prevention is better than cure and unfortunately, while we concentrate on the symptoms and ignore the cause of the disease, there will be no cure!

To quote Henry David Thoreau:

"There are a thousand hacking at the branches of evil to only one who is striking at the root." Like aids and all the other cultural and social diseases, these evils, with which we are afflicted, are incurable; but not unpreventable. I don't mean instead of - **but as well as** - doing our utmost to alleviate the present pain and suffering. The most important task is to enlighten and inspire the mass of what I term the "little people", us, you and I, the ordinary John and Jane that we see every day in the street. A call for action to all who have been conditioned by the mass media, commercial opportunists and governments into believing and accepting that this disjointed world is normality and everything that needs to be done is being done.

When the numbers of enlightened and inspired people reach the critical mass required, the power of informed people (People Power) will reinforce the few interested and capable organizations. The U.N., Amnesty international, Greenpeace, and others, who are at present attempting to implement the ideals of worldwide social justice. Until the weight of numbers, prompt, pressurize and persuade our elected representatives to legislate against, and prosecute culpable organizations and the criminals responsible for crimes against humanity, nothing will change. We are now living in a historically revolutionary period. Never before has there been such easy access to so wide a range of information. The internet and many other books are available to all who are interested in learning why the world is in such a mess. Discovering who brought it about and how this mess will only get worse if we "the little people" do nothing to change the situation. This same facility, the internet, also gives us the information and describes in detail the tools required to do just that; turn it around.

I emphasize the absolute importance and worth the individual, you the reader, to the outcome of our civilization and the survival of human life on Earth. Here is what Goethe, the great humanist, scientist and philosopher said about the importance of you the individual "

I have come to the frightening conclusion that I am the decisive element.
It is my personal approach that creates the climate.
It is my daily mood that makes the weather.
I possess tremendous power to make
life miserable or joyous.
I can be a tool of torture or an instrument of inspiration,
I can humiliate, humour, hurt or heal.
In all situations, it is my response that decides
whether a crisis is escalated or diminished,
or a person is humanized or demonised.
If we treat people as they are, we make them worse.
If we treat people as they ought to be,
we help them become
what they are capable
of becoming."

CHAPTER 8

What Kind Of World Have We Inherited?

Look around you! Haven't you ever wondered why, (in Australia in particular), this - so called - lucky country. We have a beautiful natural environment, natural resources and agriculture that produces more than we can use, with a largely happy-go-lucky population. Why is it that so many things vitally necessary for our future growth and prosperity are ignored? Why do so many things in the areas of health, education, national asset infrastructure, foreign trade and commerce, industry and agriculture, laws, taxation policies, seem to create more problems than they solve? Why does such a large proportion of the world's population live in such a sorry, sick and starving state? Are our national and international political and religious leaders so dumb, or just powerless to produce policies that lead us into a more meaningful, fruitful and peaceful world?

Certainly the God(s) of our various belief systems, over the last 5,000 years or so, have demonstrated their inability to stem the accelerating decline in social values, solve the cultural, ethnic and religious differences, or reduce the incidence of man's inhumanity to man. Have you ever thought that they may play a large part in causing the problem? The reason is that the main concern of those in control of world's finances, markets, governments and spiritual wellbeing are focused - as in most organized institutions today - be they financial, political, commercial, or religious, for the benefit of themselves and the camp followers in their particular area of activity. It has become painfully obvious that they do for the people under their control, only that which is necessary to ensure the maintenance and expansion of their questionable positions of power and influence. These separate groups work to achieve particular outcomes and create social attitudes that are conducive to their goals. However, I don't believe that there is a grand conspiracy encompassing these four groups. Rather, it is a symbiotic existence where they feed off whatever advantageous opportunities the others present to satisfy their own particular selfish agenda. It is also an unfortunate fact that these are the very groups that control the distribution of information (and misinformation). It is even more unfortunate that this covers most if not all the information available from which we form our opinions and make choices as to what we buy, who we adulate, who we worship, who we hate, who we help, who we kill and who we vote for. The fault for this cannot in anyway be attributed to us as individuals as a part of the great mass of humanity.

Let's consider the current psychological expertise, the technology, the unimaginable amount of money and effort that is spent, on weapons of mass persuasion with the sole purpose of lulling us into a false sense of security and satisfaction with the present social condition. The system works to ensure that enough of us can access an abundance of creature comforts which in turn guarantees loyalty if not total conformity to the powers that be. In the part of the world we term **the West**, we are a patriotic, flag waving, god fearing, nationalistic, group of individualists. We may organize rallies in protest and promote various social and political issues of major importance. But the power of the economic and political control is ruthlessly imposed when the present social, political or economic system is threatened. With a carrot in one hand and a stick in the other, the passive agreement of the majority of society guarantees acceptance and support for **economic rationalism**. Or, the application of **sanctions,** or **support** for this or that nation or head of state, or the **worship** of this or that God, (In other words, it is all a tragic confidence trick played out on a massive scale,) I daresay most people would react the same as I did many years ago when I was told that I was merely a product of the system, a walking talking puppet molded and shaped by the current advertising and propaganda machine. I refused to believe it; I was insulted. I could not believe that anyone could be so stupid. Until I started to give some serious thought to the kind of information being churned out by the people who control our media and other channels of propaganda; our politicians, priests, ministers, Rabbi's and Imams. It took a long time. The more attention I gave, the more seriously I addressed the assertion, brought the slow recognition that it was true. I realized that I was not alone; there were many millions like me all dancing according to these puppeteer's strings. It takes a degree of serious thought, a willingness to see our own weakness and the determination not to be jerked around by these people; the power hungry theological, political, commercial - or any other - type of mind molding opportunist. This book is my attempt to open a door to recognition for all, in revealing a few of the numerous crimes being committed that, up to now, have been so well camouflaged by the perpetrators. (the puppeteer's).

Neither you, I, or the vast majority of people, would beat up, kill, maim or rob other individuals, because we know or can imagine the pain and suffering caused. Individual moral and ethical restraint is applied, because of a personal concern in being responsible for the outcome. This is our individual conscience. 'Don't do to others what you would not like done to you'.

However, when the decisions are made by a controlling group or a management team, any action performed is then on a quite different level, and a much larger scale. It is by a controlling management unit, usually a small select group of individuals. Decisions are made in the boardroom by the 'board of directors or in 'Cabinet' or 'The Oval Office', or the Church Synod, or by Papal, Jewish and Moslem religious leaders at arms length from the individuals that form the "whole." of the population of followers. The responsibility is therefore conveniently unloaded; from the individual part, to the management which has as its driving force, the maintenance, expansion and extension of wealth and/or power of the state, corporation or religious group. There need only be one, or a small number at a meeting, with little or no conscience, to sway a decision in favour of selfish greed or power, or the fundamentalist literal interpretation of a faith. So the latent conscience of the individual is submerged and disguised in the decisions of the commercial board, the political party-room or the religious synod.

Another perspective of this phenomenon, (to borrow a phrase from Krishnamurti): is that: "The whole cannot be understood through the part". Which means that the actual mass activity or actions of any given population or group *("The Collective Consciousness"),* cannot be understood by studying the thoughts, actions, beliefs or needs of single individuals in the wider population or group.

Consider any piece of machinery, appliance, or any composite article; take any small removable part of it, such as a knob, screw, gearwheel or gauge. Viewed in isolation it has its own particular functional qualities and identity. The "whole" has an altogether different identity of its own. Into which, the part is subsumed and so it is with humanity. We, as individuals, are the parts comprising the whole of 'Humanity' which has an identity of its own. Evidence of this is seen by mass behaviour at large social gatherings, political rallies, sporting events, rock star and celebrity appearances, civil protests etc. These display the corporate or mass mind. In my terminology, it is an example of *collective consciousness* being expressed subconsciously by the group. The primary cause of the present global mess is the agenda being imposed world-wide by powerful irresponsible, immoral, and unethical activities of fundamentalist religious zealots and corporate driven "Governments". As well as the mass manipulation by profit driven trans-national financial and commercial institutions. As mentioned previously, there are a small number of people controlling these organizations (the hierarchy), that prevent the rest of humanity from enjoying the benefits of peaceful co-existence. This situation has finally become a real and present danger to the survival of many forms of life on earth; including humankind. It is nature simply following the immutable law of *"Cause And Effect"* With the benefits of hindsight, technology, science, medicine and psychology that is widely available, we now have the knowledge, ability, human and natural resources whereby the whole of humanity could enjoy the abundant (indeed overabundant) fruits of these achievements. For this, there is a desperate need for empowered, inspired and ethically motivated numbers of people.

The collective consciousness of the vast mass of little people (humanity), is the reservoir from where all knowledge and means are drawn and it is humanity collectively, that should be the beneficiaries.

It is my hope that mass education is implemented with an inspirational system designed to awaken and empower the consciousness and the conscience of this and future generations.. We can educate the uneducated and project hope to the world's countless millions of displaced, downtrodden, homeless and the hungry victims of greed. This global condition is the **effect of causes** that can and must be modified or eliminated. We can ultimately produce a world with peace and justice for all people including those who are powerless to change the present situation.

The fact is that we collectively, have been conditioned to believe competition is the key to individual *"success."* Starting in our schools; competing for the best marks to obtain the best paying jobs to buy the best cars, homes and appliances available. We are conditioned to believe that individual wealth is success and is the "*key to happiness.*" It is this belief that has fuelled a collective greed. It has also allowed individual groups of unscrupulous people to monopolize the knowledge drawn from the collective reservoir, and use it for their exclusive benefit, at the expense of all others. This is not to say that communities in the so-called "Western democratic civilized world" have not been beneficiaries. We in Western societies have been minor beneficiaries in the technological and knowledge explosion that has taken place over the last 200 years. Observation and analysis shows, that only enough creature comforts are available to some; enough to encourage our striving for more, enough to ensure our compliance to the agenda of the major beneficiaries. In the meantime, by the use of modern weapons of mass persuasion, we are brainwashed into thinking that we should willingly enslave ourselves in the effort to become a major beneficiary. Little or no thought given to those who fall by the wayside; or the countless millions at whose expense this success is achieved.

(Dwight D. Eisenhower) In his first term as US President said:

"Every gun that is made, every warship launched, every rocket fired, signifies, in the final sense, a theft from those who are hungry and are not fed, those who are cold and not clothed."

With the lies, secrecy and general lack of transparency from Governments in most of the Western world, it is difficult to differentiate between political control, the influence of the CIA, the multi-national commercial corporations and their drive for global markets or the privately run reserve banks and the economic power of financial institutions such as the IMF and The World Bank. How do we determine just who these people are? Also to what degree do religious beliefs or ethical values influence their activities? Due to years of cultural conditioning by clever social engineers, it is almost impossible for us to perceive the position, purpose and power of the individual within the scheme of things. ***the importance of our being***.

Our position is comparable to that of a microbe, being manipulated on a microscope slide in a laboratory, trying to look back up through the lens and observe the manipulator … Impossible! For the overall picture to become clear, we must mentally extract ourselves from the position of the manipulated microbe and focus objectively on the manipulators of world affairs. Only then can we realize who the real victims are in this sad human arena. They are us, and as you are reading this book, you are only a minor victim. The major victims are the uneducated,

homeless, displaced, starving, persecuted and the exploited people, barely existing in unimaginably squalor and fearful conditions

CHAPTER 9

Our Present Environment

Let's start with an average family in Australia (is there such a one?) I daresay the same applies in most of the Western world. Say an ordinary family that seems to be enslaved by an economic system over which it has absolutely no control. In the Australian vernacular, the 'typical Aussie battler' to whom the economic reality is that both parents must work to support what is considered today to be a reasonable lifestyle. The children in such families are, in many cases, a burden and in other cases, an inconvenience. This is not to say that this applies in all families or that all parents are not loving and caring people. However the following, describes in general the ***downside*** of unfortunate conditions that prevail in most western societies today; undermining well-being, happiness and confidence in the future.

Christian, Jewish and Moslem religious groups and many secular charitable institutions have addressed the problem but up to the present, they have been unable to rectify the following conditions that prompt us to ask:

Why, Nationally, in Australia, and in most Western societies, ***so many young people:***

> commit or attempt to commit suicide each year?
> Rebel and drop out of our education system?
> form various ethnic predatory gangs?
> feel no responsibility to their community?

Turn to drugs, cigarettes and alcohol?

"seem not to care" … for themselves, others, their environment, or society.

In the 10 years from 1990 to 2000, more Australians committed suicide than all the Australian soldiers killed in the second world war and the Australian Bureau of Statistics report of 8th March 2005 shows, that in Australia today, the major cause of death of children between the ages of ten and fourteen, is suicide. Why is it that there is so much negative activity, so many victims sacrificed on the altar of worldwide religious fundamentalism, political corruption and corporate greed?

Globally, the United Nations Organization figures show:

824 million people –men women and children – dying from starvation,

630 million homeless, existing in inhumane conditions in refugee camps,

40 million H.I.V infected people living and dying before our eyes, and countless numbers living under the heel of this or that political tyrant.

How this inequality was created, maintained and exacerbated, is described very clearly in following chapters. Whether in the area of politics, business, religion, education, technology or whatever, the disregard for the worldwide human condition is entrenched in the policies of the *in-power* of the day. The determination to stay in power and the tunnel vision that created the present major banking system, funnels all the money into its own drainage, to enrich those who already own just about everything. While the rest of the world's populations are ignorant of the end game being played out among the powerful international manipulators.

Not the least of which are in the U.S.A and Israel; who have elevated wholesale murder, terror and brutality to an art form; with their sophisticated weaponry, using us, - as their brainwashed assassins - willingly obeying our master's orders to overcome *'their'* perceived enemies; while insulting our intelligence with the excuse "If we don't kill them first, they will kill us".

As a result, the world is now living in fear of – so called – "terrorists" that we, as compliant servants of our masters' agenda, have inadvertently produced. This is precisely the reason that Islam along with all other religions relying on violence, are doomed in the long term, to final self destruction. How in the name of anyone's God, can one deal out death and destruction on the one hand, and expect peace, love and respect in return? The more violence that is dealt out, the greater the numbers of vengeful and violent enemies are created to resist it. I would have thought this to be axiomatic.

Mahatma Gandhi simply stated: "It is my conviction that nothing enduring can be built on violence. The only safe way of overcoming an enemy is to make them a friend" If we continue the principal of an "eye for an eye and tooth for a tooth," the world will all end up blind and toothless. As time goes on, the violence is growing like a disease reaching pandemic proportions. It has now reached the stage in the Western world, where it is now well recognized that fear is being used as a vital tool by our own unscrupulous national, religious, political and commercial groups, as a means of controlling populations and consolidating their own positions of power. Not to say that this is new, but is emphasized when required. And as stated previously, the purpose of this book is to expose the various groups and explain particular activities in which they are involved. These activities amount to gross disregard for elementary moral or social human values. Activities that collectively, if not stopped will mean the end of the human and most other species of life on earth.

It is vitally important that these groups are recognized, and the results of their activities understood. In some cases I give only an "orienting generality" where there is ample and obvious supporting evidence and leave it to the reader's own knowledge, observations and experience to fill in the things that are left un-stated. In addition to my brief references, there are literally thousands of websites that open a Pandora's Box of information on these particular identified groups. Rather than increase this small book to encyclopaedic proportions, I include further support that verifies and expands on the subject matter by way of websites,(Using internet references that illuminate in great detail the massive deception perpetrated on the whole of the so-called "civilized western world") I urge you to check these sites, if only to verify authenticity.

For the problem to have grown to the extent that we are experiencing today, it's not only our young generation that is affected, it is the vast majority of us, the general adult population in the Western, and developing world. It has not just grown amongst us like weeds in a garden. In most cases, clever social engineering skills have been used to plant and carefully cultivate political and religious beliefs. These ideas and ideals, fashions, fads, trends and brands pervade every area of our lives. All these, in order to produce the particular self serving outcomes required by these various groups.

There is both bad news and good news. The lack of understanding of why these many problems exist and the knowledge of the main players that created and are perpetuating them, lies in the *"bad news"* area. *The "good news"* is that although there is no obvious cure for the symptoms, there is a preventive measure; that if followed, will, show where the solution lies, how it can be achieved and how it is possible to greatly minimize, if not totally eliminate the causes of the problems. Contrary to the rhetoric, the actions and the hollow promises of hope from our religious and political leaders (controllers), there is a beautiful alternative path. A rational and practical solution readily available and I would like to share this invaluable knowledge with you. To make it work, a profound change (a paradigm shift) in who or what we worship, the way we learn, work, own and love is necessary. It is vitally necessary that we believe that it is possible to produce people that can recognize and will be capable of challenging and modifying this false but deep seated value system.

This existing situation is the end product of powerful interests that have manufactured our present lifestyle and worldview. The foundations of which are built on the exclusivity of our various faith systems which in turn encourages greed, competition, accumulation of group and individual wealth and power. This world-view is at present enslaving humanity. The solution, and a path out of this condition, is revealed in (Education is the Key), a later chapter.

The corporate greed of multi-national corporations, aided by the political foreign policies of governments in the more advanced nations, continue to exploit the human and natural resources in struggling developing countries. This creates a huge gap in the wealth and conditions of life between various countries worldwide. It also severely inhibits local inhabitants in the under developed countries from achieving their full potential in all fields of human endeavour. The inevitable result is that the benefits of the explosion of human knowledge acquired over the past 200 years remain beyond their reach and as time goes on the gap between the haves and the have-nots widens. How is it possible to extricate them and ourselves from this condition? From whom, when or where can we expect to salvage peace and harmony on the earth from this total mess? It is certainly not by perpetuating the same old values and beliefs that produced this present condition in the first place. The key phrase as stated previously is: "Produce the generations of capable people" and not reduce our future populations to unthinking robots. Willingly believing in and adhering to the current value systems. These manufactured and manipulated thought patterns have been the cause of our present world situation. Our political and religious beliefs and ideas are mostly absorbed from immediate and extended family, the various media "misinformation" outlets and political spin. What we get is a distorted truth. In the theological sphere it is a mystical irrational mumbo-jumbo that defies intelligent reasoning, and in the secular sphere, a rationalized and sanitized version of both government and corporate criminal activities.

It looks on the surface, as though the vast majority of people feel content with what we have. Or feel so helpless in their inability to change the situation that they lose hope and just don't care.

It is this non- caring and non-thinking state; a state of apathy, ***'ignore-ance'*** and intellectual laziness, that allows, maintains and perpetuates the present social condition. ***A passive acceptance*** of:

1). The theological myths and legends described in the Torah, New Testament and Qur'an, (the dogma and authoritarian prescriptions) as God's truth.

2). Political party propaganda.

3). Corporate globalization and economic rationalism.

4). Finance, Banking and Credit. Systems. (the debt creators).

5). The Spin Doctors: The handmaiden of the preceding four; the various Media controllers—the anaesthetizing agents - the people who create the actual nuts and bolts and the structure responsible for the numbing and dumbing of society, the "Public Relations" experts. Using Weapons of mass persuasion; skilled in the field of plausible and palatable deception. These are the five main areas in our present social system where we have been completely diverted from elementary truths and been so unaware of the crimes committed against humanity, we have been hoodwinked into acceptance. This present outcome is a stunted and disfigured parody of a truly civilized world.

Is this ***non-thinking, non-caring***, compliant, apathetic society, the best kind of world that our collective consciousness can produce? -----I think not!

The people in control in the various areas referred to above, are constantly on the ready to defend that which they have acquired. By the use of a variety of strategies, the human spirit is effectively diverted and prevented from blossoming to full potential. And, as yet, there are too few people that even recognize that we have been hijacked. Too few, that recognize the divisive structures that have been built, let alone enough people to implement an effective strategy to overcome them. When and if there are sufficient numbers of active and enlightened people in a position to pose a threat to the bastions of manufactured faith, stolen wealth and usurped power, the same weapons that have been used throughout history are brought to bear. The only difference being that today the weapons are far more damaging, sophisticated and effective. The main and most effective are ***words***. Lies and propaganda are ***(weapons of mass deception)*** and diversionary red herrings, ***(weapons of mass persuasion).*** A good example of a red herring is the war on terror. This leads us further into the mire of national, international, ethnic and cultural separation and away from cooperation and unity.

In the end, if words fail, they are backed up by force; the State police or military might which so far, has largely been used, excused and justified by the extremely devious and clever use of ----(you guessed it,) more words[7]. Here area few examples of the most useful adjectives used by media manipulators to describe and demonize individuals or groups that are, or may become a threat, You will no doubt recognize terms such as: rabble-rouser, communist, terrorist, anarchist, anti-Semite, infidel, heretic, atheist, fascist, left-wing etc. And new inventions like "hardliner." Which, on an international scale, means being one of the "axis of evil" to describe any group of nations that persist in resisting the new world order policies that are being imposed by executive power of the USA administration.

---

[7] "The Tyranny of Words") Stuart Chase.

Whatever the label, you can be sure that the particular hierarchy and the media controlled by them will when required, do their job in such a way that a large number of any population will believe and fear that the particular demonized and vilified groups pose a dire and immediate threat. And also, that no civilized society could possibly survive while these *fanatical followers* of whatever *different religious, political, commerce or financial systems exist*. These allegations are made, not without ample evidence of the collective activities of all five groups of psychic-predators that have been and are today committing crimes against humanity, (that is, crimes against us) for purposes motivated largely by greed and in many cases, misguided religious fanatical zeal.

The following chapters are a collection of essays to illustrate that there is a much better life to be enjoyed by all humanity, than the pursuit of the *false goals and gods* that we have been led to believe are the be all and end all of our existence". And if we, *'trust and obey in this life, there's pie in the sky when we die'*.

CHAPTER 10

The purpose of life

The search for both truth and the purpose of life is a dynamic exercise in which every individual should be intellectually engaged to some degree in their lifetime. Also that if you think you have found it, you haven't. However, I think I have discovered half of the exercise *(the purpose);* which is that:

Life has been created and is still being developed by a process of evolution from a primary cause. It is irrelevant whether the cause is termed God, nature, creative energy or whatever. I do not assume to know how we got here; but only to describe the distinctly discernable direction of humanity as a whole that historically indicates a purpose of our collective intellect, in a direction towards the ultimate goal. Which is: To understand the truth that underlies all things.

Let's look at some facts: we exist; and we all have life for a period of time. We all possess similar powers – in slightly varying degrees - that set us apart and above all the primates and other life forms on earth. These powers are bestowed on us by the gift of life itself and are unified within our brains (our mind).

They are the powers of intellect: reasoning, cognition (perception), curiosity, discrimination, communication, mobility and memory. When we move in a direction that causes us discomfort, our brain directs us to change direction. In the process of trial and error; over time, if we use our brains, we remember to not do this or that because of the undesired consequences. Alternatively, we learn that to move in a certain direction will result in the fulfilment of a perceived need or desire; (discrimination). **We all have**; these powers, but we **do not all use them**. These are the tools we have collectively developed in order to work towards and finally achieve the ultimate goal.

The reason that humanity has not yet reached that point is shown throughout our recorded history. This shows that civilizations has been continuously hijacked and diverted by various groups of people. By far the most obvious group has been the ancient Egyptian priesthood. Who through their ability in the areas of mathematics and astronomy acquired enormous social power. They introduced various Gods as the source of these powers and attached various religious beliefs and superstitions to persuade an ignorant primitive people to pursue activities which were believed to be in their best interest. Activities that were, in reality, in the narrow self interest of the manipulators; in this case for the priesthood, and not the broader interest of the tribe or community, and humanity as a whole.

As an example of how easy it would have been to deceive and manipulate primitive tribes of fearful people, let's take the biblical story of Abraham. Whose father —we are told - was a maker of idols in Babylon. Abraham, if the biblical description of his life is true, was anything but a good person. If he was a mythical character personified, the Hebrew tribal leaders that colluded to create and perpetuate the myth were equally discreditable.

It was through this mythical story of Abraham that a large number of people in this particular geographical area believed that God spoke to him and assured him that he, and his people, were chosen by God, above and to the exclusion of all others. They would be victorious in battle, and his descendants would rule in all the land from the border of Egypt to the Euphrates River. (GEN:15/17). This belief has involved a large number of people for about 5000 years. in countless wars; still evidenced today. These stories have been handed down to the present in the form of the biggest confidence trick ever played on humanity by Judaism, Christianity and Islam. The foundation of these three groups is based on the belief in that God of Abraham.

Since the inception of each of these religions (that incidentally, claim that this God is a God of Love and compassion), the actions of each reflects mutual hatred, cruelty and killing between each of them. This stupid internecine rivalry has had the effect of diverting and impeding humanity's advance towards the true nature and purpose of our existence.

Throughout the history of humanity, many powerful groups and individuals have seized control over the destiny of millions of people; and similar control has continued up to today; though not exclusively in the name of God. Some groups use; economic rationalism, national sovereignty, cultural survival, commercial expansion or any number of spurious reasons. Weapons of mass deception that serve to persuade large numbers of believers, that it is in their best interest, to go and kill anyone else in the world that oppose to the agenda of the controlling group.

However, in spite of these apparent political, social, and religious constraints and diversions, progressive social and intellectual development is discernable. The advancement in science, medicine, communications, are bringing larger numbers of the worlds population to a greater social consciousness. I have faith in the ability of humanity, not only to survive the tyranny of those disruptive and diversionary groups of religious, political, and commercial predators, but also to eventually triumph over them, return to and maintain our true purpose. The alternative is: ***eventual total extinction;*** and how can we be sure that it is not too late?

America with George Bush at the helm and with a long culture of militarism, tricked the world into a state of perpetual global conflict and violence on an unprecedented scale. A supposedly Christian society that he and his commercial predators so thoroughly brainwashed, that they are blind to the fact that violence only perpetuates violence. The world is now in a state of war against our perceived enemy; "terrorists." The definition of which is left to our controllers. How loose will this definition become in desperate situations?

And who is the enemy? ***US!*** or, those of us that are frustrated and brainwashed to the degree that some have been driven - or manipulated by others – their religious leaders, to willingly sacrifice their lives to oppose the political and commercial machinations of the American agenda and any other group that threatens their belief system. This type of opposition has been around for a long time[8] . The Zionist terrorist groups organized by the Stern gang, the Irgun and Haganah in Israel, helped to hijack Palestine. It is well documented that the first and most effective modern civil, (as opposed to Government) terrorists in the Middle East, were the Zionists.

Which brings us back to the story of Abraham's God: To rely on this God to save that, which is being destroyed in his name, is an exercise in futility and stupidity on a grand a scale. This is the path to oblivion![8])

---

[8]   guardian.150m.com/palestine/jewish-terrorism.htm (Google

CHAPTER 11

The corruption of Christianity

Human history has allowed very few of the ancient religious beliefs to survive. Their demise was fuelled largely by the actions of political, religious and commercial leaders whose main concerns were the acquisition of territory, wealth, and above all power. Up to today these practices continue in the form of genocide, cultural extinction, racial intolerance that are the tools of established religious, political and commercial enterprises. In many cases all traces of a conquered society's religious books, cultural practices and even buildings were destroyed in the name of conversion from their belief in "false Gods". Previous religious customs would then become heresies. What generally resulted from a conquest was at best a dilution of the conquered people's religious beliefs, rituals and practices, or at worst, an almost total annihilation of the religious belief system making it all but unrecognisable.

Christianity falls into this category and was victim of the Roman Empire under the Emperor Constantine who blended the Mithraic institutionalised pagan belief and practices of the day, with the Judeo-Christian apostolic gospel stories. In so doing, he eliminates any semblance of both the Jewish religious influence and the infant Church of the "Followers of Jesus" being established by Peter and Paul. Constantine is best known for being the first Roman Emperor to accept Christianity, while continuing his pagan beliefs. Along with his co-Emperor Licinius, he was the first to grant Christianity the status of a legalized religion through the 313 CE Edict of Milan. Although he himself was not baptized until near death The Roman Empire was expanding rapidly. Each successive emperor was challenged with meeting the soaring costs of administration and financing the legions, both for national defence and to maintain loyalty. New schemes to revise the tax structure came and went throughout the Empire's history. Large inflation rates and depressed coinage values, by the reign of Diocletian, led to one of the more drastic changes in the system. In the late third century an additional levy (tax) was imposed on land owners after the land tax had been paid. This was a separate tax and ignored the fact that taxes had already been collected, together with special tolls on money traders and companies to help increase the state revenue.

In the 4th century CE., the Emperor Constantine saw the way to strengthen political control and consolidate Roman influence throughout the Empire. The opportunity was there for the taking and only requiring a clever and powerful ruler to implement it. The Jews in Jerusalem had rejected, disowned and executed a man that many people of the time accepted as the Messiah. The message preached by his followers was one of brotherhood, love, compassion and forgiveness, which was growing in popularity among the middle class Romans, Jews and Gentiles who were struggling under the yoke of Roman oppressive taxes at the time. Following Diocletian, Constantine compounded the tax burden by making the senatorial class hereditary. By so doing, all debts and economic problems were passed from one Roman senatorial generation to the next, ruining entire families and never allowing for an economic recovery that could benefit the entire community. This shifted the responsibility for paying the expected amount of tax, from communities and individuals, to the local senatorial class. The Senators would then be subject to complete ruin in the case of tax revenue shortfall in a particular region.

This was the economic climate in which Constantine saw the opportunity to establish political unity and also religious control.. (Whether at that time, he also realised that the enormous commercial advantages that would stem from this absolute power were unlimited, we don't know). However, his acceptance and deification of Jesus as the one and only true God, the organisation and the political installation of the Roman Catholic Christian Church, was a very shrewd move that brought enormous power and wealth to the controlling body. At first this controlling body was the state. The power of state lay in the hands of the Emperors but gradually, as the clergy became more powerful, and the head of the state organised Church (the Pope), assumed equal power.

Those who control the present, control the past.

The development of the canon and theology of the New Testament was ordered by Constantine and was done purely for political expediency in order to have only one set of accepted principles of belief throughout the whole of the Roman Empire. Up to that time, the various widely spread and differing areas both geographically and ethnically led to some conflicting ideas about the actual meanings of the gospels and letters ascribed to the various biblical authors. As a natural consequence there would have been a variance of views and beliefs held by adherents in the widely dispersed areas under Rome's control or influence. A very significant reason was the difficult task of translation. Also the fact that the original message received from Jesus was mainly couched in metaphorical language, in parable or subtle terminology, as such it was open to wide ranging interpretations. As a practicing believer in the old pagan gods, Constantine had no qualms in super-imposing a great many of the pagan rituals and practices into the new belief system. This lent itself to an accommodation between the then predominant pagan religious belief and the growing popularity of the followers of Jesus.

This was nothing more than a marriage for political convenience. Both sides contributed to give birth to a new belief system that, in its final presentation, was more pagan then Christian. As an example here are just a few of the pagan beliefs that were introduced:

The priesthood and sacramental ritual of Catholicism were taken directly from the Babylonian cults together with the worship of a virgin mother-goddess. The Persian sun-worship religion, Mithraism has been preserved in exact detail in the holidays and religious customs of the Roman Catholic adherents. Doctrines and philosophies of Greek Gnosticism taught by the church fathers and adopted by early Catholic councils are still alive today. The two sacred days of Mithra the Sun God, were 25th of December (as Jesus' birthday) and Sunday (substituted for the Sabbath) in accordance to Constantine's edict of 321 CE. The Catholic Cardinal Newman gives an extended list of things "of pagan origin" which the papacy brought into the church "in order to recommend the new religion to the heathen": "the use of temples, with these dedicated to particular saints and ornamented on occasions with branches of trees, incense, candles, holy water, holydays, processions, sacerdotal (holy) vestments, the wedding ring in marriage, sacred images and the ecclesiastical chant"; also the halo in religious art.

Regarding the very controversial issue of the actual **nature of Jesus**, [9] was he divine (as God), or human? It now becomes clear that whatever was decided upon then, is still taught today and is the result a decision made by mere mortals. Whose opinions varied according to their particular personal philosophy and was never unanimously agreed upon. Nevertheless, about the year 332 Constantine, wishing to promote, organize and control Christian worship in the growing number of churches in his capital city directed **Eusebius** to have fifty copies of his version and selection of sacred Scriptures made by practised scribes and written legibly on prepared parchment. Obviously, fifty magnificent copies must have exercised a great influence on future copies, which subsequently helped forward the process of arriving on agreed laws (canon/dogma). This was enforced by decree in order that all congregations conform to the one teaching. Theologians confine the word dogma to doctrines solemnly defined by the pope or by a general council. **A revealed truth** becomes a dogma even when proposed by the Church through her **ordinary magisterium** (official teaching) position. A dogma has a twofold relation to both **(a), a divine revelation** and **(b), the authoritative teaching** of the Church.

Constantine's Sacred Scripture, contain terminology used in the sense of decrees or edicts by the civil authority of the Roman Church. Many of the decrees and edicts were strongly contested during the early formative years of Christianity in the fourth century. For example: At the first ecumenical council in Nicosia, convened by Emperor Constantine in 325 CE., the vexing question of whether Jesus was man or God was argued and decided upon. Constantine officially proclaimed Jesus divine (God in the flesh). This decision was contested and subsequently revoked ten years later by synod approval.

Arianism[10], another Christian belief first introduced early in the 4th century by the Alexandrian presbyter Arius. He proposed that Jesus was not truly divine but a created being. The fundamental premise of Arius was the uniqueness of God who is alone self-existent and immutable. Therefore, the Son, who is not self-existent, cannot be

---

9   Religious perspectives on Jesus: (Wikipedia)
10   Arianism: The Columbia Encyclopedia, Sixth Edition. 2001-07

God. Arius was an ascetic moral leader of a Christian community in the area of Alexandria. He attracted a large following through his message integrating Neoplatonism which accented the absolute oneness of the divinity as the highest perfection, with a literal, rationalist approach to the New Testament texts. Jesus was then viewed by the Arians as the most perfect creature in the material world.

When Constantine died in 337, Constans became emperor in the West and Constantius II became emperor in the East. Constans was sympathetic to the orthodox Christians and Constantius II, to the Arians. At a council held at Antioch (341), an affirmation of faith that omitted the homousion clause (like the father) was issued. In 350 Constantius II became sole ruler of the empire, and under his leadership the Nicene party (Constantine Christians) was largely crushed. The extreme Arians then declared that the Son was anomoios (unlike) the Father. These Anomoeans succeeded in having their views endorsed at Sirmium in 357, but their extreme views were overcome by the moderates, who asserted that the Son was homoiousios (of similar substance) with the Father, and conservatives, who asserted that the Son was homoios (like) the Father. Constantius at first supported the Homoiousians but soon transferred his support to the Homoios view, led by Acacius. This view was approved in 360 at Constantinople, where all previous creeds were rejected, the term ousia ("substance" or "stuff") was repudiated, and a statement of faith was issued stating that the Son was like the Father who begot him thus presenting us with the trinity, *the Father, the Son, and the Holy Ghost.* Anyone that upheld the Arian belief was then considered to be a heretic under pain of death. Although in 311CE Constantine I adopted Christianity and modified it to suit acceptable Roman cultural conditions of that time, it did not become the official religion of the Roman Empire until 438 CE. with the Theodosian Code[11]. In February 380, in the reign of Theodosius I (379-395) he and Gratian published *the Codex.* The most famous edict, was that all their subjects profess the faith of the Bishops of Rome and Alexandria and the houses of worship of the heretics were not to be called churches. Christianity was made the official religion of the Empire and all other forms of worship and religions were declared illegal.

---

[11] Medieval Sourcebook on religion: The Codex. Theodosianus

During that era when the empire was becoming Christian, emperors sought a greater share of the wealth for themselves and for the imperial Church through the control of wills and testaments. The law had also always punished violation of the tombs that lined the roads outside the city walls. The code's increasingly severe penalties for doing so suggest that the problem was getting worse. People were looting tombs for building materials and were digging up the bones of Christian martyrs for relics. In 386 an imperial decree expressly prohibited the sale of these saints' relics. "Theodosius set fanatical mobs to bash down the pagan temples of the east and required all his subjects to believe the no less remarkable doctrine of the Trinity."

Long before the Christian era, numerous variations of the trinity existed, and they were found in a host of pagan religions and mythologies. As with so many other pre-Christian traditional customs and practices, the revival of this doctrine in Constantine and Theodosius' Christian era was inevitable. It was easier for followers to see **Christianity, their new religion**, in familiar terms. All who did not profess to believe in and abide by the new code were considered heretics and severely punished. These punishments included excommunication, confiscation of property and in the extreme, death by burning at the stake. The rationale given by the church fathers for this cruel and severe treatment is that the substitution of private judgment (thinking), for the ordinary magisterium *(official spin),* had in the past, resulted in the dissolving of all sects that allowed it. Only those sects that exhibit a certain consistent discipline in which, private judgment is strictly forbidden and the ordinary magisterium is followed, according to confessions and catechisms by a trained clergy, is safe from external corruption.

The Church of Rome in the 4th and 5th centuries, seduced all the emperors of the Roman Empire into its fold. By the year 800 Charlemagne was persuaded to kneel and be crowned by the Roman Pope. From that time on, the Holy Roman Church was allowed to assume responsibility and primacy over all mortal beings including Kings. In that act church and state although still separate entities, became united in purpose and together they set about killing off all other **pagan beliefs** and superstitions, together with the various other Christian sects, such as the Gnostics, who sought knowledge rather than faith. Books were burned by the hundreds, so that, by the 7th century, in all of Christendom, no library existed with over 600 volumes. These, being void of any new knowledge, dealt mostly on the lives of people elevated to sainthood by the Church. However available information cannot be stifled completely and thanks to the Moors and other searchers for truth and knowledge in the East, Europe slowly and reluctantly absorbed new ideas. Any ideas that remotely disagreed with the new dogma, canon laws and religious teachings were viciously opposed and the cruel and brutal treatment and execution of early scientists, philosophers and astronomers are legendary. By the 9th century the popes knew their Bible was wrong, but refused to admit it. They knew the Greeks were right - the earth was spherical - just like Aristarchus of Samos said in the 2nd century BCE. Those who knew were too intimidated to speak out until 1453. It was Copernicus who first openly claimed the earth revolved around the sun just as Aristarchus said 1600 years earlier. Copernicus died just before the Church could deal with him. Protestant leaders, like Martin Luther, joined the Catholic Church in condemning the man who tried to move the earth around the sun. For the Church, the earth remained flat and unmoving for another century. In 1576 Giordano Bruno, a Dominican monk left the order and became a philosopher. He was a free thinker, agreed with Copernicus' ideas and taught on subjects such as Neoplatonism, hermetical philosophy and pantheism. For his beliefs and the crime of advancing the notion that priests had no right to use violence in attempting to convert disbelievers, Bruno was convicted of heresy by his former church. The Catholic Church locked him up for seven years in prisons of the Office of the Inquisition in Venice and Rome, and searched Europe to destroy his writings. He was offered freedom, if he would recant, but chose death before dishonour and was burnt at the stake. At his judgement he ridiculed the bishops and priests who condemned him to death with the remark: *Perchance your fear in passing judgment on me is greater than mine in receiving it.* Much later, Galileo Galilei would accept the same offer after extreme persuasion.

Galileo Galilei showed little interest in astronomy, although beginning in 1595 he preferred the Copernican theory to the Aristotelian and Ptolemaic assumption that planets circle around the earth. Only the Copernican model supported Galileo's theory, which was based on motions of the earth. He also met with serious opposition from the Catholic Church, who admonished, summoned, condemned and also compelled him to renounce his theory. In October 1632, Galileo was found guilty of heresy by the tribunal of the Holy Office in Rome. They sent him to exile in Siena and finally in December 1633, was sentenced to house arrest to his villa in Arcetri where he died January 8, 1642. Not until October 1992, did the Pope proclaim, in veiled terms and with no clear admission of wrongdoing on the part of the Catholic Church, that mistakes were made in the 1633 conviction of Galileo Galilei for heresy. For the gory details of the papal and Spanish inquisitions, see footnote[12]. The church destroyed so much knowledge that it took Western civilization almost 1700 years to arrive where the pagan Greeks were 2,000 years earlier. Why is it that we know of Copernicus and Galileo who left the sun the centre of the universe, but not Giordano Bruno? He was reputedly the last of the world's great thinkers who saw the infinite.

In 1059 Pope Nicholas presided over a meeting of the Roman Catholic Church Hierarchy (Then still called The Church of Constantine,) decreed by Apostolic authority, that he who has been elected, shall as Pope, have authority to rule the Holy Roman Church and have, at his disposal, all its resources as we know the blessed Gregory to have done before his consecration. It was not until the Pact of mutual recognition between Italy and the Vatican, signed in the Lateran Palace Rome, in 1929, that the Vatican agreed to recognize the state of Italy, with Rome as its capital, in exchange for formal establishment of Roman Catholicism as the state religion of Italy, institution of religious instruction in the public schools, the banning of divorce, and recognition of papal sovereignty over Vatican City plus the complete independence of the pope. A second concordat in 1985 ended Catholicism's status as the state religion and discontinued compulsory religious education. The Vatican is above all the seat of the central government of the Roman Catholic Church. The civil government of Vatican City is run by a Lay Governor and a council, all appointed by and responsible to the pope. The law is canon law and the courts are part of the church judicial system. Because of the Church's

---

[12]   "The Inquisitions". A timeline for the Papal persecutions.

vast interests in civil as well as spiritual affairs, an elaborate bureaucracy has been developed over centuries.

Orthodox Christianity is a generalized reference to the Eastern traditions of Christianity, as opposed to the Western traditions (which descend through, or alongside, the Roman Catholic Church) or the Eastern Rite Catholic churches. Orthodox Christianity claims to be the original Christian church founded by Christ and the Apostles. It traces its lineage back to the early church through the process of Apostolic Succession. Orthodox distinctive differences include the Divine Liturgy, Mysteries or Sacraments, and an emphasis on the preservation of Tradition, which it holds to be Apostolic in nature. Orthodox Churches are also distinctive in that they are organized into self-governing jurisdictions, which submit to the authority of the State government. In general terms, there are three main branches of Orthodox Christianity: the Church of the East, Eastern Orthodoxy, and Oriental Orthodoxy. It is estimated that there are approximately 350 million Orthodox Christians in the world.

The Roman Catholic Church, most often called the Catholic Church, is the Christian Church in full communion with the Pope, who is currently Pope Benedict XVI. It traces its origins to the original, undivided Christian community founded by Jesus, with its traditions first established by the Twelve Apostles and maintained through unbroken Apostolic Succession. The Church is not only the largest Christian Church, but also the largest organized body of any world religion. According to the *Statistical Yearbook of the Church*, the Church's worldwide recorded membership at the end of 2004 was 1,098,366,000, or approximately 1 in 6 of the world's population. According to canon law, members are those who have been baptized in, or have been received into the Catholic Church.

Martin Luther and the Great Reformation:[13]

The 16th Century experienced a religious revolution that ended the supremacy of the pope and the Roman Catholic Church in the Western World. This resulted in the establishment of the protestant church movement. Altering medieval life and ushering in the modern era of history.

---

[13]   WWW: Reformation Martin Luther: (Google)

Like Jesus, about 1500 years before him, Martin Luther could see the increasing corrupting influences that pervaded the established Church of his day. However unlike Jesus, he was highly educated. He passed the baccalaureate entrance exam to Erfurt University to study law, where he also achieved his Master's degree in philosophy before entering the Augustinian Monastery in 1505. In 1509 he was sent to teach philosophy and dialectics at Wittenberg University. While there he also achieved his doctorate in theology in 1512 and continued there, lecturing on the Bible. In 1515 he was appointed district vicar and not only the official representative of the church in Saxony, but was also the Priest at the Wittenberg city church. When preaching in Wittenberg, he observed that the number of people coming to him for confessions dropped off dramatically. On enquiring, he found that they were going to adjacent towns to buy indulgences. (mainly the St. Peter's indulgence). This practice was being used in lieu of confession to buy their salvation and was completely repulsive to him. At that time, both the papal court, and their representative in the German Church were in financial difficulties and this was the period when the sale of indulgences climbed. This practice got so bad that some priests claimed that even the souls of the dead could be redeemed by the purchase of indulgence. There was even an instruction manual for promoting the sale of indulgences issued to the church's official indulgence traders.

Luther rose in protest and wrote the famous 95 theses in 1517, which condemned this. He also condemned, not only the sale of indulgences, but other blatant unchristian-like practices and omissions in the teachings of the Church of Rome. He distributed copies to some colleagues within the Church and was supported by many of the more liberal priests, bishops and princes of various principalities in Germany. However, the main body of the church, particularly the ones that waxed rich on the indulgence scam, totally rejected his ideas and promptly declared him a heretic. Luther was called to appear by order of the Imperial Diet of Worms. He arrived as part of a triumphal procession. The emperor and church officials expected him to recant his thesis. While at the Diet, Luther's books were placed on a table. He was then asked if they were his works and whether he wanted to recant any of the information. He requested time to think, and the next day he answered with the well-known speech: "Unless I am convicted by scripture and plain reason - I do not accept the authority of the popes and councils, for they have contradicted each other - my conscience is captive to the Word of God. I cannot and I will not recant anything for to go against conscience is neither right nor safe. God help me".

Since Luther the formation of what is now termed 'the Protestant Church' spread throughout Europe. In England where for reasons that were the subject of bitter political debate, King Henry the 8th decided to divorce, putting him at odds with the Roman church in England, He established the the breakaway Church of England. In Switzerland priests such as John Calvin, and Ulrich Zwingli also rejected the strict authority over their constituencies by the Pope and broke from the Roman Church. It is interesting to note that a more radical movement grew alongside the protestant reform movement initiated by Luther, including Anabaptists, Mennonites, and others. They were re-baptized and initiated into a Christian movement that drastically rejected Catholic religious practices.

The Reformation spread from Germany into Scandinavia and central Europe, but it hardly penetrated Russia and Eastern Europe, where the Orthodox Church prevailed. Southern Europe remained loyal to Rome. After a series of religious wars from the mid 16th to the mid 17th century, most Protestants,(except the radicals) and Catholics settled for the principle that the rulers of a region should determine the religion of that region or state. Late in the 18th century, with the separation of church and state, a principle that other Protestants came to hold, began to weaken the strong Protestant influence in Northwest Europe. In the latter part of the 18th century and throughout the 19th century up to the present time Protestant missionaries have spread the movement into most of the world.

The World's Major Religions.

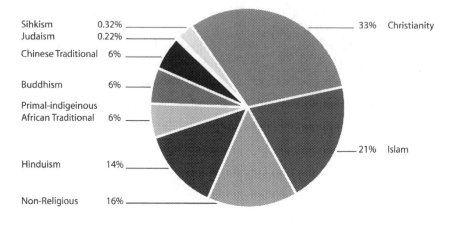

THE WORLD'S MAJOR RELIGIONS

Sihkism 0.32%	33% Christianity
Judaism 0.22%	
Chinese Traditional 6%	
Buddhism 6%	
Primal-indigeinous African Traditional 6%	
Hinduism 14%	21% Islam
Non-Religious 16%	

It can be seen from the chart that by far the majority of the worlds population (55 percent) are adherents to belief in the mythical Abrahmic God as portrayed in the Judeo-Christian-Muslim holy books. Whereas the combined alternative belief systems do not require that the rest of the world, on pain of death or hellfire, adhere to their belief, the three major ones do require the adherence of the rest, and have amply demonstrated that they believe that the laws of this God of Abraham must be obeyed. With various cruel and vicious sanctions (according to local customs) applied for disobedience. All of which sprang from the small number 0.22 of 1 percent of the current total of 6.6 billion people.

Until the rest of the world wakes up to the fact that this is the result of an obscene lie, *The Mother of all conspiracies,* the world will be locked into never ending conflict

CHAPTER 12

Virtue versus vice & nurture verses nature.

Let's face the ugly facts! We all have within us the capacity to express all and either of the two opposing forces virtue and vice. However, I think you will agree that the vast majority of people come out on the side of virtue as apposed to vice. Below are some of the things we feel and express when motivated by virtue or vice

VIRTUES	VICE
Love	Hate
Compassion	Indifference
Forgiveness	Revenge
Tolerance	Intolerance
Truthfulness	Lying
Patience	Impatience
Peace	Aggression
Humility	Arrogance
Faith	Apathy
Hope	Despair
Charity	Greed

End product

Happiness	Grief

Here we see some of them. The virtuous qualities that can enhance our lives and advance humanity and the vices that ruin our lives and threaten to destroy humanity. The present chaotic state of world affairs points to vice having the upper hand. Where, at the whim of powerful aggressive leaders, one button stands between us and oblivion. 1) How did this sorry state of affairs come about? And 2) what can you or I do about it?

In answer to the first question, how it came about is the result of blindly following the various leaders who have led us into this present state of global conflict. After having attained their position of power their agenda is always to consolidate and retain that power. Not only for themselves as individuals, but for the party or group they represent. Try to remember the many times that the actions, legislation and regulations implemented, seem to favour some small section of society over the common interest. The noble qualities of virtue are sacrificed on the altar of selfishness on the part of those in power.

We have been misled into putting our money on the wrong horse. If we continue along this crazy path, allowing these forces of corrupt power and aggression to lead us further into this man made quagmire of greed, mutual fear, separation and hate, there is little hope for good and virtue to prevail. We may protest that we do not blindly follow our leaders, but make informed decisions to support this or that political party or to believe in this or that religion. However, the big problem with this is, that most of the information we have access to and upon which we base our judgment, has been 'misinformation' (social engineering), consciously applied by those groups of people for their own self serving agenda. and unconsciously absorbed from our particular cultural environment.

Examples of the conscious social engineering experienced daily:

The *commercial predators* that prey on the young and vulnerable (particularly our immature youth) with advertising misinformation offering them credit based affluence while luring them into a lifetime of debt (and dependency). The advertisements on the box aimed at young children for this or that rubbish that does them more harm than good. *Unconscious misinformation*: is that, which we absorb through our family by our accident of birth and the culture in which we have grown. Nationalities, ethnic groups or coloured, take your pick; all different and all foster a self impression that they are superior. Small children at play don't have any enemies, that idea comes from their family, or religious, political, and national leaders. Now is the time, in the name of truth, justice and humanity, for society as a whole to realize that we can and should do something to reverse this sad and stupid state of human affairs. Do something to modify the system.

This brings us to the second question. What can we do about it? The answer lies in our willingness to become aware and our courage to question. For example, rather than believe what I have written here, it is much better for you to observe for yourself and for you personally to recognize how we are being duped and manipulated, on a daily basis by comparatively small but extremely powerful groups of greedy self-serving people. To guide your observation, please look critically at our so called education system and the virtues and vices it seems powerless to address. Look at the list of vices and see if you recognize some of them in the end product of the present primary and secondary education system? In her book Spirit Whisperers, (Chick Moorman) develops the theme of teaching to the spirit of the child. She presents various ways and means in the classroom that encourage the virtuous moral and social values of patience, humility, forgiveness truthfulness and tolerance. What we see today, is not the sum total of a completed education. The lack of emphasis on moral and social values, (none in many cases) is reflected in the behaviour of a large and growing proportion of our school leaver's. This alone, should be enough to stir us into action. And remember, it was not so long ago when children were taught (and believed), that *monarchs ruled by divine right*. We now know better!

If that is not bad enough, the leaders of our various religions and their fundamentalist followers, seem incapable of seeing or hearing the needs of the millions of both the faithful and the ignorant to deliver them from the present day evils. They are too busy defending *their* particular *concept of god* to actually see the effect that this tunnel vision is having on the wellbeing of the collective whole. By failing to challenge evil, aggressively and head on, they, and we, condone it and allow it to develop and flourish. Look at the list of vices. The three mainstream religions score seven out of ten. They are intolerance, greed, arrogance, aggression, lying and anger. You may be forgiven for asking what action can we take that will produce one virtuous person; let alone a virtuous society? The only answer is, to grow them, cultivate the process as much as possible and eliminate the weeds of vice from contaminating an otherwise healthy product. The next question that comes to mind is: How on earth is it possible, in today's political, commercial and fundamentalist religious environment? The answer is: with difficulty! The method is very simple, but the implementation is so very, very hard.

All humanity shares a common strand, a shared consciousness in the need for the collective common good. How can this consciousness, be transformed into a vision of hope in the future? We are experiencing the consequences of our past and present actions. Now is the time for transcendence. Cut the umbilicus cord of dependency on ancient theologies and prepare to blossom into a bright future. We have the knowledge, we have the tools, Just a quick glance at past and present must leave us with the conviction of the *need for change*.

How is it possible to fulfil the need? This question has been the subject of my endeavours over many years, and it was not until I became familiar with a truly amazing educational system - described in a later chapter - that is now operating and is gaining popularity around the world. This educational system follows a philosophy of natural sensitive periods of learning from birth to maturity. It is a technique that is designed to promote critical thought, independent action, self control and the value in virtue. It also contains the key elements of teaching to the spirit as all teachers are in effect, potential spirit whisperers[14].

The technique offers release from our present cultural conditioning, and release from our own ill-conceived political and religious beliefs. Once we are released from the shackles of cultural conditioning, we become free to use serious, coherent and analytical thought, encouraged to question and helped to recognise dishonesty behind any situation throughout life. If you are interested and want to know more of an education system that truly liberates our minds, I would urge and advise you most sincerely to investigate this remarkable educational system discovered and developed by Maria Montessori. The greatest gift that any parent can give their child, is intellectual freedom with an understanding of the value of virtuous behaviour in a non-sectarian and non-cultural secular context. With the type of education that stimulates

---

[14]   Spirit Whisperers: Chick Moorman

and fulfils their need to learn; the sad fact is that most individuals have never been taught the necessity, the art, or method of critical thought.

In an environment where millions of people are disinterested or incapable of analysis and rational thinking, we are all to ready to accept plausible leaders. Unfortunately, power accompanies leadership and more unfortunately, power can ultimately corrupt. Sadly, this is where we are today, and the effects are world-wide. The people who can and do think for themselves have no need for others to think for them and will be less likely to fall victim to corrupt and self-serving groups of people. The correct type of education will swell their ranks.

Nurture Versus Nature:

This is closely related to vice and virtue. In both cases, there is a distinct variation of behaviour as result of intervention (nurture). The development of any individual is greatly influenced by the type of nurture received. In the development of humanity, history has shown that, when left to our natural urges and impulses (instinct), we display every sign of our pre-historic ancestor's animalistic behaviour through our national, tribal and social group or individual approach to survival (self preservation). It could not have been otherwise, as our reactions are impulse driven; ***an instinctive compulsion*** rather than reason. ***(thought provoked action).***

The two most important of our animal instincts are "self preservation and propagation of the specie". Without these we would not have survived the rigours or the predators of our early environment. Because of these and other instinctive behaviours, patterns of behaviour developed over many thousands of years by the process of natural selection. (Evolution)

However, we as a specie, have reached a point in our development, where rational thought is vitally necessary in order to understand the role that humanity plays in this panorama of universal evolution unfolding before our eyes. We have not only survived, but conquered the ravages of predation from other species and the environment so successfully, that humanity is now at the top of the pyramid of known universal life forms. We control the destiny of all life forms on our planet as well as exercising some control over the environment. For this reason, rational thought must be, and is indeed, now being applied by a few enlightened people. It must be applied by many more if we are to avoid self-destruction. Our unsustainable treatment of available natural resources and the development and widespread use of many toxic materials, threatens our very existence. I have the utmost faith and confidence that we collectively have the means and the ability to produce solutions to these confronting environmental and social problems that we have created.

However, there is a far greater threat to our well-being and even our survival than these. We are facing the threat of widespread social ignorance and apathy. This situation has been produced over many years by a process of (social engineering) and manipulation by politicians, religious fundamentalists and commercial opportunists. We should no longer rely on our animal instincts for survival. *They are the tools of past ages of growth and are now a distinct liability and an impediment to further growth.* The tool of today is critical thought. The only solution to the problem we are now facing is the application of focused rational thinking. With our collective knowledge, if focused on today's human dilemma, we have the ability to produce heaven on earth for the whole, instead of just the very few. Even the very few that are the present beneficiaries of the earth's wealth, power and property, live in constant fear of the security of their position. How can the ignorant or the apathetic focus on anything, let alone the solution to worldwide perpetual conflict? The ignorant don't know and the apathetic couldn't care less. So where can we start to bring about a change of social consciousness? This is where the need for nurture becomes glaringly apparent.

Authority is a product of human organization. Organizations are established to achieve a collective goal more efficiently than by individual action. People who work in organizations enjoy the security they provide. They don't like change and praise the leader who brings security. The leader then thinks he has the right answer for everything. The organization then becomes bureaucratic and rigid. Eventually, in the need to protect and insulate itself, the organization like the individual, lapses into vice; greed being the first and foremost. This problem is produced by our present style of government. Although governments try to control and regulate against corrupt or dishonest operators, they are no match for unscrupulous operators. A style of government must be developed or invented that reflects in a positive and transparent manner, the goals and aspirations of society as a whole (the common good). Not only on a national, economic, political or cultural grounds, but must be globally and holistically based. There is a need for a New United Nations as a body that is committed to the welfare of humanity as a whole and not only to the most powerful nations. (a UN or a world government.) There is very little hope for this in the short term. We must plan to produce future generations of people equipped to develop a more equitable integrated and international society. In every living form the whole plan for the resulting progeny is contained in the seed. When the ground is fertile and cultivated, the seed will flourish naturally absorbing the nourishment from its environment. The resultant fruit reflects the degree of nurture provided. And so it is with human growth. The infant and young child is but a reflection of the environmental conditions in which it grows. When it comes to nurturing and nourishing our children's minds, we don't seriously consider the value or integrity of the intellectual ingredients with which we feed them. It is high time to take stock of real and basic values. To question the **real truth** behind the ideas and ideals which we pass on to children and through to future generations How many of us seriously question or look for a hidden agenda behind the religious, political and commercial cultural conditioning, we have absorbed. Reflect on the validity of the ideas that we teach our children! We are at the stage, where after 5,000 years and over 200 generations, we are still acting worse than animals towards each other. We have very strong grounds to totally reject the foundations of the various religious systems that have proved, with ample historical and contemporary evidence, to be extremely heavy, dangerous and lopsided. It has become a liability to hundreds of millions of us instead of an asset to all. But what do we do, continue to feed our young the same recipe; in other words, garbage in, garbage out?

Think, If we continue, how can there possibly be change for the better? The condition of humanity worldwide will only get worse. We must reject that which has caused so much havoc in world affairs since its inception and *adopt a system that works for us* not against us.

CHAPTER 13

Creation God and Man

Since the time our ancient ancestors evolved enough to sit around their evening camp fires and ponder the vastness of the stars above them, the rhythm of the seasons, life and death, themselves, the other animals and plants around them, humankind has been struggling to come to terms with its existence. Although humans are beginning to understand their tremendous potential they also realized that there is so much that remains a mystery to them. The more they learn the more 'horizon' become visible and what is over that horizon, they have always speculated about. Since they are oblivious to what they don't know, they have attributed all that is outside of their sphere of total understanding to some power greater than themselves. And of course it's only natural and right to do that because the power of the universe that we grew to call the vastness of space and the forces of nature were infinitely larger and more powerful than their comprehension.

Earlier humans, even some today, attribute different phenomena to different deities or gods and hoped it would be beneficial to show obeisance to the apparent power of some god, just as they would to a more powerful human. Being a tribal animal, we have the need to follow a leader like a chief, a king or sooth-seer and at times many simultaneously. Overriding earthly leaders, incomprehensible natural events occurred. This created the idea that there was an invisible power or powers outside and stronger than themselves that even earthly leaders, defy at their peril. This was the first glimmer of recognition of the laws of nature. Idols, representing the source of whatever natural phenomenon they favoured or feared, were fashioned as a means by which, in their ignorance our ancestors hoped to influence or appease.

Over thousands of years, one style of religious belief evolved in the Middle East from this idol worship; that which we call Judaism today. This occurred about 5000 years ago and was practiced differently by different tribes influenced by their political, spiritual or tribal leaders of the time. From the tribes (of Israel) that followed the Judaic faith, Christianity developed two thousand years ago and evolved into the various sects and denominations that we see today. About six hundred years later a similar religion to the then practiced Judaism and Christianity, was started by the prophet Mohammed and now known as Islam.

All three believe and pray to the same one and only all powerful God.. Instead of this fact being a leveller for the three groups, it is a matter of huge political dissent and bitter conflict, now being played out on a global scale. We have these three groups of political and spiritual leaders today, manipulating and influencing even larger numbers of people in exactly the same way; committing the same barbarism, atrocities and crimes against one another. The only difference is, now, with the astronomical advancement of science and technology, we have much more efficient ways to kill, maim and destroy. With today's expanded knowledge and intellect, it is crucial that we apply objective critical thought to **where** we came from, **what** we are doing and **how** did we get into this state of chaos.

In the hope of introducing some sanity into the existing human condition, it has become vitally important to recognize the methods used and consequences of the manipulation practiced by our political and religious leaders today. It is even more important, to know there is a way out of this condition that leads to peace and harmony with each other and nature. By comparison, the question of whether life on earth was created or evolved becomes irrelevant.

Creation:
Scientific and cosmological research has shown that the primary source of all existing matter and/or energy from the atom, to the universe and beyond. The Big Bang or whatever else we call the event or series of

events, is on a completely different scale and a totally separate sphere of activity to the life forms that evolved on this particular speck of matter in the unimaginable vastness of space many billions of years later. Life on earth is simply a by product of these events and only related to it by the co-incidental environmental changes over that time span. This created the conditions that produced and supported life about 3.5 billion years ago, allowing a simple protein-like one celled bacterial organism to form and evolve. This slow process of development has resulted in the multitude of life forms and species that we see today with mankind being the most intellectually advanced in this continuing evolution.

Our universe and countless others yet to be discovered, are all subject to unpredictable random actions by some of its parts. Such as:

1). The existence of thousands of meteorites and asteroids that create a distinct possibility of instant extinction of human, if not ALL life on Earth.
2). Solar storms, eruptions on the surface of our Sun, the effects of which we are only now beginning to understand.
3). Volcanic activity beyond human control.
Some of these actions follow observable patterns that are a part of what we term the LAWS OF NATURE; with which scientists are involved in the continuing process of discovery and understanding.

God:

Humanity's biggest mistake was to attribute that first event of creation to a God and assuming that this God has an on going concern For the day to day activities of all individual humans, plus the infinite number of other life forms. This was excusable considering our prehistoric ignorance. What is not excusable but understandable, given what we have learned of human nature, is the exploitation of that ignorance by the few for their own purposes. However none of this relates to the primary cause event which we are led to believe by our three mainstream religious leaders, is the creation of everything by the God of Abraham and that this God has the emotional psyche' of humanity; with the love, hate, greed, ambition, revenge and all the other human feelings and failings. In other words *(**man has made god in hisown image**)*. The Jews, Christians and Moslems have come to believe and accept that an unknown invisible force, exclusively partial only to *their* true believers, operates in a similar fashion to the mind of man about 5,000yrs ago, namely, God.

In view of our accumulated scientific knowledge of nature, life and the universe today, ***this concept borders on insanity.*** We will explore minutely that which is the proclaimed origin of this present Judaic, Christian and Islamic religious belief?

Man:

Let's first deal with Christianity: It began in the form of a reformation and revolutionary movement led by a Jew named Jesus, against the hierarchy of the established Judaic religion. The main reason behind the movement was that, the unacceptable and exclusive nature of this belief system, did not and could never bring about the type of world that would benefit the whole of humankind.

Jesus recognized this and tried to reform the obvious hypocrisy and greed practiced by the system's so-called believers. For that, he was executed by the Roman political machine, at the behest of the Jewish religious manipulators. He posed a threat to both and was eliminated in the cruel manner used by the Romans of that period.   Records were compiled from the various books, of the Torah, the Talmud and Christian Gospels under the direction of the Roman Emperor Constantine some 300 years after Jesus died. These are the books that comprise today's Christian Bible and were originally written by men who were concerned for the welfare and moral standards of their fellow man. The Ten Commandments are an example of their concern and wisdom. Also the teachings of compassion, love and forgiveness taught by Jesus as portrayed in the books of the New Testament. Here I must emphasize the teachings of Jesus and not all the parts that were added by over zealous followers, anxious to impress gullible and superstitious people to create the impression that Jesus was God.

Who led us up this false path in the first place? Intentionally or unknowingly the small group of leaders of the tribes of the ancient Hebrews collaborated to harness a weapon to end all weapons; the collective human spirit. This was done by the use of Abraham and his encounter with God and fostered through their self generated anecdotal history, stories, rituals and practices effectively binding them together as one. The character of Abraham was given all the strength and frailties attached to any normal individual of the times and to whom everyone could relate. The promises that God made to Abraham also applied to them would be the birthright of their future generations. The recognition of the strength of their **collective spirit**, their unity of purpose, very quickly became obvious in their victories over their neighbouring tribes

The story of Abraham, the father of Judaism, was referred to briefly in chapter five. The following serves to further explain the nature of the origin of this mythical story. The elaborate life history is woven into the plot in order to give Abraham some semblance of credibility. The allegation is that the God of his imagination spoke to him and entered into a verbal contract with him. (Gen.12: 2-3).which eventually led to him and his progeny being given all the land between Egypt and the Euphrates River. The only condition required of Abraham to seal this covenant with God, was to perform a particular pagan sacrificial rite (Gen.15: 7-20.). When any individual or group makes a claim as important as this is it not appropriate to consider that there may be a chance it could be false? Then again it may be the truth. The normal procedure is to look at the background, the known history of the person or people in order to assess their character so that we have a reasonable idea if it is the truth.

As the story goes, Abraham was born in Ur a city of the Chaldeans in Babylonia and his father was a maker and vendor of the various idols that were worshiped in those times. So it was not strange for him to invent a God. The story line is that his family left Ur and settled in Haran. Abraham and Lot left Haran and finally came to Canaan where he claims that he again spoke with this particular God.

They were a nomadic people and as there was a famine in Canaan, they wandered down towards Egypt. In those days, it was not safe for a small group to travel. They were approaching Egypt, and because his wife Sarah was so beautiful, he became fearful that Egyptians would kill him and take her. He told her to say that she was his sister. Her beauty was brought to the notice of pharaoh who took her. (Gen.12: 14-16.) And Abraham got very rich from the arrangement.

Pharaoh eventually found out and kicked them out of Egypt together with Abraham's ill-gotten gains. After returning to Canaan his nephew Lot was captured in a war between kings in the area. Abraham took 318 trained men from his household and went to his rescue, defeating his captors and capturing a great deal of goods and people. Then Melchizedek the King of Salem, who was the high priest of ***his Most High God***, blessed Abraham. For which, Abraham gave him a tenth of the loot. GEN.14:18.

By this time Sarah had not born Abraham an heir, so he slept with one of his slave girls (Hagar) with the intention of producing an heir. She became pregnant and gave birth to Ishmael. After a short time they kicked out both her and her son Ishmael. Gen.21:8. Ishmael is the biblical character upon whom the Moslem religion was founded. This is the brief outline of the man's character. He was a liar, a thief a pimp, and an adulterer. I believe the Abraham story is a myth. The tribal leaders who perpetuated it are to blame for the claim to all the land that belonged to the Canaanites, Kenites, kenizzites, Kadmonites, Hittites, Perizzites, Rephaitites, Amorites, Canaanites, Gireshites, and the Jebusites, Midianites, Edomites and the Philistines. This includes in fact, most of the known world in those days. The Jewish tribes were aggressors that conquered, raped, pillaged and plundered their neighbours in the name of their god.

Moses, the mythical hero of the exodus story, was recorded as being a murderer and a liar. The Israelite slaves were thieves Ex. 12: 35-36. They stole gold from their Egyptian masters. (Where else would slaves get gold enough for the golden calf). And what does their Bible tell us of the early activities of Abraham's people and their God? In Ps.137:7-9 God suggested that the children of the Edomites have their heads dashed against the rocks for what the Edomites had done to the Jews. Their God told Moses to take vengeance on the Midianites. Num. 31:1. His army obeyed and slew every adult male, spared the women and children and completely destroyed their cities and took all their cattle flocks and goods.Num.31:7. Moses was angry that they had spared the women and children, and he ordered all the male children be killed and told the Israelite men that they should take the virgins for themselves and kill the rest. Num. 2: 28. Prior to this, when the tribes of the exodus story were still wandering in the wilderness, Moses came down from the mountain with God's Ten Commandments and found some of his flock worshiping a golden calf. While the chisel marks on the tablet with the commandment "thou shall not kill" would have been still hot on the stone, Moses and Aaron were instrumental in killing 3000 of their own people on the spot. Ex. 32: 25. These are only a few of the many barbaric atrocities recorded in the bible, committed either at the request of, or in the name of God. What a lovely God!!? That God I could not respect, let alone worship. This is the legacy that Abraham and/or the tribal leaders of Israel gave to the world. How long will it take for the rest of the world to wake up?

In previous chapters, I referred to a path to peace and harmony. This path is the enlightenment of the general populations of all nations, to the realization of the weight of baggage (or garbage) that has been thrust upon us. Until and unless this awakening process is made widely available and jealously protected throughout civilized society, humankind remains condemned to the never-ending cycle of social conflict and mutually destructive warfare in which we have been involved over the last 5000 years.

President Bush and the Israeli Zionists escalated this to the point of perpetual global conflict using fear and terror in the attempt to gain ultimate worldwide social subservience. Ask yourself, subservience to what? Today's American way of life?

At the birth of American independence there were great philosophers, statesmen and ethical social leaders with foresight and integrity. Abraham Lincoln George Washington, Thomas Jefferson, Benjamin Franklin and the like, were the midwives that brought forth the healthy infant society and nurtured the young American dream. However history has overseen its gradual dilution, pollution and finally the total corruption of their grand dreams to the extent that it is now in the order of a nightmare!

CHAPTER 14

The way the truth and the life.
Transition, Enlightenment and Transcendence.

Through different stages of development, humankind has advanced from the primitive stone-age tribes of hunter-gatherers, through to the industrial age of machinery and mass production, up to the present. We are now at the stage of science and technology: explorers of biotechnology, astro-physics and space travel. (our micro and macro environment). Our knowledge, intellect and intelligence have grown to the stage where we are now making life saving body parts in scientific laboratories. We are designing babies at conception to be healthier and better equipped to handle the environment by Genetic engineering.

Intellectual Evolution:

From our present position with the advantage of expanded knowledge, consider these simple sequential progressive steps. Each stage of advanced knowledge is a step – a platform upon which we work - to progress to the next step. This present stage could not have been reached had it not been for the knowledge, intellect and inventions of the builders of the last step. So it continues, the dynamic expansion of humanity's knowledge, consciousness and awareness and achievement. It could not be otherwise. Our continuous search to discover the true nature of all things is inevitable. To stretch our horizons to the limits of time - past and future - to understand the universe, our environment, and to recognize the contributions - both positive and negative - by our ancestors; and their relevance to the advancing parade of mankind's intellectual evolution.

It is from this present platform, with today's intellect and using today's tools that we look at the actions and stories from our early ancestors and their theology - their concept of God, their world view - as portrayed in the Judaic Talmud, the Torah, the Christian bible and the Moslem Qur'an. Compare these to the totally different view that is presented by secular historical and scientific evidence. These three religions agree on the Judaic version of creation and the creator and is the foundation stone on which they are based. This is a belief that has far exceeded its "use by date".

The totally unacceptable immoralities, naked aggression, cruelty and greed for territory and power by the early Hebrew tribes, said to be done either at the behest of, or in the name of *god*. In addition, the information handed down in the Old Testament, is for the most part, patently self serving embellishment of the antiquated folk-lore of a primitive people.

We are asked to believe this because it's in the bible; and if we do, in the light of today's knowledge in the fields of history, physics, archaeology, anthropology, geology, astro-physics, biology, pharmaceutics and genetics, we would be no better intellectually, than our ancient and primitive ancestors in their understandable total ignorance of the elementary laws of nature. Not to mention the basic laws of science and physics.

With these tools at our disposal, and today's collective intellect and equipment, this obsolete religion and its primitive and restricted view of the environment, its tribal and socially exclusive community code of conduct, together with all the early books of the Hebrews, should be consigned to humanity's cultural scrap heap. Those who persist in promulgating and maintaining this obsolete system should be condemned for the perpetuating the crime against humanity. The one exception to this may be *"the 10 commandments"* which stand alone in glaring contrast to the behaviour of growing numbers of people in our Western (so-called) "civilised" societies today. Until now the 'fundamental' belief of the Jewish people and the State of Israel is: That they are God's chosen ones and that Abraham's covenant is still valid and entitles them to what they refer to as the land of "greater

Israel". This includes all the land from Egypt to the Euphrates River. Land in which they plundered, slaughtered and dispossessed from the local indigenous inhabitants in the name of Abraham's God.

Out of this morass of violence, deception, hypocrisy, and greed, arose Jesus. He alone had the courage to dissent to the abhorrent practices of the temple hierarchy. Jesus gave us a vision of a different path. The path to enlightenment and transition to a higher state of awareness. And finally *transcendence* to a higher state of consciousness. The ultimate understanding to be *all as one.*

CHAPTER 15

Paul's revelation

The apostle Paul was a very remarkable man. In his letters, he described himself in 1 Cor. 15:9 and again in Galatians 1: 13, as a persistent persecutor of the early Christian church; the Followers of Jesus; as they were called at that time. The early Church consisted of mostly Jewish or Jewish proselytes who he persecuted until he experienced a life changing revelation. This event caused him to understand the message that Jesus both lived and preached. From that moment until his death, Paul became the most energetic, articulate and dedicated champion of the church in its infancy. It was the life and teachings of Jesus that showed Paul in many very practical ways, that whatever God is, is to be as a servant of mankind; not the reverse as it was taught in the Hebrew Torah (of which he was a scholar) and still taught today in Jewish Temples, Christian Churches and Islamic Mosques. Congregations are urged to serve, worship and fear the God of their particular religious belief.

The lesson of Jesus' life and death was very symbolic and this message was well understood by Paul. Apparently - an epiphany - as we are led to believe, on the road to Damascus. It doesn't really matter how when or where he was enlightened, but it effected him to the degree that he understood Jesus' message and as an educated man was capable of giving very important, descriptive and illustrative messages to the Corinthians and others, in the light of it. According to the scant historical records we have, Jesus was raised in a normal, simple and not highly educated

Jewish family. He came to recognize the, blatant commercialism of usury. The injustice, cruelty and brutality of exclusivity that was being taught encouraged and practiced by the religion of his forefathers in the name of their God. The religion was very strict in the belief that only the Jewish descendants of Abraham were the beneficiaries of any advantages gained in the name of their God to the exclusion of all others. To Jesus, this concept would have been seen to be abhorrent and unfair to the rest of humanity. He was determined to change the system so as to include all of humankind. He went about preaching, with the few followers he could muster, teaching and including all outsiders to follow a different belief system to the traditional Jewish teachings of the day. He taught compassion, love and forgiveness. It was a very simple and effective path to universal peace and brotherhood.

Paul was so impressed with the message that Jesus lived and died for that he travelled far and wide preaching and writing many letters of support and encouragement to various congregations of the early church. Among these is this very descriptive and definitive meaning of love in his letter COR. Ch:13. v 4-7. Love is patient and kind; it is not jealous conceited or proud; love is not ill-mannered selfish or irritable; love does not keep a record of wrongs; love is not happy with evil, but is happy with truth. Love never gives up; and its hope, faith, and patience never fail.

This message is even more necessary today - in the light of the injustice, cruelty and brutality still occurring throughout the world - as it was in Jesus' day. Put simply, It suddenly dawned on Paul that Jesus' message was for *all humankind* and based on: *love, compassion and forgiveness from all and for all;* the *whole* of mankind. The benefits that are derived from the actions and activities of each and any should be to the benefit all and the disadvantage of none.

To follow any other way is to sin against your fellow man. Rather than recant this belief, Jesus died on the cross. Why did he die? To save us? Do you consider you are saved? Do you act any different, if you are not saved? Jesus did not die to save the individual, but to save humanity as a whole. Humanity will not be saved until individuals act to change any establishment that advocates and perpetuates selfish greed for wealth, power, territory and resources. It was that type of aggressive behaviour that earlier tribes of Israel, inflicted on their neighbours and also the Roman armies inflicted in Jesus' day.

Similar establishments exist today but are much more sophisticated and efficient. They divert the gifts that Paul mentions in CH13: v9; gifts of technology, biology, agriculture and science that have arisen from the body of humanity. They are used for the primary benefit of the few newly developed powerful organizations, financial and commercial corporations, national political controllers and misguided religious leaders. They hand out to the rest of humanity only sufficient benefits to keep them subservient to the agendas of the various leaders or groups. (The details of these groups and people are detailed in later chapters.) It is incumbent on all, (like Paul), who believe and understand the importance of Jesus' message to counter this exploitation and form an organization of ethical, rational thinking people with the necessary administrative skills and the determination to reform our theology and the society at large. If after 2000 years, *the church* has failed in its efforts to convince the majority of humanity, then it is badly in need of reform. It has not yet learnt the secret. "Go where angels fear to tread." into the world of brains and rational thought and **secularity.** *Not theology*; the world of blind faith, mysticism and myth;

I believe that in Paul's first message to the Corinthians, whose metaphorical language is so plain when he speaks of spiritual gifts in Corinthians 1 CH 12: V12-31. When he refers to "the body", he is implying the whole of the body of Christ (humanity). Though it is made up of many parts, (individuals), they form one body (the whole). If we understand Jesus' teachings, we are all of the same spirit and are as one. The rest of the passage is clear and speaks for itself. Following, in Ch.13 is the most beautiful and descriptive chapter in the Bible. Especially verses 8 -12. "Where there are prophesies they will cease; tongues will be stilled; present knowledge will pass for what we know now is incomplete.

We see (ourselves) now as a poor reflection in a mirror; *then*, we shall see face to face. *When perfection comes*, the imperfect disappears, what we know now in part *"then"* we shall know fully."

What is it that one sees in a mirror? Every piece of knowledge and every advance of science cleans away the grime of ignorance. When it is squeaky clean we will be face to face with God and know *we are as one*.

CHAPTER 16

The mind of God

When challenged on the actual existence of the God of the Abraham story, with the glaring examples of terrible personal, national social calamities and injustices perpetrated throughout the world, we ask why would such a powerful and all encompassing God allow such things to happen? The usual reply by the believers is that it is impossible for man to understand the mind of God. This means that the mind of God is too great (infinite) for our small (finite) minds to have even the smallest glimmer of understanding. I think this long-standing concept is maintained in order to confirm in the mind of the believers that God is separate from us, up there in heaven somewhere and we are down here and apart from him. An entity that everyone talks about but none can identify.

If Abraham's God is just a fabrication by Abraham, or a group of conniving fraudsters, is there an alternative entity that fits all the theological description of God, without compromising the truth? There is! The **Collective Mind** of humanity has exactly the same attributes as those which we have given to the mind of god. Also there are many metaphors and clues in the Old Testament that point to the idea of the identity of God as being collectively, ***the whole of humanity.***

First we must understand the quotation from Krishna Murti stated previously (The whole cannot be understood through the part). For example:

Take a cog, a switch, a hose or a screw from a any machine. Observed in isolation, how could anyone possibly understand the whole collective product? We as individuals are the component parts of that end product the whole of humanity. That has been described as God in many places in both the old and New Testament.

To quote just a few: Gen:3.22 God said to Adam because he ate of the fruit of **knowledge;** "man has now become as one of us (god) he must not be allowed to eat from the tree of life and live forever". Knowledge is the **catalyst** the definition of which is, (a substance that changes the state of a material without combining with it). In Gen: 1- v 37 "So God created male and female in his own image". Also from The gospel of Thomas: V 77. "Lift a stone and I am there. Cleave wood and I am there". Meaning; where **man** is acting, there is God. In Mathew 25:40 and 45, Jesus said. "Whenever you refuse to help one of the least of my brothers, you refuse to help me". In John 10:34,"It is written in your own law "that God said you are Gods". And again, in John 12: 45, Where Jesus said "whoever sees me sees him who sent me". Also John 5: 27, "and he has given the son the right to judge, because he is the Son of Man. And it is so with every individual as part of the whole of humanity. The collective mind of the whole of Humanity has exactly the same attributes as that which we have given to the mind of God.

Consider any large modern machine, the space shuttle, a large city building, the Queen Mary 2. or any complex industrial chemical or industrial manufacturing plant. Can you imagine all the science and technical expertise and components that are involved in the manufacture and construction of such a machine? To name a few: The steel; do you understand the technology that has gone into the manufacture, the shaping, the heat treatment, the welding? Some do, but not **all** of us. The electrical engineers; who understands the circuitry, the wiring of the electric motors, the switch gear and components, some, but not **all** of us. The electronics; who understands the workings of a transistor, a micro-chip, the integrated circuit, the coded keyboard, the workings of a hard disc, a compact disk or a floppy disc? Some, but not **all** of us. The computer software design and programming, Some but not all of us. What of the vast amount of highly complex technical knowledge in all fields of human endeavour that has accumulated over the last couple of hundred years alone? No single mind can begin to understand a small fraction of – what I term - the collective consciousness of humankind. Never the less, it is the small active coordinators - the individuals - that bring it together and make it all happen? The welder, the carpenter, the mechanical and electrical engineers, the assemblers, the electricians the computer operators, the concreters, the riggers, physicists, the draughtsman, scientist, and maybe hundreds more. None of these individual people have any idea of the intricacies of all the knowledge required to produce the whole. It is by the accumulated knowledge and technology that has been developed by the whole of humanity, that *it is created*.

The above are just very small examples of the collective mind of humanity. Can we even imagine the full extent of its capacity or its potential?

To use Christianity's central theme of the trinity (Father, Son and Holy spirit), *material, subtle and spirit*; we the individuals are the material and *we* make up the whole of humanity. We are transformed subtly by our experience and environment (knowledge) and to what purpose are we put? As in the example of a machine, it can be put to the beautiful purpose of bringing joy and happiness to the world, a virtual paradise or, if hijacked, it can be used to bring calamity, fear and destruction as weapons of war.

So it is with humanity. In what spirit are we being used, by whom and for what purpose?

CHAPTER 17

The identity of God

Identifying God transports theology from blind faith in myths and fables to practical conscious human reality which is, (I daresay) a basic human psychological necessity.

At this stage I remind you that, I have defined (or revealed) God as humankind, (the collective spirit of the whole of humanity). To repeat, where **God** is written it means "***the whole*** - the ***collective*** spirit - of Humanity" The following emphasises the identity of and our individual relationship to God:

There are several reasons why we should know and feel one with God. Reasons referred to directly, metaphorically, and allegorically many times in the New Testament. It is imperative that all people should embrace this concept for the following reasons. Firstly, it does not destroy ones faith in God, but focuses it in a wholesome rational direction; a state of ***inclusiveness, oneness,*** as against the exclusivity and individuality that is currently encouraged and accepted.

Secondly, it bestows enormous value on each and every one of us. If and when each of us realise that everything we do effects God, all our actions then assume a far greater degree of importance. We recognise the responsibility we have as individuals, towards each other, our community, society and the world at large. Everything we do to harm our body, mind or environment is demeaning of and an insult to God. What a beautiful belief. What hurts me hurts God. Not that this knowledge will stop all or any of us from smoking, taking drugs or stealing, lying, cheating and killing. However, when our spiritual and moral background is such that we practise the values of virtue over vice, from early childhood, at home, school, Sunday schools, Synagogues and Mosques, and learn that our actions not only effects ourselves, but effects the whole of humanity, then *IT will be done on earth as it is in heaven.* Our present actions are not only an insult to God, but a deterrent to the advancement of our community, society and civilization as a whole. What a beautiful concept. *What hurts me hurts god and whatever harm I do to myself or others, harms god.*

Let's explore the above, using the *misinterpreted theological terms* with which we are familiar. It is easy to perceive that virtuous behaviour is godlike, and vicious behaviour is satanic. Take love as one very small example:

Love of man for a woman and vice-versa is perfectly natural, and in the natural course of events, leads to sexual activity and, if it feels good for both individuals, great; so long as it does no harm.

Question: How can virtuous behaviour do harm?

Answer: In many ways: For instance, with young unmarried people, it can result in unwanted pregnancy, abortion or unwanted children, family upheaval or a lifetime of personal hardship. On a small scale this only affects a few individuals but on the larger national and social level, it has massive effects. Sex outside of marriage creates a jealous spouse, leading to violence, family break-up and harmful individual effects on family members.

Question: On the national social level, what is our response?

Answer: Harm minimization. As in the contraceptive pill, condoms, social security payments for young single parents, the family court with all the family pain, social, community and national economic costs of broken homes, neglected children and thousands of homeless people. What a mess!

We, and future generations must not only learn the value of godlike virtue, but develop the wisdom to recognize and avoid the Satanic consequences that may stem from all or any of our actions by learning to avoid the seduction of materialism. (*lead us not into temptation*.) Conversely, whatever we do to help and advance our position individually, without harming others, not only elevates ourselves, but also our society and God. We should treat our body as a temple, which is the actual embodiment (incarnation) of the power from whence we sprung, whether created or evolved.

In the grand scheme of the universe, were we created or did we just evolve? This question really becomes irrelevant compared to the importance of focusing on our present global chaotic state. We are in a state of distraction, division, confusion and diversion in which the reality and the enormity of deception is hidden. While this remains, we are under constant threat of imminent extinction by self destruction. The goal that should be the ultimate triumphal reward for our existence, will forever elude us. Ask yourself again, in what spirit **selfish** or **collective,** are we now being used; to what purpose, and by whom? The spirit is the thought, the motivating purpose of action which we may say, reflects the spirit within any object or being. If the social object, (the human mind) is hijacked, then, its original purpose is thwarted and directed to the self serving purposes of the hijacker. History shows that when small powerful groups or individuals pursue self serving agendas, it is at the expense of the rest of society.

CHAPTER 18

To be one with God

How Can One Perceive Oneself To Be One With God?

This I find, is a difficult concept to explain. There are several reasons that are convincing enough to arrive at the following logical conclusions even though I draw some of my evidence from the Old Testament writings. Gen:1-27 and Gen: 3-22.

As an individual I am the image of God. Gen 1:27. However, there are about 6 and a half billion of me that make up the group that is humankind. That is **we.** You and I are a part of the group and have identities of our own, but as the whole cannot be understood through the part, the whole has its own identity. For instance, as a very simple example:

Take a normal house-brick; the materials of which it is made are identified as clay and straw. These undergo a subtle change when molded and baked. The identity then becomes a brick, and its spirit is identified by its use, (which is determined by the user) man, who possesses the virtuous ability to enhance or the vicious ability to spoil and destroy.

I perceive everything to exist in three forms; material, subtle and spirit. The basic brick consists of earth and straw, (a) the material, plus (b) being shaped and baked (the subtle change), make the brick the end product of (a) plus (b). Plus (c) (the motivating thought), or the *spirit* behind the use for which it was created. How any particular creation is finally used however, will vary according to individual control of it. It can be beneficial, as in a structure, or destructive if used as a missile. With humankind, you and I, the individual is (A), the "material". The "subtle" transformation is (B) the acquisition of knowledge. GEN: 3-22. The (structure) of which we are a part, is the whole of humanity. (C), "*the spirit* in action", is evidenced by our actions and reflected in the state of our world today.

We all have within us all the vices and virtues. One may argue that these are very subjective terms that can alter and can change according to time and place. In narrow terms this maybe so. But broadly, I think it will be accepted that virtue is that which enhances and improves, and vice is that which harms and impedes humanity's slow progression towards happiness, peace and harmony between all peoples.

Taking the analogy of the brick further, the material in the brick, clay and straw as their own separate identities are relatively ineffectual. Apply a subtle change such as molding and baking "a", the material and its identity then assumes a very effective form that can be put to a variety of uses. The spirit would normally be determined by the actions of the creator but if hi-jacked, it is the user that determines the spirit in which it is used. Some build beautiful houses, politicians, military leaders and religious fanatics build walls to keep people in or out. Or use as weapons. The spirit of the user (virtuous or vicious) is recognised in the action.

Single individuals, are the material that make up "the whole of humanity" this *material* is totally ineffectual until *knowledge,* (the subtle transformation) takes place. Now comes the tricky part! With what spirit is this product (the individual) used? I am sure we have all heard the term value adding. This is precisely what has been applied throughout history that allows intelligent people to do unintelligent things. We are experiencing the results of this today, here and now.

The world is now dependant on various leaders and *groups* that have the ability to deceive and further transform, manipulate and control large segments of the material (humanity), to act and to be used according to a particular leader or group's agenda. A good example is, President George W. Bush, Prime Minister Tony Blair and other national leaders, who were able to utilize hundreds of thousands (a very large portion of the available material) of men and women, send them thousands of miles across the globe to deliver death dealing shock, awe and terror to millions of other individuals in order to achieve their particular agenda. Some will remember Adolph Hitler in Nazi Germany and Joseph Stalin in Communist Russia, who similarly deceived, manipulated and controlled.

It is very easy to see that these massive resources could have more easily been used to build and produce things to alleviate world poverty if they had not been hijacked by greedy commercial interests. *Power, wealth and mass-media control* are the *weapons of mass deception* that enable these various groups to manipulate whole populations. In the areas of conflict, cruelty and destruction *we humans* have not changed since the beginning of recorded history. Although *(we the whole)*, cannot be understood through the individual part, it doesn't mean that an individual cannot influence the whole. Many famous individuals throughout history have made great contributions to our advancement from the primitive caves to modern castles and skyscraper buildings. We have come from the horse drawn carriage, to traversing far flung planets. From the club, spear and boomerang to nuclear and cluster bombs; from our total ignorance of the laws of nature to science, genetics and quantum mechanics; from primitive outlines on cave walls to the exquisite paintings and sculptures that now decorate our world; from the ancient rams horn and the flute to the great variety of musical instruments of today. If it was not for the efforts of these few individuals in the past, *the products of past accumulated collective consciousness*, we would not have acquired the intellectual capacity and advanced knowledge that we have today. It will only be through the efforts of the few today that higher levels may be reached in the future.

In only one area of the above has the advance of our collective intellectual activity met with consistent, stubborn and violent opposition by religious leaders and this area is science. In particular, scientific discoveries of natural laws which contradict the perception of God as portrayed by the Church.

People like Galileo, Copernicus, Archimedes, De Vinci and Darwin were ruthlessly persecuted, regardless of truth or proof. Anyone that discovered a fundamental law of nature that threatened the theological hierarchy's powerful grip on that relatively ignorant and superstitious group of people under their sway met with a similar fate. Slowly but surely, truth does prevail. It is evident today that, many people are no longer willing to make that leap of faith into a belief that is so unbelievable. However, It is not so difficult to make a leap of recognition. Recognition of a concept that eliminates ones faith in a false god and illuminates ones faith in the collective spirit of humanity, which is described as god many times in the bible. However, it is not just the expansion or extension of knowledge that is required. That leap takes one out of the dimension of the physical, material and spiritual confines of the past cultural conditioning, into a new or different dimension.

We use the term "outside the square" and unless we recognise this difference, no matter how much knowledge we accumulate, we are only making the square bigger. This different dimension that I refer to is to go out of the door of one room and into another. It is what I believe to be a transcendence of consciousness from: Me and my somewhat dubious relationship with an external God", to: Me, and my direct connection with the Collective consciousness of my fellow man (the whole of humanity). It is a spiritual connection that does not exist outside of humanity and cannot exist beyond our collective selves. It is to be at one *(atone)* to or with God. It is as if - I, humanity and God - are collectively saying, "the only evidence of your being is my being". When one arrives at this state of consciousness, the whole terminology of the old room is easily understood. It is an attempt to justify the baggage of ancient mythology and ignorance.

Ignorance is static. It must change, it resists truth, it is anchored firmly in the past and goes nowhere. Ignorance through the ages has led to chaos, destruction, inhumanity and confusion, which is what we still have today. Not until we break the stranglehold of ignorance, will we be free.

Simply put: The unit of mankind (the individual), is transformed through knowledge and forms the collective (whole of mankind) that produces all human action.

This action reflects the collective spirit of mankind in our inexorable journey towards the absolute truth of all creation. We may never achieve this, but it is in our nature to try.

Part Two

Table of Contents

CHAPTER 1

Damage control required

The inherited behaviour and ethics handed down from the various customs religions and traditions of our ancient forebears have had a profound effect on the values, beliefs and behaviour of their progeny and is manifestly evident in today's society.

As mentioned in previous chapters it is obvious that the competitive greed and scramble for material acquisition by the wealthy and powerful groups in our world today, has overcome the collective human love and compassion.

In the effort to justify their behaviour powerful opportunistic groups have flooded the various media outlets with clever advertising and imagery, glamorizing the lifestyle of the rich and famous. Along with this comes a distinct and relentless bombardment of the message that you too can achieve this exalted position of *success.*

Unfortunately the idea of success has been falsely equated with the acquisition of money and material goods. It seems that whole populations in the Western World has been seduced by this and have succumbed to the idea that the possession of lots of goods and money for oneself automatically brings happiness.

A radical change from this present state of selfishness, to a state of universal love, compassion, peace and prosperity is desperately needed. The people that would benefit most from this change would be the displaced, the disempowered, the misled, and the gullible people of the world. This incidentally, happens to be the vast majority of the world's population. Up to the present time, this great majority, have been successfully governed and contained (albeit with growing difficulty) and also, used and abused by political, theological, commercial and financial parasites and predators.

The muffled and mixed objections voiced by the few social and religious charitable organizations amounts to little less than tacit agreement with these values and at times actually aiding and abetting the behaviour of particular political or secular groups. I have previously described the development of the various religions as controlling organizations that dispense rigid systems of belief, as the fundamental source of much of the social cultural conflict in the world. The following is a list of the various *'secular'* groups that are also responsible for a variety of crimes against humanity. Their activities are highlighted by the physical damage inflicted on our environment and populations as well as the global ecology on which our existence and the existence of all living creatures depend. Surely these activities are crimes against humanity and it is important that they are exposed. There is an urgent need from every quarter to prevent these criminal activities from continuing before it is too late.

The Secular List:
1). Political: Arms Manufacturers. (The state killing machine).
2). Commercial: Multi-national corporations, trade and pharmaceutical monopolies.
3). Financial   : Banks and the debt creators.
4). The Media : The numbing and dumbing agencies.

These various groups of the powerful and wealthy have successfully flourished in the social environment which has been designed to further their own ambitions Whether it is individual, corporate, national or culturally motivated it has the same result. The ascendance and maintenance of the ruling group at the expense of the common good.

The following chapters contain many examples of corporate crimes where inhumane treatment and environmental plunder is used for the sole purpose of increasing profits. The result of which serves to widen the gap between the haves and have-nots, creating resistance movements that are today so easily branded as terrorist groups. The Industrial revolution that started in Britain called for a great number of people to be educated. This gave birth to a whole class of people that did not exist before, commonly called, the working class. The concept of individual "success" is subtly linked to material possessions and monitory wealth and over time, the urge to meet these false values, subliminally inculcated into our culture. In the case of commercial, wholesale, retail, manufacturing and service industries, the profits go back to the companies in the form of massive benefits to the CEO's, directors and to a lesser extent, the shareholders. In the armaments industry, profits are shared between a very few particular manufacturing companies, individual selected dealers and higher echelon individuals in the governments worldwide. The various Government agencies that sell these instruments of death and destruction to tyrants, dictators and demagogues to maintain their positions of power are actually accessories to their crimes.

From **"The Rogue Economy"** Loretta Napoleoni.[15]

"Do you realize that between the spreading of democracy and the rising of slavery there is an almost perfect correlation? If the number of democratic countries increases so does the global pool of slaves and that today the price of a slave is a fraction of what was during the Roman Empire?

Do you know that the fall of the Berlin Wall boosted the global sex industry? That piracy is on the rise everywhere so is money laundering, a multi billion business involving banks and international organizations?

Are you aware that house prices are skyrocketing because of declining interest rates, not because banks are suddenly good Samaritans but only because Western salaries have plummeted and that the Western middle class is poorer than ten or twenty years ago? Do you remember that terrorism made more victims in the Western world during 1970s and 1980s, and that the number of hijacked planes steadily decreased since the end of the 1980s? Do you know that Saddam Hussein was not involved with Bin Laden, and al Zarkawi was not a member of Al Qaeda and that all the reasons to wage war with Iraq were completely false? Are you aware that the so called dietetic foods make us fatter because fat has been replaced with carbohydrates which unfortunately, contain more calories?"

---

[15] :www. Rogue Economics » Home

CHAPTER 2

Political power and the war mentality.

How good people are persuaded to do bad things:
First, provide us with an enemy. Then convince us that we are not safe
until the enemy is obliterated. And just who is it that must do the
obliterating, US (while standing a good chance of being obliterated
in the meantime). We are the ordinary John and Joan's, the Ali and
Aliya's, the Rafi and Rebecca's the little people that have been culturally
conditioned and suitably brainwashed to believe that our leaders, both
secular or religious, are looking after our interests and have our welfare
and the wellbeing of our community at heart.

I approach this particular chapter with mixed feelings. Politics and
politicians are, intertwined, polluted and corrupted by strong influences
within the other four areas of power. Although the politicians appear
to control the executive power of the state they are subject to covert
manipulation by powerful forces in the national and international
commercial, financial, media, and religious areas and any one of these
can determine the future of any political party. The combination of
any two or three of the above is enough to guarantee government
compliance to their agenda.

Governments must appear to their constituents to be strong and
in total control of any situation that arises from day to day. However,
instead of introducing legislation to benefit the wealth and prosperity
of the people at this point in history most of the legislature seems to be

designed to smooth the path of big business in order to expand their wealth and power. This is at the expense of the general community. To suggest that the overtly dominant powerbrokers are our law-makers is to ignore their political rhetoric and non transparent activities that contain hidden agendas that to many politically sophisticated people, seems so glaringly obvious. Government by an Oligarchy is a government in which a small group exercises control (often for corrupt and selfish purposes). This accurately describes the condition in the United States under the Bush regime. The Neo-conservative forces in America are the World's commercial and economic power-brokers. Who are these oligarchs and how powerful are the organizations run by them? To name a few: The Central Intelligence Agency (CIA), the National Endowment for Democracy (NED), Freedom House, the Zionist lobby, the World Bank, the IMF and their collaborators. All in the one bag branded NEO-CONS. They seek to install their brand of democracy and free trade worldwide by interfering, coercing and de-stabilizing political structures of foreign nations that oppose their agenda. Oligarchy is in fact a corrupt activity, the definition of which is: "The misuse of public (governmental) power for illegitimate, usually secret, private, or group advantage."

Throughout the history of early civilization, through the feudal system and on to agrarian national economies, the powers of state lay in the hands of Royalty, the aristocracy and in some cases the priesthood. However, with the rise of industry and technology these powers have gradually been eroded in favour of powerful industrialists, technocrats and financiers that have eventually usurped government. All forms of government are susceptible to various forms of corruption. The most common are patronage, lobbying, embezzlement and cronyism. Corruption also often facilitates criminal activities such as drug trafficking, money laundering, and criminal prostitution. It is not restricted only to any or all of these activities especially where the CIA branch of the US Government is concerned. It seems that internationally many major political parties of the West have succumbed to the influence of some of the above pressures and have therefore become unrepresentative clones and drones governing us on behalf of the USA and global corporate capital[16] . In Australia there was

---

[16] Google: The Israeli spy ring

a real concern and growing opposition to the blind faith and allegiance displayed by our incumbent conservative political party; particularly in its acceptance and willingness to follow the U.S government's criminal foreign policies. A typical example is shown in this observation by political scientist C. Douglas Lummis:

"Public opinion polls worldwide, show that the majority of people believe that the war on Iraq was carried out only to achieve the economic goals of the large Oil Companies. And had nothing to do with WMD as has been shown by the inability of the United States and United Kingdom to locate any real evidence of them since the beginning of hostilities in Iraq." And will any U.S citizens be made to face an International War Crimes Tribunal over Iraq? Not anytime soon, as the U.S is no longer a signatory to the International Criminal Court in the Hague. Congress passed and George W Bush signed, sealed and delivered the American Servicemen's Protection Act (ASPA), which not only bars any U.S. co-operation with the International Criminal Court, but also bars U.S. military aid to other countries unless they agree to shield U.S. troops on their territory from ICC prosecution. It also bans U.S. troops from taking part in UN peacekeeping operations unless the UN Security Council explicitly exempts them from possible prosecution and authorizes the President to use force to free U.S. prisoners hauled before the ICC which is located at The Hague. In other words the US can with impunity, invade a NATO ally to free U.S citizens charged with War Crimes."

The actions of the US government have thoroughly demonstrated its goal of worldwide military, political and commercial supremacy. Its various international activities in the recent past (since 1990's) have shown that the national borders, cultural differences, ethnic groups, social public opposition, other political systems, or religious beliefs are seen only as a challenge to be overcome using any means at its disposal.

Dick Cheney, Donald Rumsfeld, Richard Perle, Elliot Abrams, Paul Wolfowitz, Ben Wattenberg, are part of the advocacy group known as "The Project for the New American Century" or PNAC. It is this group that called for some major new policy directions, the uppermost being "establish full military control of the Middle East." Wolfowitz, among various appointments was President of the World Bank, where, under a cloud of scandal he was replaced. He was later appointed to Chairman of the Secretary of State's International Security Advisory Board (ISAB) that deals with advice to the Department of State in the area of political-military issues. He is said to have planned the invasion of Iraq as early as 1997, almost six years before the actual hostilities. His objective, of course, was oil and the security of Israel. The PNAC are part of a group of Jewish American/Israelis who integrate and enter government for the sole purpose of influencing and supporting the pro-Israeli foreign policy of the US. They and their Christian partners, are known as neo-cons whose main activity is on lobbying and furthering the Israeli hold and expansion in Palestine. Some of them are dual citizens and a few serve in the US military. Whether their motivation is anger at the Muslim world seen as a religious and territorial enemy or a deep-rooted reaction to the Holocaust, or the culmination of European anti-Semitism, their reactionary militarism becomes a world-threatening force answerable only unto itself. Hence the concern.[17] (The footnote references and the information to which they are linked is considered by the editors of the New York Times and other mainstream US. news media, as not advisable for the public to know.) These covert groups, particularly the CIA, do all in their power to oust foreign leaders whose policies do not suit our Western brand of democracy. In other areas, they do the opposite by supporting and supplying military equipment to cruel despotic tyrants and dictatorships regardless of the human misery that these leaders may be inflicting on their own people. For example, arming and supporting

---

[17] "Encyclopedia of religion and War".) By Gabriel Palmer Fernandez. www./globalissues.org/Geopolitics ICC.asp - 14 Oct 2004 – All this information is now easily accessed on the net in: "CIA and the Church committee" and also, "CIA and drugs". Also on DVD. an expose' on fraudulent governments "Truth, Lies and Intelligence".]

Saddam Hussein in the war against Iran.[18] The Destabilization of the elected Allende government in Chile and installing General Pinochet, supporting Osama Bin-Ladin in Afghanistan to fight the Russians and the many attempts to de-stabilize the operation because of a desire not to offend their Pakistani and Afghan allies. The main reason why this is not more widely known is that the main players in the U.S. media have always worked to protect the Agency and to keep the American public in the dark as to the nature of its activities (as documented in great detail in Carl Bernstein's article in the October 20, 1977, issue of the newssheet Rolling Stone titled "The CIA and the Media": How America's Most Powerful News Media Worked Hand in Glove with the CIA (and why the Church Committee Covered It Up").Referring to the armed interventions in Guatemala, Congo, Cuba, Nicaragua, Angola, Libya, Philippines, Panama, and the Dominican Republic. Foreign journalists on the spot contend that the colour-coded popular "revolutions" that ousted Milosevic in Serbia, Shevardnadze in Georgia, and the Kuchma crowd in Ukraine were also made in the USA by the CIA. The IMF also played a major role in crippling Argentina. Yet it refuses to accept responsibility for the chaotic and catastrophic economic crisis over the past 10 years. Worse, it continued to insist that the Argentinean government budget for a surplus while millions suffered increasing poverty and even hunger in this major agricultural exporting country.

In Uruguay, legislators recently passed a law blocking for three years, access to hard currency held in high-interest accounts with the country's two state banks. Faced with the prospect of the law's approval, United States promised a $1.5bn emergency loan to help it deal with its economic crisis and enable the continuity of these accounts. This was the first time that Bush administration agreed to provide direct support to a country in economic trouble. Washington DC has made it clear that the loan was intended to tide Uruguay over, only until the IMF comes up with its own loans. In this case, the neo-con cabal, acted as a proxy for the IMF for their own benefit.

In the USA, that once beautiful "Land of the Free and Home of the Brave," the arms and weapons industry underpins all manner

---

[18] (For a graphic example, of this on the GOOGLE, enter "thanks for the memories Saddam Hussein").

of activities. If corporate objectives and financial influence or what is, in reality the economic occupation of a country is resisted, the heavies enter the game. The establishment of the neo-cons' political agenda follows the same recurring script. Where American business interests abroad are restricted or perceived to be under threat by a popular or democratically elected leader or party, (like Hugo Chavez in Venezuela) supported by the people because of policies of land reform, strengthening unions, redistribution of wealth, nationalizing foreign-owned industry, and regulating business to protect the local workers, consumers and the environment. The socially beneficial type of people's democracy, being outside the influence of the "new world order", cannot be allowed to flourish in any way shape or form. Twice they have managed to force new national elections and twice he has been re-elected. There is the ever-present fear that an example of good governance in the true spirit of fairness and shared wealth would expose the sham of our enslavement to the present economic system imposed by big business. It would constitute a step in the direction of a cure from the disease with which we are now afflicted. Once this cure can be seen to be successful it would spread and finally expose the fabric of lies and deceit that we have been fed.

Like a well-oiled machine on behalf of American business, and often with their help, the CIA mobilizes opposition. First, it identifies right-wing groups within the country (usually the military), and offers them a deal: "We'll put you in power if you maintain a favourable investment climate for us."

The Agency then hires, trains and works with them to overthrow the existing government - usually a democracy or socialist leaning democracy - or where there is even a hint of socialism. It uses every trick in the book. Propaganda, stuffed ballot boxes, purchased elections, extortion, blackmail, sexual intrigue, false stories ridiculing and vilifying opponents in the local media, infiltration and disruption of opposing political parties, kidnapping, beating, torture, intimidation, economic sabotage, death squads and even assassination. They will do whatever it takes. Alongside and underneath their visible structure the CIA is a veritable menagerie of secret planning cabals and operational units that try to put the contending strategies of different power centres of capital into effect. Do you ever wonder how all those so-called "colour coded revolutionary" banners, posters, flags and protesters suddenly appear? This is the principal charge of the CIA, the biggest snake in the pit.

The "Agency" is precisely that! It is the active force that puts the plans and schemes of the most powerful Wall Street, financial, commercial, armament, and oil interests into operation. Ten Years of economic sanctions, and attempts to de-stabilize the secular government of Saddam Hussein in Iraq failed to get the desired results. Finally the vilification and outright lies about the regime were used as an excuse for the U.S (Bush and his cronies) to wage an illegal pre-emptive war. After five years of emphatic denial by President Bush that there were no prisoners kept outside the USA apart from Guantanamo Bay, he finally admitted that the CIA detained prisoners in countries where the international laws on humane treatment and torture were not strictly applied.

Within the CIA the lines between the U.S. State and private corporate power are totally blurred and have melded into one gigantic force. If not checked this will lead us all to extinction. Their covert operations, para-military, dirty tricks department — call it what you will — has for at least 40 years been well documented. Enough information has been sourced showing significant CIA activity in the area of drug trading that shows that a large part of its funding is derived through the sales of heroin and cocaine. The real drug lords are the CIA.

The CIA supported the Mujahadeen rebels [who in 2001 were part of the "Northern Alliance" fighting the Taliban which became the core of the new Afghani government following the U.S. attack on Afghanistan in late 2001]. The CIA, were heavily engaged in drug trafficking while fighting against the Soviet-supported government and its plans to reform the very backward Afghan society. The Agency's principal client was Gulbuddin Hekmatyar one of the leading drug-lords and a leading heroin refiner[19]. The CIA supplied the trucks and mules, to carry arms into Afghanistan, and used them to transport opium to laboratories along the Afghan-Pakistan border. The crop provided up to one half of

---

[19] Google: Meet Mr. Blowback, Gulbuddin Hekmatyar. CIA op. and homicidal thug. (Gary Leupp)

the heroin used annually in the United States and three-quarters of that used in Western Europe.

U.S. officials admitted in 1990 that they had failed to investigate or take action against the C.I.A's drug and arms trafficking. With the C.I.A and other U.S. agencies actively engaged in destabilizing governments, to suit America's agenda for economic supremacy, what can the United Nations and other Western governments do about these conflicts?

Consider these conflicts:

Religious supremacy: As in Northern Ireland, Indonesia, Philippines, Afghanistan, Iran, Lebanon, Sri Lanka, Kashmir, Israel/Palestine, India?

Ethnic cleansing: as in Rwanda, Bosnia, Kosovo, Somalia and Sudan etc.?

Geo-political control: as in India, Pakistan, Nigeria, Sudan, Vietnam, Cambodia, Laos, Chechnya, Afghanistan, Kazakhstan and the many other sovereign states.

Do we really know just how many of these conflicts have been supported or orchestrated by the CIA? Particularly when we discover the extent of involvement of the Bush family and their secret business activities over the last eighty years. The following is just a small excerpt from "watch.pair. the Bush family." (A website that may serve to arouse your curiosity).

After 60 years of inattention and denial by the U.S. media, newly-uncovered government documents in The National Archives and Library of Congress reveal that Prescott Bush, the grandfather of President George W. Bush, served as a business partner and U.S. banking operative for the financial architects of the Nazi war machine from 1926 until 1942, Congress then took aggressive action against Bush and his 'enemy national' partners. The documents also show that Bush and his colleagues, according to reports from the U.S. Department of the Treasury and FBI, tried to conceal their financial alliance with German industrialist Fritz Thyssen, a steel and coal baron who, beginning in the mid-1920s, personally funded Adolf Hitler's rise to power by the subversion of democratic principle and German law. Moreover, Bush was managing director of the Union Banking Corporation, the American branch of Hitler's chief financier's banking network. Other companies where Bush was a director - and which were seized by the American government in 1942, under the Trading With the Enemy Act were, a shipping line which imported German spies, an energy company that supplied the Luftwaffe with high-ethyl fuel and a steel company that employed Jewish slave labour from the Auschwitz concentration camp. "Furthermore, the declassified records demonstrate that Bush and his associates, who included E. Roland Harriman, younger brother of American icon W. Averell Harriman and George Herbert Walker, President Bush's maternal great-grandfather, continued their dealings with the German industrial barons for nearly eight months after the U.S. entered the war. The federal government did not crack down on the Bush-Harriman/Nazi operation until 1942.

After the war, Congressional investigation revealed that Fritz Thyssen's German Steel Trust, Germany's largest industrial corporation, which interlocked with Union Banking Corporation, produced a high percentage of Germany's national output of metal products and explosives. The Union Banking Corporation was run for the 'Thyssen family' of 'Germany and/or Hungary, nationals of a designated enemy country.'

Prescott Bush, the grandfather of George W Bush, was not only a good friend of Allen Dulles (CIA director), president of the Foreign Relations Council and international business lawyer, he was also a client of Dulles' law firm that had the miraculous ability to scrub the story of Bush's treasonous investments in the Third Reich out of the news media, where it might have interfered with his political career not to mention the presidential careers of both his son and grandson. Like all the other Bush scandals, they were swept under the rug. These revelations were virtually ignored by virtue of the confidential censorship of the corporate media. There are a few, even on the left, who question the current relevance of this information. However, Prescott Bush's dealings with the Nazis do more than illustrate a family pattern of genteel treason and war profiteering. From George senior's sale of missiles to Iran, while at the same time selling biological and chemical weapons to Saddam Hussein, to George junior's crazy activities in crony capitalism, in present-day Iraq. Junior knew that Saddam had been given biological weapons, Daddy has the receipts.

CHAPTER 3

Weapons of Mass Deception

Michael Hasty, points out classic examples of corruption in the high echelons of power in the United States of America. He also graphically details the use of ridicule as an effective weapon extensively used by the corrupt, to dismiss the truth.

Michael Hasty is a writer, activist, musician, carpenter and farmer. In January 1989, he was the media spokesperson for the counter-inaugural coalition at the senior George Bush's Counter-Inaugural Banquet, which fed hundreds of Washington DC's homeless in front of Union Station, where the official inaugural dinner was being held. (The following was first published in the Online Journal). Hasty wrote about Conspiracy Facts:

Just before his death, James Jesus Angleton, the legendary chief of counter-intelligence at the Central Intelligence Agency, was a bitter man. He felt betrayed by the people he had worked for all his life. In the end he had come to realize that they were never really interested in American ideals of "freedom" and "democracy", they really wanted "absolute power."

Angleton told author Joseph Trento that the reason he had been given the counter-intelligence job in the first place, was by agreeing not to submit "sixty of Allen Dulles' closest friends" to a polygraph test concerning their business deals with the Nazis. In his end-of-life despair, Angleton assumed that he would see all his old companions again "in hell."

"The transformation of James Jesus Angleton from an enthusiastic Ivy League cold war warrior, to a bitter old man, is an extreme example of a phenomenon I call a *paranoid shift*.

I recognize the phenomenon, because something similar happened to me".

Michael Hasty never actually met James Jesus Angleton even though he worked in the C.I.A. While Michael worked as a low level clerk as a teenager in the '60's.their paths never crossed. He recognized the symptoms of "paranoid shift," because of similar concerns occurred to him during the U.S debacle in Vietnam. He became completely paranoid after the disillusionment of learning that the U.S foreign policy story was a lot more complicated and devious that what he had previously believed. He goes on to say that over the next 30 years, even with being a radical, he still held some faith in the basic integrity of a system where power ultimately rested with the people, and if enough people decide and voted, they could change the system. But when he could no longer believe that this was necessarily true his personal paranoia was confirmed. What tipped him over the edge was William Blum's book, "A Rogue State: A Guide to the World's only Superpower." In which Blum warns of how the media will make anything that smacks of conspiracy theory an immediate object of ridicule. This prevents the media from ever having to investigate the many strange interconnections among the ruling class. For example, the relationships between the boards of directors of media giants, and those of the energy, banking and defence industries. These unmentionable topics are usually treated with what Blum calls the media's most effective tool-"silence". In the event of somebody asking questions, all you have to do is say, "conspiracy theory," and any allegation instantly becomes too frivolous to merit serious attention. On the other hand, since his paranoid shift, whenever the words "conspiracy theory" come up, (which seems more often, lately) it usually means that someone is getting too close to the truth. September 11th - was the date his paranoia actually shifted, though he states that he didn't know it at the time. He also says:

"Unless you're paranoid, it doesn't make any sense at all that George W. Bush, commander-in-chief, sat in a second-grade classroom for 20 minutes listening to children read a story about a goat, after being informed that a second plane had hit the World Trade Centre. Nor does it make sense that the Number 2 man, Dick Cheney-even knowing that "the commander" was on a mission in Florida, nevertheless sat at his desk in the White House, watching TV, until the Secret Service dragged him out by the armpits.

Unless you're paranoid, it makes no sense that Defence Secretary Donald Rumsfeld sat at his desk until Flight 77 hit the Pentagon well over an hour after the military had learned about the multiple hijacking in progress. It also makes no sense that the brand-new chairman of the Joint Chiefs of Staff sat in a Senate office for two hours while the 9/11 attacks took place. He had left explicit instructions that he was not to be disturbed - and he wasn't. In other words, while the 9/11 attacks were occurring, the entire top of the chain of command, of the most powerful military in the world, sat inert at various desks. Why weren't they in the "Situation Room?" Don't any of them ever watch "West Wing?" In a sane world, this would be an object of major scandal. But here on this side of the paranoid shift, it's business as usual.

Years, even decades before 9/11, plans had been drawn up for American forces to take control of the oil interests of the Middle East for various imperialist reasons. And these plans were only contingent upon "a catastrophic and catalysing event," like a *new Pearl Harbour*, or Tonkin Gulf to gain the majority support of the American public to set the plans into motion. When the opportunity presented itself, the guards looked the other way ... and Presto ..., the path to global domination was open. Simple, as long as the media played along. And there is voluminous evidence that this was the case.

Number one on the "Project Censored" annual list of under-reported stories in 2002 was the Project for a New American Century, (now the infrastructure of the Bush administrative team) whose report, published in 2000, contained a "Pearl Harbour" quote. Why is it so hard to believe serious people; who have warned us repeatedly, that powerful ruling elites are out to dominate "the masses?"

"Did we think Dwight Eisenhower was exaggerating when he warned of the extreme "danger" to democracy of the military industrial complex?"

Were Teddy and Franklin Roosevelt, or Joseph Kennedy just being class traitors when they talked about a small group of wealthy elites who operate as a hidden government behind the government? Why can't we believe James Jesus Angleton - a man staring eternal judgment in the face - when he says that the founders of the Cold War national security state were only interested in "absolute power?"

More disturbing are the many eerie parallels between Adolph Hitler and George W. Bush:

- Wearing uniform (which no previous American president has ever done while in office)
- Government by secrecy, propaganda and deception.
- Open assaults on labour unions and workers' rights.
- Pre-emptive war and militant nationalism.
- Suspiciously convenient "terrorist" attacks, to justify a police state.
- A conservative authoritarian style with public appearances in military uniform and the suspension of liberties.
- The fantasy of economic growth based on unprecedented budget deficits and massive military spending.
- A cold, pragmatic ideology of fascism including the violent suppression of dissent and other human rights with the use of torture, assassination and concentration camps.
- And most important, is Benito Mussolini's preferred definition of *"fascism"* as "corporatism, because it binds together the interests of corporations and the state."

By their deeds, you shall know them. The most perplexing part is probably the same question that plagues most of us. Why don't other people see the connections? Being paranoid we have to figure out with an answer that fits into our system, why more people don't see these connections. Fortunately, there are a number of possible explanations. First on the list would have to be *advertising*. This is what Marshal McLuhan, the guru of the modern electronic media, called the *"cave art of the electronic age."*

Joseph Goebbels who was the head of Hitler's propaganda machine gave credit for most of his ideas on how to manipulate mass opinion to the American (modern in 1936) commercial advertising and public relations techniques. However, the new science of public relations available to the corporate empire today, makes the Goebbels operation look primitive by comparison. The precision of communications technology and graphics; the century of research on human psychology and emotion and the uniquely centralized control of triumphant post-Cold War Empire of monopoly capitalism, have combined to the point where "the manufacture of consent" can be set on automatic pilot. (This is further illustrated in a later chapter on the Media). A second major reason people won't make the paranoid shift is that we are too fundamentally decent. We can't believe that the elected leaders of our country, the people we've been taught through twelve years of public school to admire and trust, are capable of sending our young soldiers to their deaths and slaughtering tens of thousands of innocent civilians, just to satisfy their greed - especially when they're so rich in the first place. Besides, America is good and the media are liberal and overly critical. Third, people don't want to look like fools. Being a "conspiracy theorist" is like being a creationist.

Of course, people sometimes make mistakes, but our military and intelligence community did the best they could on and before September 11, and anybody who thinks otherwise is a "conspiracy theorist." Lee Harvey Oswald was the sole assassin of JFK, and anyone who thinks otherwise is a conspiracy theorist.

Perhaps the biggest hidden reason people don't make the paranoid shift is that knowledge brings responsibility. If we acknowledge that an inner circle of ruling elites: *Control* the world's most powerful military and intelligence system, *controls* the international banking system, *controls* the most effective and far-reaching propaganda network in history, *controls* all three branches of government in the world's only superpower and *controls* the technology that counts the people's votes, we might then be forced to conclude that we don't live in a particularly democratic system. And then voting, making contributions and trying to stay informed wouldn't be enough. Because then, the duty of citizenship would go beyond serving as a loyal opposition, to serving as a "loyal resistance"- like the Republicans in the Spanish Civil War, except that in this case the resistance to fascism would be on the side of the national ideals, rather than the government. A violent insurgency would not only play into the empire's hands, it would be doomed from the start.

Forming a non-violent resistance movement, on the other hand, might mean forsaking some middle class comfort, and would doubtless require a lot of work.

It would mean also educating ourselves and others about the nature of the truly apocalyptic beast we face.

It would mean reaching across turf lines and transcending single-issue politics, forming   coalitions and sharing data and names and strategies, and applying energy at every level of   government, local to global.

It would mean probable civil disobedience, at a time when the Bush, Blaire, Howard regimes are starting to classify that action as terrorism

It would mean being wise as serpents, and gentle as doves and would also require a critical mass.

It would mean, in the end, organizing a progressive confederacy to govern ourselves, just as the revolutionary founders of the U.S. formed the Continental Congress. But as a paranoid I'm ready to join the resistance. And the main reason is, I no longer think that the conspiracy is much of a theory.

The US House of Representatives Select Committee on Assassinations found:

That the murder of John Fitzgerald Kennedy was probably the result of a conspiracy and that seventy percent of Americans agree with this conclusion is not a "theory." It's fact.

That in America, the more TV you watched, the less you knew. Also, a recent survey by international scholars found that Americans were the most "ignorant" of world affairs out of all the populations they studied. This is not a "theory." It's fact.

That the Council on Foreign Relations has a history of influence on official US government foreign policy;

That, in the early 1970s, the newly-formed Trilateral Commission published a report which recommended, "in order for globalization to succeed," American manufacturing jobs had to be exported, and American wages had to decline, which is exactly what happened over the next three decades; and that, during that same period, the richest one percent of Americans doubled their share of the national wealth, is not "theory." It's fact.

That, beyond their quasi-public role as agents of the US Treasury Department, the Federal Reserve Banks are profit-making corporations, whose beneficiaries include some of America's wealthiest families; and that the United States has a virtual controlling interest in the World Bank, the International Monetary Fund, and the World Trade Organization, the three dominant global financial institutions, is not a "theory." It's fact.

That the international oil industry is the dominant player in the global economy; and the Bush family has a decades-long business relationship with the Saudi royal family, Saudi oil money, and the family of Osama bin Laden;

That, as president, both George Bushes have favoured the interests of oil companies over the public interest; and both George Bushes personally profited financially from Middle East oil.

That American oil companies doubled their records for quarterly profits in the months just preceding the invasion of Iraq, is not "theory." It's fact. That "Rebuilding America's Defences," the Project for a New American Century's 2000 report, and "The Grand Chessboard," a book published a few years earlier by Trilateral Commission cofounder Zbigniew Brzezinski, both recommended a more robust and imperial US military presence in the oil basin of the Middle East and the Caspian region.

That, in the 1960s, the Joint Chiefs of Staff unanimously approved a plan called "Operation Northwoods," to stage terrorist attacks on American soil that could be used to justify an invasion of Cuba; and that there is currently an office in the Pentagon whose function is to instigate terrorist attacks that could be used to justify future strategically-desired military responses, is not a "theory." It's fact.

That the FBI has completely exonerated - though never identified the speculators who purchased, a few days before the attacks. (Through a bank whose previous director is now the CIA executive director), an unusual number of "put" options, and who made millions betting that the stocks in American and United Airlines would crash, is not a "theory." It's a fact.

That the US intelligence community received numerous warnings, from multiple sources, throughout the summer of 2001, that a major terrorist attack on American interests was imminent;

That, according to the chair of the "independent" 9/11 commission, the attacks "could have and should have been prevented," and according to a Senate Intelligence Committee member, "All the dots were connected;" That the White House has verified George W Bush's personal knowledge, as of August 6, 2001, that these terrorist attacks might be domestic and might involve hijacked airliners; that, in the summer of 2001, at the insistence of the American Secret Service, anti-aircraft ordnance was installed around the city of Genoa, Italy, to defend against a possible terrorist suicide attack, by aircraft, against George W Bush, who was attending the economic summit there; and

That George W Bush has nevertheless regaled audiences with his first thought upon seeing the "first" plane hit the World Trade Centre, which was: "What a terrible pilot," is not "theory." It's a fact.

That, on the morning of September 11, 2001: standard procedures and policies at the nation's air defence and aviation bureaucracies were ignored, and communications were delayed; the black boxes of the planes that hit the WTC were destroyed, but hijacker Mohammed Attar's passport was found in pristine condition.

That high-ranking Pentagon officers had cancelled their commercial flight plans for that morning; George H.W. Bush was meeting in Washington with representatives of Osama bin Laden's family, and other investors in the world's largest private equity firm, the Carlyle Group; the CIA was conducting a previously-scheduled mock exercise of an airliner hitting the Pentagon; the chairs of both the House and Senate Intelligence Committees were having breakfast with the chief of Pakistan's intelligence agency, who resigned a week later on suspicion of involvement in the 9/11 attacks; and

That the commander-in-chief of the armed forces of the United States sat in a second grade classroom for twenty minutes after hearing that a second plane had struck the towers, listening to children read a story about a goat, this is not "theoretical," these are facts.

That the Bush administration desperately fought every attempt to independently investigate the events of 9/11, is not a "theory." Nor finally, it is not in any way a "theory.

That the one single name that can be directly linked to all the following: The Third Reich, the US military industrial complex, Skull and Bones, Eastern Establishment Good Old' Boys, the Illuminati, Big Texas Oil, the Bay of Pigs, the Miami Cubans, the Mafia, the FBI, the JFK assassination, the New World Order, Watergate, the Republican National Committee, Eastern European fascists, the Council on Foreign Relations, the Trilateral Commission, the United Nations, CIA headquarters, the October Surprise, the Iran/Contra scandal, Inslaw, the Christic Institute, Manuel Noriega drug-running "freedom fighters" and death squads, Iraq-gate, Saddam Hussein, weapons of mass destruction, the blood of innocents, the Savings and Loan crash, the Bank of Credit and Commerce International, the "Octopus," the "Enterprise," the Afghan Mujahaddin, the War on Drugs, Mena (Arkansas), Whitewater, Sun Myung Moon, the Carlyle Group, Osama bin Laden and the Saudi royal family, David Rockefeller, Henry Kissinger, and the presidency and vice-presidency of the United States, is: George Herbert Walker Bush. "Theory?." To the contrary; it is a well documented, tragic and (especially if you're paranoid) terrifying fact.

CHAPTER 4.

Dodgy Diplomacy

In the past America's military power was largely hidden behind the screen of diplomacy, **albeit of a very dubious kind.** However, since the status of the oligarchy in the USA was elevated to self proclaimed vigilantes, and their pursuit of terrorism and territorial and economic control became world wide, diplomacy is only a stop-gap procedure. If diplomacy fails, try national de-stabilization and regime change. If that fails, apply sanctions. If the threat of force fails, invade. The big problem with that strategy is that the line of last resort can, by the use of any perceived or contrived provocative situation become the action of first response - i e: armed intervention or pre-emptive attack. For example: The contrived Tonkin Gulf incident as the excuse for the U.S. involvement in Vietnam. The latter, led to the destruction of the whole social infrastructure and fabric of society as we see in Iraq today.

Squillions of dollars and vast human resources in the technologically advanced nations of the world are diverted to the arms industry. While a large proportion of the world's population remains in abject poverty. This is not just a crime, it's an obscenity.

If only a small fraction of this human effort and money was siphoned off and directed into global social infrastructure, education and international community projects; transparently prioritized to help most needy nations first, there would then be no need for the balance to be spent on manipulating, controlling and killing large numbers of people. It could water barren areas, eliminate the hunger and abject poverty, educate and uplift the poor worldwide and there would then be no need for national defence. This would enable every one on earth to live the quality of life that one attributes to their own idea of Heaven. Not everyone's idea of heaven is the same. The rich would not only still be comparatively rich, but also secure.

Again, the quote from President Eisenhower during his first term in office:[20]

"Every gun that is made, every warship launched, every rocket fired, signifies in the final sense, a theft from those who hunger and are not fed, those who are cold and are not clothed." One may think that the billions of dollars given in foreign aid over the last few years is an extremely charitable gesture, but in effect, it is just taking money from the poor in rich countries, (taxes) and giving it to the rich in poor countries (graft and corruption). Evidenced by the extensive use of Swiss and other non-disclosure banks that are havens for money hungry tyrants around the world

in which to hide their ill gotten gains. However, over the last few years, documented evidence of a few cases has been made available to public scrutiny. Switzerland is confronting the largest dirty money investigation in its history after disclosures that $654 million has been found in accounts in the names of the former Nigerian dictator Sani Abacha, his family and associates. Uri David who controls engineering and property companies in London, has had a Swiss bank account frozen containing $60m that is suspected to be part of the $4.2bn -yes, billion - stolen by General Sani Abacha and his family during his brutal five-year rule. An international hunt to recover the money has taken place since Abacha's death in 1998. Another right wing regime supported by the U.S known worldwide for its enormity was the Marcos Government in the Philippines.

---

[20] (Dwight D. Eisenhower, From a speech before the American Society of Newspaper Editors, April 16, 1953 thirty-fourth president of US 1953-1961)

Finally, the Marcos regime was brought down by people power, the action of over a million unarmed people:

In The Rogue State. William Blum[21] states:

"Don't forget, that while wanton destruction of towns, cities and villages is a war crime of long standing, the bombing of cities from airplanes goes not only unpunished but virtually un-accused. Air bombardment is state terrorism, terrorism by the rich. It has burned up and blasted apart more innocents in the past six decades than have all the anti-state terrorists who ever lived. Something has benumbed our consciousness against this reality. In the United States we would not consider for the presidency a man who had once thrown a bomb into a crowded restaurant, but are happy to elect a man who once dropped bombs from airplanes that destroyed not only restaurants, but also the buildings that contained them and the neighbourhoods that surrounded them. I went to Iraq after the first Gulf war and saw for myself what the bombs did. Wanton destruction is just the term for it. Round and round they go, and never seem to learn. Regime change plans, whether by CIA operations or by pre-emptive war, almost always go badly. American intervention abroad – installing the Shah of Iran in the fifties, killing Diem, in South Vietnam in the sixties, helping Osama Bin Laden and Saddam Hussein in the eighties, and propping up dictators in many Arab countries – has had serious repercussions for American interests, including the loss of American life."

No.1 on the list of secular criminal activities is State *arms manufacturing* industry.

And leading the world by a very big margin is America, Illustrated by the following chart.

---

21   William Blum HOME PAGE: and follow the links

Global Distribution Of Military Expenditure In 2005

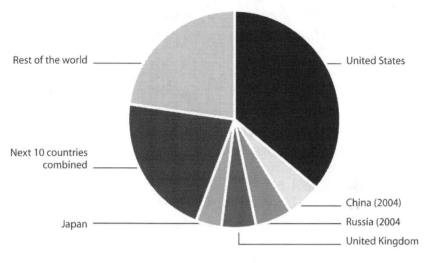

GLOBAL DISTRIBUTION OF MILITARY EXPENDITURE IN 2005

Rest of the world — United States

Next 10 countries combined —

Japan — China (2004)

Russia (2004

United Kingdom

Source: Center for Arms Control and Non-Proliferation, 2007

In Context, the U.S. Military Spending: Versus Rest of the World.[22]

Who benefits most from wars?

1). The arms manufacturers. Continuing war means continuing enormous profits.

2), The banks and financial institutions that finance the wars, and

3). Our current political leaders whose primary interest is staying in power.

---

[22] The U.S. data is from 2005. Using US spending for that year, we can compare US military spending with the rest of the world: The US military spending was In the order of $424 Billion almost two-fifths of the total almost seven times larger than the Chinese budget, the second largest spender and twenty-nine times as large as the combined spending of the six "rogue" states (Cuba, Iran, Libya, North Korea, Sudan and Syria) who spent $14.65 billion. It was more than the combined spending of the next 14 nations. The six potential "enemies," Russia, and China together spent $139 billion, Just 30% of the U.S. military budget

How do they do this? By creating in us a fear and hatred of the enemy and then having established that fear, proclaim, that they are the only ones able to save us. Who else can save us from this invented imaginary fear, but our leaders? They have us exactly where they want us, supporting their grasp on power. In the U.S. particularly, a very large part of the national economy is devoted to the armament industry. Compared to the rest of the world the numbers are indeed staggering. They are very busy manufacturing missiles, ships, planes and rockets that deliver biological weapons, nuclear bombs, cluster bombs, napalm, land mines and who knows just what type and even more devastating death dealing devices are in the pipeline. Today, *pre-emptive attack is justified* and governments of particular nations, forty-nine countries in all, some of them so small that they can't be seen with the naked eye and are euphemistically called the coalition of the willing. They include Britain, Australia, Denmark, Bulgaria, Costa Rica, Micronesia, Palau, Afghanistan (*Afghanistan?* They must be joking!). These and more, have all been persuaded by various means, *including coercion and bribery*, that this war is vitally necessary for their survival. The glaring and relentless lies and false accusations against the Saddam Hussein regime and the horrible mess that Iraq has become, shows how a lie will eventually come back to bite you. The US has become a pariah state in the eyes of most of the world's peace loving people. The arsenal of death dealing equipment by the US and its NATO allies is so huge, that other nations not in close alliance with them feel threatened. The outcome is that both China and Russia feel impelled to continue to build up their military capability in order to have some sort of chance of defence in the event that they may be targeted by the US.

The question now is, can Obama repair the damage? Division of people requires borders (fences) creating suspicion that breeds enmity. This creates friction, which breeds fear of aggression and it's this fear that creates the need for defence. A classic example of how separation can affect a community is, the annexation and division of sections of Palestine by the creation of Israel. We should first consider the geo-political conditions that prevailed in the Middle East at the time of this event. In the area of Palestine and the other neighbouring states, such as Iraq, Saudi Arabia, Jordan, Syria, Lebanon, this whole area was (prior to the First World War), known as Mesopotamia. After the defeat of Turkey in that War[23], Mesopotamia was officially conceded to the conquerors Britain and France, as mandated territory.

They arbitrarily created the particular borders according to military alliances and promises made to the various local tribal leaders, by the legendary Lawrence of Arabia in return for their efforts in defeating the Turkish forces. After the Second World War, the area of Palestine was still maintained as British Mandated Territory. My parents and grandparents were born and raised in Mesopotamia in the portion of the old Ottoman Empire now known as Iraq. They lived in a small village near the city of Kut al-Amara about 100kms South of Baghdad, on the Tigris River.

My extended Jewish family, were the caretakers and stewards of the tomb of Ezra (the judge and scribe of the Torah and Old Testament) who had the misfortune to die there. The Village that grew around the tomb was known as, Al'Uzair (Ezra's tomb in English). It was and still is a holy shrine for pilgrims both Jews and Moslems. They had lived in peace and friendship with one another in this area since time immemorial. This lasted through the Turkish occupation as part of the Ottoman Empire through the defeat of the Turks by the British and continued up to the end of the Second World War. This ended when the State of Israel was declared in 1947. The British concession to the Jewish demands for statehood only came after Jewish armed groups carried out a series of skirmishes and terrorist attacks on both British military and civilian targets. These activities and political negotiations finally forced the division and territorial boundaries.

The geographical and political separation of Jew and Moslem in the Middle East (the State of Israel), made the separation official. Since that time the Palestinian intefada, the protests against the encroachment and occupation of their homeland, by European Jewish settlers created the environment where peace could not be sustained.[24] Where there are deep cultural divisions between people that are fuelled by both their political and fundamentalist religious leaders on both sides, tolerance is not an option. In Iraq before the invasion Saddam Hussein ruled with

---

23   Dissolution of the Ottoman Empire: (Wikipedia)
24   Ref. http://timelines.ws/countries/PALESTINE_A_2000.HTML

an iron fist. Although he was Sunni, the policy was flexible enough to accommodate and control the other Islamic sects within the country; Shiite being the pre-dominant. The law prevented the various factional groups from forming militias to promote and enforce their particular version of Islam on the rest of the community and this law was firmly enforced. I have spoken to a few Iraqis that fled the intolerable conditions that developed since the first invasion in January 1991 and their view was that they were much better off under Saddam's regime. They had laws along secular lines and as long as you abided by the law life was sweet. Iraq is a classic example of the results creating conditions that foster sectarian and cultural separation.

And so it continues on an international scale with borders, separation, suspicion, enmity and aggression. This is bad enough on issues of culture or national sovereignty, but when it comes to blatant outright invasion for purely political need to guarantee supply of another nations resources, it closely resembles piracy. Whichever way you look at it, it's daylight robbery. Unfortunately the actions of America in Iraq, and Israel in Palestine and Lebanon, have de-stabilized the whole area of the Middle East.

This situation further impoverishes the rest of the world. It consumes a great deal of money and the loss of innocent lives. The cost in money, energy, human and natural resources by the top four countries alone defies imagination. If it were to be made available to eliminate division and barriers globally, it could totally eliminate national social and ethnic enmity and poverty. However, in the case of fanatical religious difference this would require a specific and enlightened form of education over the time span of at least a number of generations.

The advancement of civilization depends upon universal education.

If anyone is still of the opinion that our American friends could not possibly deliberately allow the killing of 3000 [mostly] white people in New York on 9/11/2001, consider their past record of murderous deeds: A hundred thousand in the Philippines(1900), a million Koreans (1950), several million Vietnamese,(960) thousands of Latin Americans [1900- 2006], many thousands of Africans and thousands of Kosovo's, (1990s). How many brown innocents died as a result of the Gulf of Tonkin lie? How many brown innocents died as a result of US. intervention in Panama, Nicaragua, Guatemala, El Salvador, Chile, Grenada?

To emphasize the extent of political and commercial deception, the Halliburton story tells it all. How their commercial hands fit the State's gloves. Their right hand fits the political glove and the left, the military glove. They have both hands in the public purse and why is no one in the government screaming fraud?

The Halliburton Contracting Corporation, with illegal help of the U.S. government has reaped gigantic profits from the wars and foreign policies produced by the Bush family and their cronies. All involved in fraud, bribery and gross corruption. Check their web sites as they are so extensive and detailed.[25] The following is an abridged CBS report on the commercial advantage granted to the company that was controlled by Dick Cheney before he became Vice President.

Almost as soon as the last bomb was dropped over Iraq, the United States began the business of rebuilding the country. As it turns out, the U.S. will have spent approximately $25 billion to repair Iraq by the end of 2008 and many billions will be needed after that. The earliest contracts were given to a few favoured companies. Some of the biggest winners in the sweepstakes to rebuild Iraq have one thing in common: lots of very close friends in very high places. One such is Halliburton the Houston-based energy services, and construction giant. Dick Cheney, the former "CEO", was vice president of the United States.

Even before the first shots were fired in Iraq, the Pentagon had secretly awarded the Halliburton subsidiary, Kellogg Brown & Root, a two-year no-bid contract to put out oil well fires and to handle other unspecified duties involving war damage to the country's petroleum industry. It is worth up to $7 billion. Under normal circumstances, the Army Corps of Engineers would have been required to put the oil fire contract out for competitive bidding. But in times of emergency when national security is involved, the government is allowed to bypass normal procedures and award contracts to a single company without competition. That is exactly what happened with Halliburton. The

[25] Ref.:"Haliburtoncontracting".dear-free-world.blogspot.com/2004_05_01_ archive.html There are many links that expose this corporation

Pentagon came to Halliburton because the company already had an existing contract with the Army to provide logistical support to U.S. troops all over the world.

This is how they describe themselves: "Let me put a face on Halliburton. It is one of the world's largest energy services companies, and it has a strong engineering and construction arm that goes with that. You'll find us in 120 countries. We've got 83,000 people on our payroll, and we're involved in a ton of different things for a lot of wonderful clients worldwide."

According to Bob Grace, President of GSM Consulting, a small company in Amarillo Texas, Halliburton had assets pre-positioned, and had capability to get sub-contractors to do the various types of work that might be required in a hostile situation. GSM worked for the Kuwait government after the first Gulf War and was in charge of fire-fighting strategy for the huge Bergan Oil Field, which had more than 300 fires. In September 2001, when it looked like there might be another Gulf war and more oil well fires, he and a lot of his friends in the industry began contacting the Pentagon and their congressmen. This is his story:

"All we were trying to find out was, who we present our credentials to," says Grace. "We just want to be able to go to somebody and say, 'Hey, here's who we are, and here's what we've done, and here's what we do. They basically told us that there wasn't going to be any oil well fires." Grace produced a letter from the Department of Defence saying: "The department is aware of a broad range of well fire-fighting capabilities and techniques available. However, we believe it is too early to speculate what might happen in the event that war breaks out in the region." It was dated Dec. 30, 2002, more than a month after the Army Corps of Engineers began talking to Halliburton about putting out oil well fires in Iraq. "You just feel like you're beating your head against the wall," says Grace. He was told: "The mission at that time was classified, and what we were doing to assess the possible damage and to prepare for it was classified. Communications with the public had to be made with that in mind."

"I can accept confidentiality in terms of war plans and all that. But to have secrecy about Saddam Hussein blowing up oil wells, to me, is stupid," says Grace. "I mean the guy's blown up a thousand of them. So why would that be a revelation to anybody?"

Grace says they're charging $50,000 a day for a five-man team. I know there are guys as well-qualified as the guys over there that'll do it for half that." Grace and his friends are no match for Halliburton, when it comes to landing government business. Last year alone, Halliburton and its Brown & Root subsidiary delivered $1.3 billion dollars worth of services to the U.S. government. Much of it was for work the U.S. military used to do itself with military personnel and equipment. A Halliburton spokesman describes the type of work involved: "We are building base camps, providing goods, laundry, power, sewage; all the kinds of things that keep an army in the field." Charles Lewis, the executive director of the Centre for Public Integrity, a non-profit organization that investigates corruption and abuse of power by government and corporations stated: "There's no other word for it, It's a sweetheart deal".

"The trend towards privatizing the military began during the first Bush administration when Dick Cheney was secretary of defence. In 1992, the Pentagon, **under Cheney**, commissioned the Halliburton subsidiary Brown & Root to do a classified study on whether it was a good idea to have private contractors do more of the military's work. Of course, they said it's a terrific idea, and over the next eight years, Kellogg, Brown & Root and another company got 2,700 contracts worth billions of dollars, They helped to design the architecture for privatizing a lot of what happens today in the Pentagon when we have military engagements." Two years later, when he leaves the department of defence, Cheney is "CEO" of Halliburton. Thank you very much. It's a nice arrangement for all concerned."

Lewis says: "The best example of these cosy relationships is the defence policy board, a group of high-powered civilians who advise the secretary of defence on major policy issues - like whether or not to invade Iraq. Its 30 members are a Who's Who of former senior government and military officials". There's nothing wrong with that, but as the 'Centre for Public Integrity' recently discovered, nine of them have ties with corporations and private companies that have won more than $76 billion in defence contracts and that's just in the last two years. "This is not about the revolving door, people going in and out, there is no door. There's no wall. I can't tell where one stops and the other starts. I'm dead serious. They have classified clearances, they go to classified meetings and they're with companies getting billions of dollars in classified contracts and their disclosures about their activities are classified. Well, isn't that what they did when they were inside the government? What's the difference, except they're now in the private sector."

Richard Perle resigned as chairman of the defence policy board last month after it was disclosed that he had financial ties to several companies doing business with the Pentagon but Perle still sits on the board, along with former CIA director James Woolsey, who works for Booz Allen and Hamilton; the consulting firm that did nearly $700 million dollars in business with the Pentagon last year. Another board member, retired four-star general Jack Sheehan, is now a senior vice president at the Bechtel corporation which just won a $680 million contract to rebuild the infrastructure in Iraq. That contract was awarded by the State Department which used to be run by George Schultz, who sits on Bechtel's board of directors. "I'm not saying that it's illegal. These guys wrote the laws. They set up the system themselves, for themselves so of course it's legal," says Lewis. It just looks like hell. You have folks feeding at the trough, and they may be doing it in red white and blue and we may be all singing the "Star Spangled Banner," but they're doing quite well from the trough." And - abra kadabra – magically, corruption is made to appear legal. Halliburton has done extremely well. So far, the company has earned almost a billion dollars on the oil well fire contract alone, and will earn many more billions providing logistical support for U.S. troops stationed in Iraq. As for Vice President Cheney, he says he had nothing to do with the Army Corp's decision to give the no bid contract to Halliburton. Cheney also insists he cut all financial ties to the company three years ago. However, Senate democrats challenged that assertion, saying that the Vice President still gets hundreds of thousands of dollars from his former company each year - they also call for congressional hearings on Halliburton's contracts."

With this type of morality at the helm of the ship of state, what can you expect from the rest of the crew on the bridge? As the old song title goes, "Let's make hay while the sun shines."

Again I urge you to look and observe the condition of the world as a whole, the BIG picture. Consider where the whole population of the world could be today, if all the science and technology, the talents and inventions of humanity's accumulated knowledge arising from our collective consciousness - humanity's collective efforts - were directed to the uplifting of all. Rather than to the extremely small proportion of humanity in the Western developed world and their corrupt mates in Third World and developing countries.

I personally, can't get over this. By various means they usurped control of most of the world's resources and productive capacity for their own ends. To add insult to injury, waste astronomical sums of our money (taxes), to protect their stolen assets.

There are many examples of corporate crimes where inhumane treatment and environmental plunder have been used for the sole purpose of increasing profits. The result of this is to widen the gap between the haves and the have-nots. It also creates resistance movements that, in today's political climate, can easily be branded as terrorists.

The history of the rise and rise of the corporate world, started largely with the "Industrial Revolution" in Britain. This brought about the need for people to be educated in the making, the use and maintenance of machinery and the skills of accounting and the numerous other areas of work that arose. It also gave birth to a whole class of people that had previously not existed; The **Working Class**. Whole populations of poorly but adequately educated people that were encouraged to believe that, if they worked hard and diligently, they too could achieve the life style of the mill owners, merchants or shopkeepers. All they needed was enough money and possessions and they could be successful. To the poor this is the key to happiness. Present day social engineering has subtly and subliminally inculcated these false values into our culture. Unfortunately this has been largely at the expense of the billions of people in the under-developed world and also to the environment of our planet.

In the case of commercial, wholesale, retail, manufacturing and service industries, the profits go back to the individual companies in the form of massive benefits to the directors, CEO's and to shareholders. However, in the government controlled armaments industry, apart from the pennies that are made by the various selected dealers, the big profit is with those in power. Where words and diplomacy fail to achieve any objective, it's the bully-boy with the most armament power that wins the day. The various governments that supply these instruments of death and destruction to tyrants, dictators and demagogue's to maintain their positions of power are actually accessories to their crimes and should be held accountable.

CHAPTER 5

Power and The Global Corporate Mind.

Commercial and Industrial Multi-national Corporations:
How does the corporate or commercial mind view the marketplace?
The particular view depends on which rung of the commercial ladder
you are on. For example, producers, traders, wholesalers, retailers and
some that are none of these, but deal on the fringes of all of them. The
parasites; the paper shufflers that use the marketplace like the parlour
game Monopoly, buying and selling things that they don't see, smell,
touch or taste, even selling things they haven't yet bought, known as
forward selling. Commodities such as international currencies, stocks
and shares, commodity futures, local government service and public
utilities such as suburban waste collection and disposal, water supply
and energy (electricity) generation and supply.

Some of the business phraseology used is: Supply and demand,
economic rationalism, market forces, user pays, cost effective,
intellectual property and the bottom line. These are euphemisms for
screw the cost down to the absolute minimum and rake in the absolute
maximum the market will bear. With no or very little thought given to
the economic, social and ecological harm that their activities cause. In
the world of big business it's the law of the jungle – dog eat dog - and
survival of the fittest.

Commerce, Consumerism and Outright
Piracy: *(forgive us our trespasses)*.

The following chapters show how capitalism is eating itself.

(Capitalist cannibals)

If the arms industry is not doing enough to destroy people and populations, commercial corporate greed is adding to our problems. This chapter exposes some of the modern day robber barons who are raping the environment, pillaging our resources, ruining our health and locking up an unimaginable amount of our wealth. This is only the tip of the iceberg. Many of the large commercial enterprises have coalesced into only a few very large sub-groups such as: Multinational mega-corporations dealing in pharmaceuticals, oil, arms, chemicals, drugs, bio-technology, agriculture, municipal and local government services etc. By virtue of their power and financial resources, they have usurped the so-called democratic election process by strong lobbying and the devious use of a magical tool, *the media.*

It is the media that creates voting patterns and, in most cases, influences our world view. Also, by clever use of the media, lobby groups infiltrate the halls of power with un-elected people, with the use of presidential or ministerial appointments and advisers. (Cronyism). In reality, the people who are then represented are the powerful and wealthy - who are virtually (to coin an appropriate phrase,) able to "get away with murder" by covering up any criminal or socially detrimental results of their activities. On the local retail scene, consider:

Safeway's / Woolworth's.

As an advertising gimmick, Woolies, that great Australian retailing icon, advertised widely that on the 23rd Jan 2007, they would donate the takings from all their stores to support drought relief (an estimated $3 million dollars), suggesting that we do the right thing and shop that day at one of their supermarket stores. However, a very thoughtful and knowledgeable (now retired) Church of Christ Minister, was prompted to comment. "Is this the same Woolworth's that:

Paid its CEO $12 million a year ... (Age 3.12.06) Continues to do deals with a multimillion dollar meat supplier with a history of bribes and kickbacks, which led to the sacking of a Coles CEO ... (SMH 15.1.07)

Was fined $7 million for anti-competitive liquor dealing ... (The Australian. 23.12.06)

Was fined $9million for price fixing in the bread market. (The Australian. 1.2.06)

Consumer Affairs Victoria took out a court order "forcing the company to immediately cease fundraising until it complied with the law" ... (Age 8.12.05)

Is now one of the largest, if not the largest gaming and liquor suppliers in Australia, taking $1 billion dollars from hotels with 12,000 gaming machines ... (AFR 31.10.05). is one of the largest tobacco pushers in the market. Tobacco contributed to some 19 000 deaths last year-400 per week ...(The Australian. 16.6.06). And is now one of two petrol/diesel suppliers in Australia who are cornering the market, driving all independent operators to the wall, including many rural suppliers!

On the international scene:

The following particular corporations[26] carry out some of the most criminal human rights abuses of modern times, yet it is increasingly difficult to hold them to account. Economic globalization and the rise of trans-national corporate power have created a favourable climate for corporate criminals. They are motivated principally by profit and the rule of supply and demand. Their only loyalty is to themselves and the stockholders. Several of the companies below are being sued under the Alien Tort Claims Act. This is a law that gives citizens of any nationality the right to sue in US federal courts for violations of international rights or treaties. When corporations in the US. act like criminals, people have the right and the power to stop them. Leaders and multinational corporations alike are accountable for the accords they have signed.

Around the world, in Venezuela, Argentina, India and the United States, citizens are stepping up to test their democratic right to hold corporations accountable to international law. However, can you

---

[26] Reprinted with permission from Global Exchange, www.globalexchange. org."

imagine just how far a private citizen would get, up against the financial and political muscle of any of these giant corporations?

The following fourteen corporations are only the tip of an iceberg that shows the lengths that these corporate cannibals will go to turn a profit.

1).Caterpillar:

For years the Caterpillar Company has provided Israel with the bulldozers used to destroy Palestinian homes. Despite worldwide condemnation, Caterpillar has refused to end its corporate participation in house demolition by cutting off sales of ***specially modified*** D9 and D10 bulldozers to the Israeli military. In a letter to Caterpillar CEO James Owens, the Office of the UN High Commissioner on Human Rights said: "allowing the delivery of your bulldozers to the Israeli army in the certain knowledge that they are being used for such action, might involve complicity or acceptance on the part of your company to actual and potential violations of human rights ..."Peace activist Rachel Corrie was killed by a Caterpillar D-9, military bulldozer in 2003. She was run over while attempting to block the destruction a family home in Gaza. Rachel's family filed suit against Caterpillar in March 2005 charging that Caterpillar knowingly sold machines used to violate human rights. Since her death, at least three more Palestinians have been killed in their homes by Israeli bulldozer demolitions.

2). Chevron:

This petrochemical company is guilty of some of the worst environmental and human rights abuses in the world. From 1964 to 1992, Texaco (which transferred operations to Chevron after being bought out in 2001) unleashed a toxic "Rainforest Chernobyl" in Ecuador. Their many criminal acts were:

    a). To leave over 600 unlined oil pits in pristine northern Amazon rainforest and dumping 18 billion gallons of toxic production water into rivers used for bathing water. As a result, local communities suffered severe health effects, including cancer, skin lesions, birth defects, and spontaneous abortions.

    b). To organize the violent repression of peaceful opposition to oil extraction. In Nigeria Chevron hired private military personnel to fire on peaceful protestors who opposed oil extraction in the Niger Delta.

c). Additionally Chevron is responsible for widespread health problems in Richmond, California, where one of Chevron's largest refineries is located processing 350,000 barrels of oil a day. The Richmond refinery produces oil flares and toxic waste in the Richmond area. As a result, local residents suffer from high rates of lupus, skin rashes, rheumatic fever, liver problems, kidney problems, tumours, cancer, asthma and eye problems.

d). The Unocal Corporation which recently became a subsidiary of Chevron is an oil and gas company based in California with operations around the world. In December 2004, the company settled a lawsuit filed by 15 Burmese villages, in which the villagers alleged Unocal's complicity in a range of human rights violations in Burma, including rape, summary execution, torture, forced labour and forced migration.

3). Coca-Cola Company:

This company is perhaps the most widely recognized corporate symbol on the planet. It also leads in the abuse of workers' rights, assassinations, water privatization, and worker discrimination. Here are some of their activities between 1989 and 2002:

a). Eight union leaders from Coca-Cola bottling plants in Colombia were killed after protesting the company's labour practices.

b). Hundreds of other Coca-Cola workers who have joined or considered joining the Colombian union SINALTRAINAL, have been kidnapped, tortured, and detained by paramilitary mercenaries hired to intimidate workers to prevent them from unionizing.

c). In India, Coca-Cola destroys local agriculture by privatizing the country's water resources. In Plachimada, Kerala, Coca-Cola extracted 1.5 million litres of deep well water, which they bottled and sold under the names Dasani and Bon-Aqua. As a result, the groundwater was severely depleted affecting thousands of communities with water shortages and destroying agricultural activity. The remaining water became contaminated with high chloride and bacteria levels, leading to scabs, eye problems, and stomach diseases in the local population.

4). DynCorp:

Private security contractors have become the fastest-growing sector of the global economy during the last decade: a $100-billion-a-year mostly unregulated service industry. DynCorp, one of the providers of these mercenary services, demonstrates the industry's power and potential to abuse human rights. While guarding Afghan statesmen and African oil fields, training Iraqi police forces, eradicating Colombian coca plants, and protecting business interests in hurricane-devastated New Orleans, these hired guns bolster the security of governments and organizations at the expense of many people's human rights. DynCorp's fumigation of coca crops along the Colombian-Ecuadorian border, led Ecuadorian peasants to sue DynCorp in 2001. Plaintiff s argued that DynCorp knew, or should have known, that the herbicides were highly toxic. In 2001, a mechanic with DynCorp blew the whistle on DynCorp employees in Bosnia for rape and trading girls as young as 12 into sex slavery. According to a lawsuit filed by the mechanic, "employees and supervisors were engaging in perverse, illegal and inhumane behaviour in purchasing illegal weapons, women, and forged passports." DynCorp fired the whistleblower and transferred the employees accused of sex trading out of the country, eventually fi ring some, but none were prosecuted.

5). Ford Motor Company:

Among automakers, Ford Motor Company is the worst. Every year since 1999, the US Environmental Protection Agency has ranked Ford cars, trucks and SUVs as having the worst overall fuel economy of any American automaker. Ford's current cars and trucks have lower average fuel efficiency than the original Ford Model-T. Ford is also in last place when it comes to vehicle greenhouse gas emissions. According to a recent report by the Union of Concerned Scientists, Ford has "the absolute worst heat-trapping gas emissions performance of all the "Big Six" automakers. Despite the company's recent green-washing PR campaign, its record has actually worsened. According to Ford's own sustainability report, between 2003 and 2004, the company's US fleet-wide fuel economy decreased and its CO2 emissions went up. Ford has also lobbied against lawmakers' efforts to increase fuel economy standards at the national level and is also involved in a lawsuit against California's fuel economy standards.

6). Freeport McRan Copper and Gold Inc:

This is the largest mining company in West Papua. Freeport first came to West Papua in 1967 when they received the very first mining contract issued by the Suharto government. The construction of the mine required moving millions of tons of earth from the top of the jayawijawa mountain. They also built a giant aerial tramway to carry the ore to a concentrator that converts it into liquid slurry which then flows down a 100 km pipeline to a specially constructed export port at Amamapare on the Arafura Sea. Freeport's operations have grown from an initial 10,000 hectares to the most recent 2.6 million hectare mine at Grasberg. This expansion was sustained by investment from another trans-national, Rio Tinto which now has a 40% interest in Freeport operations. Freeport is now the largest gold mine and third largest copper mine in the world.

Freeport's environmental and social impact: In 2001 it produced 1.4 billion pounds of copper and 2.6 million ounces of gold with estimated reserves of 52 billion pounds of copper and 64 million ounces of gold. This production, has cost the local people dearly in terms of loss of land, environmental destruction and human rights abuses.

a). Large areas of rainforest are being cleared to establish the mine and important rivers are being polluted by the 200,000 tons of tailing sand produced by the mine each day. By the time the mine ceases production the adjacent Wanagong valley will be filled to a depth of 450 meters and the 114 hectare Carstensweid meadow will be covered by 250 meters of waste rock.

b). Downstream, the tailings cause severe flooding and erosion. The toxic minerals in the water contaminate fish and mollusks in the river and are polluting nearby coral reefs.

c). The local people are deeply affronted by the destruction of Jayawijaya Mountain (also called Mt Grasberg). In their cosmological beliefs, Jayawijaya is the head of their sacred mother. To them Freeport has already cut off their mother's head by reducing the top of the mountain to a plateau and it is now digging into her heart.

7). KBR (Kellogg, Brown and Root):

This is a Subsidiary of Halliburton Corporation; KBR is a private company that provides military support services. It is notorious for questionable bookkeeping, dishonest billing practices with US taxpayer dollars and no-bid contracts. Their dubious accounting in Iraq came to light in December 2003 when Pentagon auditors questioned possible overcharges for imported gasoline. In June 2005, a previously secret Pentagon audit criticized $1.4 billion, in "questionable" and "unsupported" expenditures. In 2002 the company paid $2 million to settle a Justice Department lawsuit that accused KBR of inflating contract prices. Many third-country national (TCN) labourers have been hired by KBR to "rebuild" Iraq. Generally hailing from impoverished Asian countries, they have unexpectedly become part of the largest civilian workforce ever hired in support of a U.S. war. Once abroad, the workers find themselves with few protections and uncertain legal status. They often sleep in crowded trailers and wait outside in scorching heat for food rations and lack adequate medical care and putting in hard labour seven days a week, 10 hours or more a day.

8). Lockheed Martin:

Lockheed Martin is the world's largest military contractor. Providing satellites, planes, missiles and other lethal high-tech items to the Pentagon, keeps the profits rolling in. Since 2000, the year Bush was elected, the company's stock value has tripled. As the Centre for Corporate Policy, the website www.corporatepolicy.org notes, it is no coincidence that Lockheed VP Bruce Jackson—who helped draft the Republican foreign policy platform in 2000, is a key player at the Project for a New American Century (PNAC), the intellectual incubator of the Iraq war.

Lockheed Martin is not the only defence contractor that goes behind the scenes to influence public policy, but it is one of the worst. Stephen J. Hadley, who stepped into Condoleezza Rice's old job as Assistant to the President for National Security Affairs, was formerly a partner in a Washington DC law firm representing Lockheed Martin. He is only one of the beneficiaries of the so-called revolving door between the military industries and the "civilian" national security apparatus. These war profiteers have a ***profound and illegitimate influence*** on the country's international policy decisions.

9). Nestle` USA:

The problem of illegal and forced child labour is rampant in the chocolate industry, because more than 40% of the world's cocoa supply comes from the Ivory Coast. This is a country in which the US State Department estimates had approximately 109,000 child labourers working in hazardous conditions on cocoa farms. In 2001, Save the Children Canada reported that 15,000 children between nine and twelve years old, many from impoverished Mali, had been tricked and sold into slavery on West African cocoa farms, many for just $30 each. Additionally, violations of labour rights are reported from Nestle factories in numerous other countries Nestle, the third largest buyer of cocoa from the Ivory Coast, is well aware of the tragically unjust labour practices taking place on the farms with which it continues to do business. Nestle and other chocolate manufacturers agreed to end the use of abusive and forced child labour on cocoa farms by July 1, 2005, but they failed to do so. They are also notorious for the aggressive marketing of infant formula in poor countries in the 1980s. Because of this practice, Nestle is still one of the most boycotted corporations in the world, and its infant formula is still controversial. In Colombia, Nestle replaced the entire factory staff with lower-wage workers and did not renew the collective employment contract. In Italy in 2005, police seized more than two million litres of Nestle infant formula that was contaminated with the chemical isopropyl-thio-xanthone (ITX).

10). Philip Morris USA:

Philip Morris International, aka The Altria Group Inc. Among tobacco companies, they are notorious for their diversification. Altria Corporation owns a total of 43 companies: 24 cigarette and tobacco brands, Alpine Basic, Benson & Hedges, Bristol, Bucks, Cambridge, Chesterfi eld, Cambridge, Classic, Collector's, Commander, English Ovals, F6, Lark, L&M, Marlboro, Merit, Next, Parliament, Players, Saratoga, Virginia Slims, and West. Plus an additional 9 Food & Beverage Company Brands: Dame, Jacobs Coff ee, Kaffee HAG, Kool-Aid, Kraft Foods, Boca Burger, Lindens Bagels, Maxwell House, Milk,

Nabisco, Onko, Oscar Mayer Meats, Post Cereals, Philadelphia Cream Cheese, Shake n Bake, Splenda, Suchard, Tang and Vegemite.

Documents uncovered in a lawsuit filed against the tobacco industry by the state of Minnesota, showed that Philip Morris and other leading tobacco corporations knew very well of the dangers of tobacco products and the addictiveness of nicotine. To this day, Philip Morris deceives consumers about the harm of its products by offering light, mild and low-tar cigarettes that give consumers the illusion these brands are healthier than traditional cigarettes. The company says it doesn't want kids to smoke, yet it spends millions of dollars every day marketing and promoting cigarettes to youth. Overseas, it has even hired **underage Marlboro girls** to distribute free cigarettes to other children and sponsored concerts where cigarettes were handed out to minors. As anti-tobacco campaigns and government regulations are slowing tobacco use in Western countries, Philip Morris has aggressively moved into developing country markets where smoking and smoking-related deaths are on the rise. Preliminary numbers released by the World Health Organization predict, global deaths due to smoking related illnesses will nearly double by 2020. More than three-quarters of those deaths will occur in the developing world.

11). Wal-Mart:

Wal-Mart is the biggest corporation in the world. It owns 5,100 stores worldwide and employs 1.3 million workers in the United States and 400,000 abroad as well as millions more in the factories of its suppliers. Many people have heard of the way Wal-Mart steamrolls its way into every possible town, destroying local supermarkets and countless small businesses.

Wal-Mart has a long track record of worker abuse, from forced overtime, sex discrimination, illegal child labour and relentless union busting. Wal-Mart also notoriously fails to provide health insurance to over half of its employees. Who are then left to rely on themselves or taxpayers to provide for a portion of their healthcare needs through government Medicaid.

Less well known, is the fact that Wal-Mart maintains its low price level by the use of substandard labour conditions in the overseas factories that produce most of its goods. The company continually demands lower prices from its suppliers, who, in turn, make more outrageous demands on their workers in order to meet Wal-Mart's requirements. In September 2005, the International Labour Rights Fund filed a lawsuit on behalf of Wal-Mart supplier sweatshop workers in China, Indonesia, Bangladesh, Nicaragua and Swaziland. The workers were denied minimum wages, forced to work overtime without compensation, and were denied legally mandated health care. Other worker rights violations that have been found in foreign factories that produce goods for Wal-Mart include; locked bathrooms, starvation wages, pregnancy tests, denial of access to health care. Employees are fired and blacklisted if they try to defend their rights. Numbers 12, 13 and 14, are described in the next chapter covering the pharmaceutical industry and are reprinted with permission from Global exchange

CHAPTER 6.

The Pharmaceutical Industry:

More Classic Examples Of Greedy And Irresponsible Chemical Corporations:

These companies, including Glaxo-Smith-Kline, Roche, Dow, Merck, Pfizer, Monsanto and others, supply a large variety of their products to most of the independent sovereign states that occupy the continent of Africa. Unfortunately they are at a price unaffordable to afflicted people.

The largest consumer - South Africa – has started to use much cheaper generic brands of a number of drugs including those required for the treatment of HIV AIDS and are now being sued by one or more of these companies disputing South Africa's right to import and license the generic versions of the expensive patented HIV/AIDS drugs. If it is successful, the lawsuit will also prevent South Africa from licensing the local production of the same drugs. South Africa has 2.4 million people with AIDS and an additional 4-5 million infected with HIV. It simply cannot afford to buy the drugs necessary to treat those people. AIDS is a disease that requires several different medicines for each individual. No single drug fights AIDS symptoms because each symptom must be treated separately. The staggering figure of thirty-nine pharmaceutical companies, are now suing the South African Government.

To put it into perspective a review of the pharmaceutical production process indicates that generally, US- and European-based companies do research and development in collaboration with government-sponsored research agencies. Pharmaceutical companies will then patent a particular medicine under a registered name such as, Panadol (patented by Glaxo-Smith-Kline). The generic drug is much less expensive and can be made by anyone. Generic versions of HIV-AIDS drugs are on offer at a fraction of the cost of patented brand-name drugs.

12). Dow Chemical:

Has been destroying lives and poisoning the planet for decades. The company is best known for the ravages and health disaster for millions of Vietnamese and U.S. Veterans caused by its lethal Vietnam War defoliant, Agent Orange. Dow's "invent first, ask questions later" standard of business led the multinational company to develop and perfect Napalm, a brutal chemical weapon that burned many innocents to death in Vietnam and other wars. In 1988, Dow provided pesticides to Saddam Hussein despite warnings that they could be used to produce chemical weapons. In 2001 the company inherited the toxic legacy of the worst peacetime chemical disaster in history when it acquired Union Carbide Corporation (UCC) and its outstanding liabilities in Bhopal, India.

This disaster, as the 'Students for Bhopal' website recounts: "On December 3rd, 1984, thousands of people in Bhopal, India were gassed to death after a catastrophic chemical leak at a UCC pesticide plant. More than 150,000 people were left severely disabled. Of whom 22,000 have since died of their injuries in a disaster now widely acknowledged as the world's worst ever. It refuses to address its liabilities in Bhopal or even admit its existence and continuing Union Carbide's tradition of profiting from extreme corporate irresponsibility. In India, Dow's subsidiary faces manslaughter charges and is considered a fugitive from justice for a pending criminal case related to the 1984 chemical explosion. Dow and U/C's lack of accountability in the disaster continue to affect the lives in Bhopal to this day.

World wide Dow is involved in human rights abuses, environmental destruction, water and ground contamination, health violations, chemical poisoning and chemical warfare. Dow Chemical's impact is felt globally from their Midland, Michigan headquarters to New Plymouth, New Zealand. In Midland, Dow has been producing chlorinated chemicals, burning and burying its waste including chemicals that make up Agent Orange. In New Plymouth, New Zealand, 500,000 gallons of Agent Orange were produced and thousands of tons of dioxin-laced waste were dumped in agricultural fields. Dow's toxic legacies of human rights abuses traverse to agricultural fields in Central America where Dow exported EPA-banned pesticide DBCP for use on banana and pineapple crops. As a result, thousands of banana workers were exposed to DBCP and became sterile. In retail markets across the world Dow's dangerous chemicals are present as common household solvents, plastics, paints and pharmaceuticals.

13). Monsanto:

By far, the largest producer of genetically engineered seeds in the world, dominating 70% to 100% of the market for crops such as soy, cotton, wheat and corn. The company is also one of the most flagrant abusers of the human rights of food sovereignty, access to land, and health. Monsanto promotes mono-culture—the practice of covering large swaths of land with a single crop. This practice pushes out subsistence farms and destroys arable land by drastically decreasing soil, water quality for years and draining soil of key nutrients. The company also undercuts food prices by flooding countries like Mexico, India, and Brazil with cheap, genetically modified foods, resulting in the displacement of millions of farm workers, who are forced to migrate to cities or work as landless peasants or share croppers.

According to the India Committee of the Netherlands and the International Labour Rights Fund, Monsanto also employs child labour. In India, an estimated 12,375 children work in cottonseed production for farmers paid by Indian and multinational seed companies, including Monsanto. A number of children have died or became seriously ill due to exposure to pesticides. Monsanto's yearly profits are $5.4 billion. It is also the world's leading producer of the herbicide glyphosate, marketed as Roundup. Roundup is sold to small farmers as a pesticide, yet in the long run, harms production. The toxins accumulate in the soil and the plants eventually become infertile, forcing farmers to purchase genetically modified "Roundup Ready" Seed, which is able to resist the herbicide. This then creates a cycle of dependency on Monsanto for both the weed killer and the only seed that can resist it Both products are patented and sold at inflated prices. Documentary evidence shows that Human exposure to the pesticide causes cancers, skin Disorders, spontaneous abortions, premature births, and damage to the gastro-intestinal and nervous systems. Another Monsanto strategy designed to capture a market is: "Terminator Technology" together with the US Department of Agriculture, the Monsanto subsidiary, "Delta and Pine Land Co.", has developed genetically modified "Terminator technology" or "gene protection system" that triggers seed-sterility in crops. This creates a biological lock against seed-saving and replanting. The farmer then must buy seed for next season's crops from them. Patents are being sought in 87 countries. Monsanto has, on various occasions, claimed either that the technology does not exist, or that it is not yet in use in its commercialized lines.

14). Pfizer:

One of the largest and most profitable pharmaceutical companies in the world with revenues of $52.5 billion in 2004. In addition to Viagra, Zoloft, Zithromax, and Norvasc, Pfizer produces the HIV/AIDS-related drugs Rescriptor, Viracept and Diflucan (fluconazole). Like other drug companies they sell these drugs at prices poor people cannot afford and aggressively fight efforts to make it easier for generic drugs to enter the market. They have even cut off drug shipments to Canadian pharmacies that sold Pfizer drugs to patients in the United States for costs more affordable than those offered in US pharmacies. To ensure its profits Pfizer invests heavily in US campaign contributions. Though it can't seem to afford to offer life-saving drugs at affordable prices, it was able to scrounge up $544,900 for mostly Republican candidates in election cycle 2006 and $1,630,556 in the 2004 election cycle.

Drug companies' refusal to put human beings' health ahead of their own greed and profits is especially deadly for people with HIV/AIDS. AIDS killed 3.1 million people in 2004. This shocking death rate could be greatly reduced if treatment was made available to people who cannot afford it. Pfizer and other drug companies have refused to grant generic licenses for HIV/AIDS drugs to countries like Brazil, South Africa and the Dominican Republic, where patients are forced to pay $20 per weekly pill for drugs like fluconazole though the average national wage is only $120 per month.

Instead of helping eradicate the world's worst pandemic in history, the World Trade Organization has made matters worse. Beginning in

1995, the agreement on Trade-Related Aspects of Intellectual Property Rights (TRIPS) protected companies by stopping WTO member countries from making generic versions of their drugs. Because of public pressure the WTO announced a new agreement in 2003 to allow poor countries to access cheap generic antiretroviral drugs, but in practice, the drugs are just as inaccessible to poor countries as they were before. Pfizer it seems, also values shareholder profits before safety standards. In Europe in 2005, it withdrew from scientific studies of a new class of AIDS drugs called CCR5 inhibitors, choosing instead to rush its own untested CCR5 inhibitor onto the European market without full information about the drug's side effects.

As previously mentioned, Dow Chemical Company in August 4 1999, announced that it would acquire the Union Carbide Corporation, creating the world's second largest chemical company. It could be described ecologically as a "union made in hell." Prior to this they gained notoriety in the 1960s as a manufacturer of the herbicide known as a new class of AIDS drugs called CCR5 inhibitors choosing instead to rush its own untested CCR5 inhibitor onto the European market without full information. They were found to have toxic dioxin contaminants which have been blamed for causing health disorders and birth defects in both the victim Vietnamese population and U.S. war veterans that delivered it. Its formula has also been found to have carcinogenic properties primarily affecting females.

An April 2003 report paid for by the National Academy of Science concluded that during the Vietnam War over 6,000 spraying missions in Vietnam and Cambodia were carried out by the US. Over 15 million litres were used, 3,181 villages were sprayed directly, and between 2.1 and 4.8 million people "would have been exposed during the spraying." Dow and Monsanto were the two largest producers of Agent Orange for the U.S. Military and were named in a law suit along with eight other companies. A number of lawsuits by American GI's have been won in the years since the Vietnam War.

DOW and Union Carbide:
Three organizations representing survivors of the criminal and inhumane use of Agent Orange have sent a memorandum to the chief executive officer of Dow Chemical reminding him of liabilities arising

from the Bhopal disaster. They hold Union Carbide responsible for the deaths and injuries caused by the accident. For years the Survivors' organizations have called upon the corporation to release precise details of the chemicals released during the accident and results of tests conducted by Union Carbide to assess the effects of methyl-iso-cyanate on animals (one of the toxic components released). This information has been withheld by Union Carbide because the company claims it is confidential business information. However, such data was urgently needed for effective treatment of those who remain ill.

CHAPTER 7

The Water War

The Water Privatization Scam:
The world's "multinational water mafia:" [27]

Suez, Vivendi and a handful of companies, mostly based in France and England, dominate the water multinationals. Based on the number of projects the top five are Suez-Lyonnaise des Eaux (France), Vivendi (France), Aguas de Barcelona (Spain), Thames Water (Britain) and SAUR International (France). They undertake a wide variety of operations such as telecommunication, energy and waste in addition to their water-related specialties. The top two, Vivendi and Suez capture about 70 percent of the existing water market share. They also work together through joint ventures thereby creating oligopolies. Not only do they lobby their own governments, but also have close links with global water NGOs such as Global Water Partnership and World Water Council. The privatization of water has had a disastrous impact on the human right to clean water. The French company Suez is one of the worst perpetrators of this abuse, followed closely by Bechtel. The billions of dollars in profit made by these companies is at the expense of poor people living in countries where thousands lack access to potable water. Because of private water contracts negotiated at government level, they are hit with skyrocketing water prices. Suez goes by many

---

[27] (Google.): "Water privatisation" alerts and updates extensive global area information on a daily basis.

names around the world Ondeo, SITA and others in order to mask its worldwide net of controversial activities.

The majority of water consumers all over the world believe water is a human right. This is the reason that water distribution companies are classified as public utilities. Government agencies monitor their operations and regulate their rates and charges to consumers. However, the privatization program of international financial institutions such as the World Bank, the Asian Development Bank (ADB) and the International Monitory Fund (IMF), target the services sector for conversion to corporate profit driven enterprises. So the civil society in Asia-Pacific region and elsewhere are angrily protesting against privatization of water services because of the detrimental impact of this on the water sector in so many areas.

The Philippines:[28]

Manila, after seven years of water privatization under a Suez company (Maynilad Water), a study showed that water rates increased in some neighbourhoods by 400 to 700 percent. These studies also showed that the negligence of the company resulted in cholera and gastro-enteritis outbreaks that killed six people and severely endangered the lives of 725 in Manila's Tondo district. The news reports about the death of four people and the hospitalization of 200 more in Manila, due to contaminated water are greatly saddening and extremely alarming. Doctors who attended to the victims, suspect a cholera outbreak via the water system in the area which could easily extend to other localities that are part of the same deteriorating pipe network. Yet even as its clients die, fall ill, suffer water shortages, pay exorbitant rates and put up with other abuses, Maynilad refuses to accept the responsibility for the general breakdown of its operations. The closed-door arbitration process between government and Maynilad continues, still, is unable or unwilling to establish Maynilad's obvious role in the decline of Metro Manila's water situation. The Philippines is the classic example: Many people and communities are demanding that the Asian Development Bank (ADB)review not only its water policy but also its overall lending strategy that traps governments into poverty-inducing measures such as the privatization of water utilities. The Philippine experience demonstrates how Banks use the debt of its developing

28   civilsociety/WaterforthePeopleNetworkAsia

member-countries to give them the leverage to aggressively push for severe conditions. Prerequisite to the loan approval are conditions that tightly secure the loan repayment and guarantees a no loss situation to the private company. With water supply being capital intensive, privatization as a loan condition, created an environment enabling trans-national corporations to takeover water supply systems that were previously government utilities. The Philippine experience demonstrates the so-called "private sector participation" (PSP) in providing water services as promoted by the water policy and enforced by the Asian Development Bank's "conditionalities." Individuals, particularly the poor, will always be at risk. After eight years of having profiteering private corporations in Metro Manila's water distribution system, the undue burden was passed on to the hapless consumers. Tariffs escalated so fast: Manila Water's unit rate now reads 700 percent higher than in 1997, while The "West Zone" operator (Maynilad)'s tariff, has increased by 500 percent. More than 700 people were victims due to contaminated water. Seven of them died from a cholera outbreak in the west zone of Metro Manila alone. The West Zone operator (Maynilad) is itself in hot water. It is continuously embroiled in controversy over its rate increases and mismanagement. Yet be settled, is an anomalous corporate rehabilitation plan that obligates the government to shell out public funds amounting to $53-million.

Bolivia[29]:

Another Suez company (Aguas de Illimani) left 200,000 people without access to water and caused a revolt when it tried to charge between $335 and $445 to connect a private home to the water supply. Countless people were unable to afford this charge in a country whose yearly per capita GDP is $915. Unfortunately, the IMF and World Bank have played a key role in pushing water privatization all over the world. Many countries have been required to open up their water supply to private companies as a condition for receiving IMF loans. The World Bank has approved millions of dollars in loans for the privatization of water systems. In 1996 the Water War politicized the failures of the Goni Govt. privatization program. The euphemistically dubbed "capitalization," was nothing less than the fire sale of state assets, exacerbating the financial crisis of the state. Bolivia's borrowing

[29]   citizen.org/documents/Bolivia

from 1997 to 2002 increased dramatically from 3.3 to 8.6 percent of its Gross Domestic Product. The International Monetary Fund's demands for regressive changes to the tax structure and reductions in public expenditures to mitigate the budget deficit set the stage for further political crises. The World Bank denied a $25 million loan guarantee to Cochabamba, Bolivia, unless the local government sold its public water system to the private sector. It was subsequently sold to the Bechtel Corporation. Two years prior to this deal, the same World Bank officials threatened to withhold $600 million in international debt relief unless Cochabamba's water system was privatized. Bolivia is the poorest country in South America. Immediately after Bechtel bought the municipal water supply, the American firm raised prices two hundred percent and cut off water access to the people too poor to pay. Families needed to pay about one quarter of their salary for their water. When the company refused to lower its rates, there was a general strike, a stand-still in the transportation service, demonstrations and riots in the streets, resulting in mass arrests, hundred of injuries, and at least one death. After only four months, Bechtel fled to the United States and filed a twenty-five million dollar suit against Bolivia. This is to be tried behind closed doors in a secret trade court at World Bank headquarters in Washington D.C.

Canada[30]:

The ill effects of this approach were seen in the 1998 case in which the U.S. Company Sun Belt sued the Canadian government for $10 billion for violating the North America Free Trade Agreement (NAFTA). The grievance was that the government of British Columbia prohibited the mass export of its potable water when Sun Belt wanted to export it to thirsty California

Mexico:

In another case, Metalclad successfully sued the Mexican government for $16.5 million after Mexican authorities barred the operation of the company's hazardous waste treatment and disposal facility in San Luis Potosí state. The company claimed that was an unjust expropriation.

---

[30] cbc.ca/news/features/(link to water, and water privatization) 30 Metalclad fiasco in mexico: (google).

These and many other NAFTA cases are omens of what Central and South America can expect from the FTAA[31].

The effects in developing countries:
Ghana:

In 2001[32], due to IMF and World Bank policies, the privatized water fees in Ghana increased by 95 percent. New loan conditions threaten even more increases to bring prices up to a "market rate." "The current water tariff rates are already beyond the means of most of the population in Ghana. Rudolf Amenga-Etego, the National CAP (C.E.O) of Water in Ghana, says: "How will the population possibly be able to absorb a so-called 'market price' in the context of privatization?" Privatizing public services like water is a growing trend and Ghanaians have already seen huge rate increases," Wenonah Hauter, Director of Public Citizen's Critical Mass, Energy and Environment Program said: "We are concerned about the growing trend toward privatization in the United States and want to see its impacts elsewhere." Several recent Public Citizen Reports have concluded, that the end results of privatization contracts in the U.S. have been "less than positive" for consumers and local governments

Indonesia:

After a privatization promise to "stop leakages" in Jakarta water reticulation system in 1999, the company increased prices and decreased the water pressure resulting in the water not reaching outlying areas. In 2004 the Bill of Water Resources was finally passed in Indonesia. This had been postponed several times due to objections by farmers, city consumers, religious and community organizations, NGOs and academics. Their objections were based on aspects of the law that set the agenda for the privatization and commercialization of water. Articles in the law provide for control of drinking water plus water resources such as ground and river water and parts of rivers; affectively giving control of water for agricultural irrigation, energy and industry to the private sector. The law dominantly favours corporate economic interests and is strongly influenced by the World Bank and the IMF.

---

[31] Metalclad fiasco in Mexco
[32] tradewatch.org/pressroom/release.cfm?ID

New Guinea:

Privatization caused people who could not afford the price, were forced to drink pond water. Consequently many were infected with "guinea worm." This is a worm that can come out anywhere on your body at any time. The weakest countries are the most vulnerable and the least able to provide proper oversight. Corporate hypocrisy has reached new heights when this "public health emergency," that is a by-product of privatization, is being played up and used as an excuse by the World Bank and the IMF to justify further water privatization.

Over 1 billion people in the world today are without readily available drinkable water[33].

This provides the climate for commercial predators to enter and capture a market place. More than 200 water privatization projects have been funded through The World Bank, The Asian Development Bank or the IMF. However altruistic and beneficial it may initially sound, recent experience has shown that – as always – profit comes before people. The U.S. government and trans-national corporations insist on privatization and neo-liberal policies in the management of water. The main tool to push the privatization agenda is the Free Trade Area of the Americas (FTAA). Under the terms of the FTAA, foreign investors will be able to sue and demand compensation from governments for any law or rule departure that affects their profits. This could mean costly economic sanctions to any country that revokes privatizations of aqueducts or tries to limit or prevent the international trade in water, even if such attempts are motivated by environmental or public health reasons.

Such investor protections already exist in the North American Free Trade Agreement (NAFTA), covering Canada, the United States and Mexico. The treaty defines water as a tradable good, allowing all levels of governments- from Puerto Rico to Hawaii and from Chiapas to Alaska- to sell their water resources to the highest bidder under threat of being sued by private companies.

Most importantly, ordinary people affected by these developments such as the residents of Cochabamba, Bolivia, New Guinea, Indonesia, Ghana, Alexandria township, South Africa and the subsistence farmers

---

[33]   Dirty Aid Dirty Water. (Google)

of Andhra Pradesh, Bangladesh and India, are opposed to this corporate piracy!!

Further points on multinational corporate led water privatization:

Their geographical target is urban consumers; but 90% of water poor live in rural areas.

When multinationals come in, rate increases equal more expensive services (ask the Bolivians and Philippino's). There is *no* accountability to consumers, *only* to shareholders.

It reduces local control and public rights, fosters corruption, is difficult to reverse; can leave not only the rural poor but also the urban poor with no access to clean water. It also undermines water quality and can compromise the ecosystem's need of water The investor protections provided by NAFTA and the proposed FTAA do not even exist in the World Trade Organization. (WTO). At this time only sovereign states can present grievances to the WTO, but this will change if the Multilateral Agreement on Investment (MAI) is approved.

With the MAI, trans-national corporations will be able to use the WTO to sue any member country that limits their activities and/or profits. With neo-liberal globalization a massive increase is expected in activities that consume fresh water such as manufacture, monoculture based agribusiness and urban expansion.

The CIA in the US claims that by 2015, water will be one of the major causes of international conflict. The United Nations forecasts that the demand for the liquid will exceed the supply by 56 percent in 2025 if current trends continue. According to the World Bank, the next world war will not be over oil but over water. Yet the World Bank and IMF still insist on prescribing liberalization of this sector for most of the developing nations!

Do you think "multinationals want to get involved to help solve the water and sanitation needs of the poor?," and after reading the above, would you trust a multinational on this? The Water Wars have begun. And as the oil reserves run out, the multi-national corporations fight for control of what's left.

CHAPTER 8

Logging

This is another problem area that is seriously threatening the world's ecology. Here are a few details of international logging operations in the Amazon rain forest in Brazil, Australia, Africa, Myanmar (Burma), and West Papua:[34]

Brazil:[35]

The Brazilian Government is attempting to introduce legislation that could reduce the Amazon forest to 50% of its size. The following, gives some facts regarding the importance of retaining 100% of what now remains: 20% of the oxygen that we breathe on this earth, is generated within The Amazon rainforest 30% of the world's freshwater is contained within the Amazon basin, 60% of the cancer-fighting drugs used today are derived from plants that can only be found within the Amazon rainforest. The area to be deforested is four times the size of Portugal and would be mainly used for agriculture and pastures for livestock. All the timber is to be sold to international markets in the form of wood chips, by large multinational companies. The truth is that the soil in the Amazon forest is useless without the forest itself. Its quality is very acidic and the region is prone to constant floods. At this time more than 160,000 square kilometres deforested for the same purpose, are abandoned and in the process of becoming deserts. This

---

34 Rain Forest destruction worldwide: (google)
35 Ref. "Amazonian rain forests" (Wikipedia)

proposal is in the short-term interests of a few and in the long term interests of none.

Africa:

The vast majority of tropical moist and tropical rainforests exist in west and Central Africa. However, those are rapidly vanishing, according to the F.A.O, Africa lost the highest percentage of rainforests during the 1980s of any bio-geographical realm, a trend that continued from 1990-1995. Although 1997 was a year of extensive publicity, the outlook for Central and West Africa's rainforests is not promising. Many countries have agreed in principle to conventions of biodiversity and forest preservation, but in practice these concepts of sustainable forestry are not enforced. Most governments lack the funds and technical know-how to make these projects a reality and "paper parks" are common. Funding for most conservation projects comes from foreign sectors and 70-75% of forestry in the region is funded by external resources. Additionally a population growth rate is exceeding 3% annually. This, combined with the poverty of rural peoples, makes it difficult for the government to control local subsistence clearing and hunting. Equally challenging is the tremendous debt obligations facing the governments of these countries. Already terribly poor (16 of the world's 20 poorest countries are in Africa) and by 1996 African countries with tropical rainforest had accumulated a Foreign Loan Debt of more than US$177 billion, an almost insurmountable sum considering the low annual GDPs of most member countries. The easiest, most expedient way for such governments to service these debt payments is to sell their forest products and resources. Recently several organizations including the UN have put pressure on African governments to abandon tax incentives that encourage deforestation and provide virtually no return to most African people. In addition, the region with its biodiversity and varied landscapes has excellent potential for eco-tourism. Finally, the region's biological wealth offers tremendous potential for bio-prospecting for potentially useful drugs, food sources and other pharmaceutical products.

MYANMAR: (BURMA)

The following report is taken from forestry monitor, 'Global Witness' concerning deforestation in the military ruled state of Myanmar:

Myanmar's Forests are being ravaged by logging due to the great demand of China's growing economy.[36] China borders Myanmar's North-eastern states, and has boosted its economic influence with its smaller neighbour in recent years, with Beijing seeing friendship with Myanmar strategically important. Especially since the Chinese government in 1998 imposed a nation-wide ban on logging in China on ecological conservation grounds. "It appears that China's concern for the ecology is limited to their own country.." The report said, that in 2001, legal timber exports were just over 688,000 cubic metres, while China alone recorded imports of 850,000 cubic metres, the report also suggested rampant illegal felling of trees. This has led to large scale environmental destruction estimated at a minimum of 500,000 cubic metres a year and is apparently controlled by armed ethnic groups. The military rulers have so far failed to stem the flow of timber exports and have tried to cover up the full extent of the volume. With the military strangle-hold on all facets of Myanmar life, it would be hard to believe that the military generals are not the final beneficiaries of this ecological crime. In the long term this is unsustainable. Drug traffickers have invested in logging to launder money and logs have been hollowed out to conceal drugs and some drug eradication schemes have been used to justify large-scale logging by providing farmers with alternative income. There is an argument for sustainable commercial logging, however, the greed of the people behind these present rapacious practices, if allowed to continue will only add to the worldwide destruction of forests that produce oxygen and reduce carbon dioxide.

West Papua:[37] (West Irian)

West Papua's great natural resources have attracted some of the world's largest oil and mineral corporations. They include Mobil, Esso, Shell, BP, BHP and Freeport. In addition it has one of the largest tracts of tropical rainforests left in the world. Even in the 1930's the Dutch were extracting high quality oil from the Sorong area and Dutch geologists discovered the deposits which were later developed by the

36   news.mongabay.com/2005/1031-global_witness.html
37   eco-action.org/ssp/resources.html

Freeport mine. These resources were also known to the Indonesian government and foreign mining interests. Indeed the dispute over Papua between 1949 and 1962 and US support for Indonesian control can be partly understood as a struggle for these resources West Papua contains 30% of Indonesia's remaining forests and, with the over-logging of Kalimantan and Sumatra, it is rapidly becoming the main source of Indonesian timber. By 2002 the Indonesian Government had given out potential forestry concessions over 22 million hectares - 30% of West Papua's land area. Besides these areas where companies can officially log, there are many areas where illegal logging occurs. Indeed an estimated 70% of all timber exported in Indonesia is cut illegally. In spite of the fact that the export of unprocessed logs was officially banned in the 1980s, un-sawn logs are still exported from Papua. The Asian Development Bank (ADB)warned in May 2001 that "overexploitation and poor management imperils Indonesia's forestry resources" while Indonesia's largest donor group, the Consultative Group on Indonesia (CGI), has linked the payment of billion-dollar loans to reform in the forestry industry. Under Suharto, tribal communities had no legal claim on their land and logging concessions were entirely controlled by the government. Logging companies often employed the police and army to suppress local protests. The army itself and retired officers are heavily involved in running logging companies. A glaring example is the company P.T. Hanurata, which is still jointly controlled by the Suharto family and the Indonesian army Special Force Command (Kopassus). In one notorious case, people in the Asmat area were forced by the army to log trees in the early 80s for no payment. More recently Korean, Malaysian and Chinese logging companies have moved into Papua. China is a major market for Papuan timber since it has already reduced its own logging to prevent China's future environmental problems. Relatively little has changed in Indonesia after Suharto, but the autonomy law for Papua does say that any future use of customary land requires a permit granted by the affected community and also allows Papuan communities to challenge permits granted by previous governments. Also, as of early 2003, the autonomy law has not been implemented.

Australia:

Gunns Limited: Australia's Biggest Destroyer of Native Forests.[38]

This is the largest native-forest logging company in Australia and the largest hardwood-chip company in the world. Gunns receives the overwhelming majority of logs destined for sawmills and woodchip mills from Tasmania. It owns all four export-woodchip mills in Tasmania. It exports more woodchips from Tasmania than are exported from all mainland states combined. Gunns exports over four million tonnes of native-forest woodchips each year.

The vast majority of the logging operations on public land in Tasmania consist of clear-felling and burning. They own over two thirds of the eucalypt sawmilling industry in Tasmania, and two major eucalypt veneer mills. They are also the driving force behind the destruction of old growth forests in places such as the Tarkine, the Styx, the South-West wilderness and the North-east Highlands. Gunns have also cleared many thousands of hectares of native forest including rainforest on its private land. After these forests are chipped the land is converted to timber plantations. They use poison baits (carrots) to kill wallabies and possums that browse on the seedlings established in place of the cleared forests. The poisoned carrots also kill other wildlife ('non-target' species) such as bettongs, quolls and owls.

Wood chipping:

The company derives most of its profits from export wood-chip. Export wood-chippings accounts for over 90% of the old-growth logs extracted from logged forests on public land. It also owns two woodchip mills at Bell Bay (north of Launceston), one at Hampshire (south of Burnie), and one at Triabunna (East Coast). The Hampshire mill generates the woodchips that are piled on the wharf at Burnie. Many of these are rainforest woodchips (predominantly myrtle). The woodchips are sold to paper-making companies in north Asia – mostly in Japan. Gunns' customers include Mitsubishi, Nippon and Oji. In 2000, wood-chipping in Tasmania reached record levels, according to the Australian Bureau of Statistics. However, since 2001, (when Gunns became a virtual woodchip monopoly in Tasmania), Gunns has refused to supply data on wood-chipping (for 'business-confidentiality'

---

[38]   www. corpwatch: tasmania logging

reasons). It seems that there is no end to the cavalier attitude to human and environmental danger displayed by corporate greed in the pursuit of profit.

CHAPTER 9.

The battle for the consumer dollar.

Together with political, financial, pharmaceutical, water and timber predators detailed in previous pages, there are a host of predatory trans- national corporations with a vast array of products competing for market share of six and a half billion people. To these corporations, we are the world's marketplace.

Ajinomoto Corporation is a glaring example of how the pharmaceutical industry produces its own market. This company produces food additives, many of which make us sick while also producing medicines in order to keep us alive. What a business? They are the worlds' largest producer of free glutamic acid and also the world's largest producer of "monosodium glutamate". In addition, this company also has a financial interest in Memantine (Namenda), the first drug developed for people with advanced Alzheimer's disease.—A drug which according to the AARP (AARP Bulletin / July-August 2004, p 13), "blunts the brain chemical glutamate [glutamic acid] which can accumulate abnormally and kill brain cells". It's hard to not get paranoid about the food industry and pharmaceutical companies when we read something like this. They have two separate revenue streams flowing into to the same bank.

Further, information on the subject of harmful and dangerous chemical products in processed foods such as M.S.G.(Mono-sodium-glutamate) reveals that It is slowly poisoning us. John Erb. a research assistant at the University of Waterloo in the US. made an amazing discovery while going through scientific journals for a book he was writing called "The Slow Poisoning of America". In hundreds of studies around the world scientists were creating obese mice and rats for use in diet or diabetes test studies. No strain of rat or mice is naturally obese so the scientists have to create them. They make these morbidly obese creatures by injecting them with MSG when they are first born. This triples the amount of insulin the pancreas creates and causes rats, (and humans), to become obese. There is even a title for the race of fat rodents they create: "MSG-Treated Rats". If this shocks you, go to your kitchen and check the cupboards and the fridge. MSG is in most items! The Campbell's soups, the Hostess Doritos, the flavoured potato chips, Top Ramen noodles, Betty Crocker Hamburger Helper, Heinz canned gravy, Kraft salad dressings, most frozen prepared meals; especially the healthy low fat ones. (This applies to the US and one would assume that it would follow that all of the major international supermarkets would be similarly stocked). The items that didn't have MSG, had something called Hydrolyzed Vegetable Protein which is just another name for MSG. It was shocking to see just how many of the foods we feed our children everyday are filled with this stuff . They hide MSG under many different names in order to fool those who catch on but, it doesn't stop there. Not according to John in his book, that is an expose` of the food additive industry, in which he states that MSG is added to food for the addictive effect it has on the human body. Even the propaganda website sponsored by the food manufacturers lobby group supporting MSG, explains that the reason they add it to food is to make people eat more. (Lead us not unto temptation).

A study of elderly people showed that people eat more of the foods to which MSG is added. The Glutamate Association Lobby group says eating more is beneficial for the elderly. But what does it do to the rest of us? The phrase, 'bet you can't eat just one', takes on a whole new meaning where MSG is concerned and we wonder why the Western World's population is overweight? The MSG manufacturers themselves admit that it addicts people to their products. It makes people choose their product over others, and it makes people eat more of it than they would if MSG wasn't added. Not only is MSG scientifically proven to cause obesity, it is an addictive substance like a nicotine for food! Since its introduction into the our food supply sixty years ago, MSG has been added in larger and larger doses to the pre-packaged meals, soups, snacks and fast foods we are tempted to eat everyday. In America the FDA has set no limits on how much of it can be added to food. They claim it's safe to eat in any amount. How can they claim it is safe when there are hundreds of MSG related scientific studies with titles like the following?

1). The monosodium glutamate (MSG) obese rat, as a model for the study of exercise in obesity". Gobatto CA, Mello MA, Souza CT, Ribeiro IA. Res. Com. Mol. Pathol-Pharmacol. 2002

2). "The period and subsequent development of obesity". Tanaka K, Shimada M, Nakao K, Kusunoki Exp Neurol. 1978 Oct.

Yes, that last study date was not a typographic error, it **was** written in 1978.

Medical researchers and food manufacturers have known these MSG's side effects for decades.

There are many more studies that link MSG to Diabetes, Migraines and headaches, Autism, ADHD and even Alzheimer's. Just what is the extent, or the limits of its side effects? What can we do to stop the food manufactures from dumping fattening, addictive and potentially harmful MSG into our food supply and causing the obesity epidemic we now see?

The US government, (George W. Bush and his corporate crony puppeteers), pushed a Bill through Congress called the "Personal Responsibility in Food Consumption Act" also known as the "Cheeseburger Bill"[39]. This sweeping law bans anyone from suing food manufacturers,

wholesalers and distributors. Even if it comes out that they purposely added an addictive chemical to their foods. The Bill was rushed through in both the House of Representatives and at the Senate early in 2004. It was important that Bush and his corporate supporters get it through before the media lets everyone know about MSG, the intentional Nicotine for food. The food producers and restaurants have been adding this to their products for years, and now we are paying the

---

[39] "Cheeseburger Bill" news.bbc.co.uk/2/hi/americas/3500388.stm

price for it. So be discriminating at your supermarket. Our children should not be cursed with obesity and other symptoms of diseases of unknown origin caused by the vast array of Chemical food additives. So far, we have dealt with,

1) Weapons of mass persuasion (the media). And,
2) Weapons of mass destruction; (nuclear bombs and depleted uranium).

The only items left are the products spawned from politicians going to bed with chemical companies and these are,

No.3) Weapons of mass extinction. These are herbicides (such as agent orange) which is carcinogenic (cancer causing) and teratogenic. (Teratogenesis is a medical term from the Greek, literally meaning **monster-making**. It has gained a more specific usage for the development of abnormal cell masses during foetal growth (pregnancy), causing physical defects in the foetus. Although the third category, "mass extinction" may sound rather extreme, when you list the global activities in which the industrial, commercial, pharmaceutical and financial giants are engaged, it is regrettably a very accurate description.

What can we do about these problems?

The first important step is to create public awareness.

a) Awareness of the dangers, and
b) Awareness of our potential to stop them

It is important to know the strength and ability of you and I, the misguided, misinformed, but thoughtful and educated public. Our potential power is in our knowledge and our numbers. When the number of enlightened people reaches the critical mass, the great hope, is that this potential energy is sufficient to depose those that have caused the problems and those who have allowed such depletion of world resources and degradation of political social integrity to exist. Our great need is to develop people of honesty and integrity to guide us on the path of peace, security and social justice for **all humanity**.

As the great prayer goes: "Give us this day our daily bread" **So long as it doesn't poison us.**

We are all subjected to the wide use of false information, clever and misleading advertising and packaging. This has become the norm and not considered a crime in the Western world today. The use of chemical preservatives in our food, dangerous chemical pollutants in the air we breathe, false and misleading labelling and naming of food products is a regular feature. In fact, with the use of media advertising, all or any deceptive ploy is considered to be fair game as long as it increases market share. This type of 'integrity in the global market place is the integrity that provides unconscionable producers, wholesalers and retailers the opportunity to gouge large profits from consumers while undercutting local producers with cheaper imports.

A good example of such a product marketed with integrity is frozen fish, imported from Vietnam under the names of Pacific Dory, Deep Sea Dory and Basa[40]. It retails in Australian stores at less than half of the price of the clean and green Australian variety bearing the similar name, John Dory. The origin of the pacific Dory, deep sea Dory and Basa is the Mekong River and is now Australia's biggest-selling fish.

The problem, according to the chairman of the Australian Fish Names Committee, Roy Palmer, is that Pacific dory has never seen the Pacific or any other ocean for that matter, it is nothing like a dory. Large quantities are raised in cages suspended under houseboats and barges in the crowded and polluted waters of Vietnam's Mekong River. The same snap-frozen and imported fish, is being sold as a popular line in Australian supermarkets under the deceptive marketing label, freshwater fillet. It is Pangasius bocourti, one of twenty-one species of freshwater catfish found in the Mekong basin and in a move designed to curb deceptive naming practices by fishmongers and supermarkets, was last year, christened Basa under the Seafood Services Australia's uniform fish names process.

Managing director of the Sydney Fish Market, Grahame Turk commented; "Basa's success in the marketplace has been a key factor in fish imports from Vietnam doubling in 2002-03 and then doubling again last year," An estimated 300,000 to 400,000 Vietnamese are involved in the government-owned Basa fishery. According to Grahame Turk, who is also deputy chairman of the Australian Seafood Industry Council, they produce more Basa than Australia's total seafood production of

---

[40]   (Google) Australian Seafood Industry Council. "Vietnam's basa production

550,000 tonnes a year. Vietnam's annual Basa production is expected to reach 1 million tons within five years." Vietnam's catfish exports have already decimated the local catfish industry in the US where producers are fighting back. According to the American domestic fishing lobby, there is no Basa-farming standard among Vietnamese processors.

Therefore, no distinction in the marketplace between professionally farmed product and caged fish from Mekong houseboats and barges. The sewage systems along the Mekong cannot keep pace with rapid development, consequently, run-off from the river's hinterland is polluted by sewage, fertilizers and pesticides.

American industry sources claim that large stocks of Basa in cages are fed through holes cut in the floors of houseboats where the human waste also goes straight into the river. Food for the fish includes vegetable and crop waste, rice bran and animal waste." The Mekong and associated aquaculture ponds have a high silt concentration, say the Americans, also it is common Vietnamese practice to soak the basa fillets in sodium tripolyphosphate (STPP), a chemical used as a preservative and seafood texturizer. This means that consumers who purchase Basa by weight from supermarkets need to be wary, because fish treated with STPP retains more water.

In August, the American states of Alabama, Mississippi and Louisiana suspended the sale of all Vietnamese aquatic products, following the discovery of the antibiotics ciprofloxacin and enrofloxacin in Basa imports. These are prohibited in western countries because of the risk of their transferring resistant micro-organisms to humans. They are used by the producers to combat salmonella and other disease in fish. The antibiotics can also lead to the development of the infectious disease campylobacter, which can cause diarrhea, abdominal pain, fever, nausea and vomiting.

Between the food, beverage, pharmaceutical and tobacco companies, or the political structures behind the arms manufacturing and war, one wonders who are the more dangerous to society. While we're on dangers to society, here are a few facts on the *mining, storage and the disposal of uranium* and radio active waste, that all should know.

Uranium:

The ore is mined in both open cut and underground mines then milled and leached in a uranium mill. The mill is a chemical plant designed to extract uranium from ore. Usually, it is located near the mine to limit transportation. A leaching agent is used which not only extracts uranium from the ore, but also removes several other constituents like molybdenum, vanadium, selenium, iron, lead and arsenic. The uranium must then be separated out of the leaching solution. The final product produced from the mill, commonly referred to as "yellow cake" (U_3O_8 with impurities) and is packed and shipped in casks. Mill tailings are normally dumped as a sludge in special ponds or piled and abandoned. The largest such piles are in the US and Canada and contain up to 30 million tonnes of solid material. In Saxony, Germany the Helmsdorf pile near Zwickau contains 50 million tonnes, and in Thuringia the Culmitzsch pile near Seelingstadt contains 86 million tonnes of solids.[41]

Open-cut mining operations expose potential pollution to the atmosphere. In the case of uranium, normally mined by open cut method, radium is the most important radioactive pollutant. The uranium mill tailings decay producing radon gas. Radon gas is invisible, odourless and heavier than air. Other potentially hazardous substances in the tailings are selenium, molybdenum, uranium and thorium. The mill tailing residues all adversely affect public health. Four principal ways that the public can be exposed to the hazards from this waste are: One, the diffusion of radon gas directly into air when tailings are used as a construction material or backfill around buildings, breathing the air containing radon increases the risk of lung cancer. Two; Radon gas can diffuse directly from the piles into the atmosphere where it can be inhaled, and also small particles can be blown from the piles and inhaled or ingested. Three; Radioactive products in tailings decay, producing gamma radiation which poses a health hazard to people in the immediate vicinity and finally, the dispersal of tailings by wind or water, or by leaching, can carry radioactive and other toxic materials into surface and groundwater that may be used for drinking.

The World Health Organization (WHO) says radon causes up to fifteen percent of lung cancers worldwide. In an effort to reduce the

---

[41]   Ref: "Decommissioning projects Europe". Google

rate of lung cancer around the world, the World Health Organization is launching a new international radon project to help countries increase awareness, collect data and encourage action to reduce radon-related risks. The U.S. EPA is one of several countries supporting this initiative and is encouraged by the World Health Organization's attention to this important public health issue.

Dr. Michael Repacholi, the coordinator of the WHO Radiation and Environmental Health Unit, said: "Radon poses an easily reducible health risk to populations all over the world, but has not, up to now, received widespread attention," He went on to say. "Radon in our homes is the main source of exposure to ionizing radiation and in many cases accounts for fifty percent of the public's exposure to naturally-occurring sources of radiation." The toxic waste of the uranium mining activity, if abandoned and left untreated, has a radio-active life of 240,000 yrs. This is why all uranium producing countries have a heavy moral and social responsibility to ensure that two things happen.

1). Uranium must be safely extracted.
2). The waste product must be safely stored.

Otherwise it should be left in the ground. However where trade and commerce are involved, profit comes before security, morality and ethics

Depleted uranium "D U":
As if the previous examples are not bad enough. The introduction of depleted uranium weaponry, used by America and probably supplied to its allies (NATO countries, Australia and Israel), also creates a serious global health threat from exposure to long term radiation. The current fear of the in power people today is the logistics of distribution and safe keeping of the multitude of very lethal weaponry. If, or when any may fall into the hands of terrorists, they could be used against us. Depleted uranium weaponry currently in use by the US military:

David Bradbury a highly respected Australian journalist and filmmaker recently produced a film on the use of depleted uranium by US military and NATO forces in recent wars. He was interviewed on ABC program "speaking Out," on Sunday the 6th Nov. 05. In this interview, he revealed that D.U treated bullets, bombs, missiles and land mines have been used in the first and second gulf wars, also in Afghanistan and the Balkans. He gave some of the facts relating to the nature of these weapons:

They produce radio active residue, the half-life of which, is 4.5 billion years.

They generate heat up to 5000 degrees C. They vaporize target material into radio-active Uranium Oxide particles that are highly carcinogenic.

2,500 tons were used in both Iraqi wars and still counting.

1,000 tons in Afghanistan and

80 tons in the Balkans.

Captain Douglas Rokke[42], an air officer in the Vietnam War, was commissioned to decontaminate and ship back to America, two armoured tanks used in Iraq for future development of depleted uranium weaponry. In the process he, and about fifty of his team, developed radio-active blood poisoning. In July 2004, on trying to obtain medical records of troops involved in Iraqi operations that are normally stored in St. Louise Missouri, he found that they had mysteriously disappeared. All he was told is that one day there was a fire that destroyed the lot. He states that there is no known masking agent that will decontaminate the soil, materials, equipment and structures affected. He now has 5,000 times the safe level of radiation in his body. This is a terrible indictment on criminal inhumane use of depleted uranium by the US military.

A secret 20 year treaty was signed between Australia and America that could allow the US. to further develop this weaponry in the Southern hemisphere in Queensland Australia[43].

Some facts on equatorial separation:

It is a fact that meteorological movements in the North and South hemispheres are separate with very slight interaction in the equatorial

---

[42]   Google):View topic – Depleted Uranium Munitions and You Talisman Sabre and Australia's Guam connection

[43]

area. The Earth is a spinning globe where a point at the equator is travelling at around 1100 km/hour but a point at the poles is not moved by the rotation. This fact means that air-born particles moving across the Earth's surface are subject to Coriolis forces that cause apparent deflection of the motion. The Coriolis force deflects to the right in the Northern hemisphere and to the left in the Southern hemisphere when viewed along the line of motion and very little equatorial interaction. This tends to isolate air-born pollution between the North and South hemispheres. At the moment the population is living in a comparatively clean and green environment. Why on earth would any Australian Federal Government want to bring a more potent form of radiation from the northern hemisphere, to the Southern hemisphere? Particularly to Queensland, an area that is subject to regular cyclonic activity. Our politicians profess great indignation against Afghanistan, Columbia and other opium and similar drug producing countries. … on moral grounds! If so, why? The same moral indignation is not exercised where uranium is concerned. This is a material that poses a far greater danger to humanity's survival than drugs ever would. . . .*but wait, there's more*:

Dioxin the indiscriminate killer[44]:

One of the biggest threats to public health produced by chemical companies is the substance known as Dioxin. This is the most toxic chemicals known to man. Its potency is second only to radioactive waste. Dioxin is created as an incidental by-product into the environment and its contamination becomes very wide spread. Small traces of this substance can in fact be found in the clothing you wear, in the food you eat and in the toys that your children play with. Dioxin is very long lasting and has the ability to accumulate in living tissue. It is present in your body from the moment that you are born to the moment you die. There is no safe level of Dioxin that a person can be exposed to. The smallest amounts have bean proven to significantly increase the chances of developing cancer, as well as various other health defects. The longer we sit and wait the more serious the problem will become. Dioxin is a threat to our society and as such it heeds to be dealt with immediately. Dioxins and furans are some of the most toxic chemicals known to science.

[44] What are Dioxins and Furans? "Dow Chemicals information"

A draft report released for public comment in September 1994 by the US Environmental Protection Agency clearly describes dioxin as a serious public health threat. The public health impact of dioxin may rival the impact that DDT had on public health in the 1960's. According to the EPA report, not only does there appear to be no "safe" level of exposure to dioxin, but levels of dioxin and dioxin-like chemicals have been found in the general US population that are already at or very close to levels associated with severe adverse health effects."

Dioxin is a general term that describes a group of hundreds of chemicals that are highly persistent in the environment. The most toxic compound is - 2 3 7 8-tetrachlorodibenzo-p-dioxin or TCDD. The toxicity of other dioxins and chemicals like PCBs that act like dioxin are measured in relation to TCDD. Dioxin is formed as an unintentional by-product of many industrial processes involving chlorine such as waste incineration, chemical, pesticide, wood pulp manufacturing and paper bleaching. Dioxin was the primary toxic component of Agent Orange. It was found at Love Canal in Niagara Falls NY and was the basis for evacuations at Times Beach, MO and Seveso in Italy. Dioxin[45] is formed by burning chlorine-based chemical compounds with hydrocarbons. The major source of dioxin in the environment comes from waste-burning incinerators of various sorts and also from backyard burn-barrels. Dioxin pollution is also affiliated with paper mills which use chlorine bleaching in their process and with the production of Polyvinyl Chloride (PVC) plastics and with the production of certain chlorinated chemicals (like many pesticides). In addition to cancer, exposure to dioxin can also cause severe reproductive and developmental problems (at levels 100 times lower than those associated with its cancer causing effects). Dioxin is well-known for its ability to damage the immune system and interfere with hormonal systems.

Exposure to dioxin has been linked to birth defects, inability to maintain pregnancy, decreased fertility, reduced sperm counts, endometriosis, diabetes, learning disabilities, immune system suppression, lung problems, skin disorders, lowered testosterone levels and much more.44 How are we exposed to dioxin? The major sources

---

45   Internet Explorer For an detailed list of health problems related to dioxin, "The People's Report on Dioxin":

are in our diet. Since dioxin is fat-soluble, it bio-accumulates -(97.5%) - climbing up the food chain and it is mainly found in meat and dairy products; milk, chicken, pork, fish and eggs in that order. In fish alone the dioxin levels in fish are 100,000 times that of the surrounding environment. The best way to avoid dioxin exposure is to reduce or eliminate your consumption of meat and dairy products by adopting a vegan diet. According to a May 2001 study of dioxin in foods, the category with the lowest [dioxin] level was a simulated vegan diet with 0.09 parts per thousand. Pure vegans have been found to have very low levels in comparison with the general population. This indicates the lower contribution of dioxin in these foods to the human body. In EPA's dioxin report, they refer to dioxin as hydrophobic (water-fearing) and lipophilic (fat-loving). This means that dioxin, when it settles on water bodies, will rapidly accumulate in fish rather than remain in the water. The same goes for other wildlife. Dioxin works its way to the top of the food chain.

Health experts have long warned of the dangers of high-fat foods that can lead to heart disease or cancer. New studies show that each fatty bite may also carry a dose of other highly toxic chemicals.[46] According to these studies, man-made toxic chemicals including traces of highly carcinogenic dioxin, is being released into the environment and turning up in fast-food and grocery store staples such as meat, fish and dairy products. Some industrialized countries show levels of over 200% more than the U.S. government safety standards. Arnold Schecter is a scientist who has been involved with dioxin and PCB studies in Russia, China, Cambodia, the Middle East and Vietnam as well as the United States. He points to the widespread contamination by dioxin. "These synthetic chemicals have been found from penguins in Antarctica, in the rain that falls in South East Asia and the milk of a nursing mother in Germany", Despite his gloomy conclusions, he remains hopeful and says that the problem can be overcome. "For the most part, these synthetic chemicals are historically new and have only been around the later half of the 20th century". When released into the atmosphere, once an animal has ingested these toxic chemicals that are

---

[46]   How Toxic is Your Diet?: "Inter Press Services" Washington, Nov. 20 (IPS)

in the environment as a by-product of incineration, they accumulate in the fat.

We should take every step to stop putting dioxins into our environment and our food supplies. This trend can be reversed in industrialized countries. You can avoid the intake of dioxins, (to a certain extent), by eating food that is low in fat, but it is more desirable to avoid producing dioxins in the first place. Two recent studies on the subject conducted by Schecter, have been published in the British journal Chemosphere in which he states: "Dioxins, and dioxin-like substances like PCBs and furans, are getting into food supplies at levels that are highest in high-fat foods, and lowest in low-fat foods such as fruits and vegetables. Besides cancer, minute amounts of these chemicals have been shown to lead to nervous system and liver damage as well as mimicking hormones that disrupt reproduction and human development," He points to a study in Japan and Taiwan of persons who ingested rice oil that had been contaminated with PCBs and furans (similar toxic substances) during the 1960s and 1970s, suffered from a combination of higher cancer mortality, increased frequency of lung infections, numbness and other nervous system effects. According to Schecter, "It is known that every person in every industrialized country has dioxins in their blood ... but since about 96 percent of the general population's exposure to dioxins is through food, we wanted to see if certain kinds of food contained more dioxins than others. From ice cream and fish bought in the grocery store to Kentucky Fried Chicken and McDonald's Big Mac, all samples collected from across the United States contained trace amounts of dioxin that well exceed many government regulations. While vegetables and fruits also contained trace amounts of these chemicals, the amount was significantly less than in high fat foods." Advocacy groups such as the American Public Health Association (APHA) believe that in light of these new scientific findings, governments should be doing more to protect people's health.

In Australia in 2006, Sydney Harbour was closed to commercial and recreational fishermen. People have fished Homebush Bay and the Parramatta River that runs into the harbour for at least 100 years. The reason for closure was that the whole area was heavily contaminated with Dioxin.

Union Carbide has been producing plastic film and other P.C.B products at Rhodes on the bank of the river for forty-five years and Timbrol, (also a chemical company) before them, on the same site for thirty years. No wonder after a total of seventy-five years, the riverbed heavily contaminated. Also, the whole of the landsite has been passed for housing development. The land was bought by the NSW government in the 1990's. The government is now faced with an enormous cost of de-contamination if, in fact, it is actually possible. Developing countries can avoid this problem completely by *not* allowing the same pollution creating industrialization as we have in the developed world.

According to the studies, developing foetuses and infants are most at risk from the effects of dioxins. Birth defects, learning disabilities and other development problems have been linked to dioxin exposure because these chemicals "mimic" or "block" oestrogen and progesterone, natural hormones which instruct the body on how it should develop. In just six months of breast feeding, a baby in the United States will, on average, consume the EPA's maximum lifetime dose of dioxin. Breast milk contains high levels of fat.

"The amount of this chemical required to disrupt normal development could be as low as one part in a trillion, says Michael Jacobson. This is the equivalent of a single drop of liquid placed in the centre car of a 10-kilometer long cargo train. Dioxins are also highly persistent in the environment and extremely resistant to chemical or physical breakdown" There are many methods that can be used to reduce the emissions of Dioxin. However, they will only be possible if enough people get involved. Research, has determined that the emission of Dioxin into the environment may eventually decrease as a result of government intervention. However, a "decrease" in emission is not good enough. There is no safe level of Dioxin. As long as this substance continues to be emitted it will continue to pose a serous threat to the health of all living creatures.

CHAPTER 10

Money, Banking and Globalization.

The history of money[47]:. How Money Is Created, Used, And Abused.

This information has been hidden, disguised and deliberately withheld from public knowledge. The details of this gigantic scam are not widely known nor understood, but when its effect on the wellbeing of the whole of Western society is realized, only then can it be dealt with effectively. This knowledge will add another strong reason to help bring about sufficient social pressure to free our hostage world. Money and its value is not a mystery. It is only a tool we use for an agreed value for various commodities. However, what is mysterious is exactly how it is provided and distributed. The responsibility for this has been acquired by a group of people we call financiers and bankers who, in carrying out their responsibilities, are in a position to secretly gouge a very large proportion of the national wealth without being exposed.

When we explore the history of how this situation developed, the explanation is so simple that it is almost unbelievable. Because of the very great impact that the fraudulent misuse of money has had in bringing so much pain and suffering to this world, you had better believe it. It is a story of the naivety and gullibility of some and the greed of others who held power at a particular period of history. How is the value of money affected? The value is affected when we add anything

---

[47]   (Google)Excepts from "XAT The History of Money 1,2 and 3" (accessed Oct.2008):

to an item or commodity that we buy and resell. Even if it is only the sale price, without actually **value adding,** (which is the term currently used for re-working to improve it,) this then becomes its value. We have not actually made anything, we have only changed the rate of its exchange for an item of similar value. Before money was developed the simple barter system was used. Such as, exchange of one item for another at an agreed value, (say 20 cobs of corn for one pair of sandals). This worked well until the means of production advanced to the stage where the sandal maker wanted corn, but the corn producer didn't need sandals. To overcome this problem an independent and neutral article was needed to represent a particular rate of exchange for each and every item of trade. Necessity is the mother of invention so it is said, and in various parts of the world different articles were used to facilitate trade. In China Jade was used. In most pacific islands, cowry shells, in other places precious stones. Through natural evolutionary intellectual growth similar solutions to the problem were found throughout the world in totally independent areas. It seems that money was created to overcome a problem that confronted the development of communities everywhere. However, again to quote an old adage, "One door closes, another door opens ". As the problem in commodity trading was solved, the door to the manipulation of money was opened. A particular type of social predator was created; The Financier, **The Money Changer**. We find in all societies throughout the history of the Western World that some people will lie, cheat, even kill in order to accumulate wealth and power. This creation of money also brought with it the disease of greed. Another old saying is that "money is the root of all evil." This is wrong; it is the **abuse of money** that is the problem. We take for granted that money is here; we all use it and we all are able to acquire it by selling our labour or making something to sell or trading in various ways. We never give much thought to just where it comes from, who makes it, who distributes it, how it is distributed and why. In other words no one asks the **"how when where and why" of money.** The popular conception that the Government makes and distributes it according to the needs of the community and international trading is quite wrong. When I tell you that **private enterprise controls the printing, distribution, the lending and the rates of interest charged on all the money in circulation today** you probably won't believe it.

This situation has been the cause of wars, the downfall of governments, depressions and revolutions, all in order to gain or keep control of the issuance of money. In the early days the Crown had the control and the battle between them and powerful commercial interests for control alternated and was finally won by private business. It is almost unimaginable that privately owned companies should be allowed to have this power but it is an inescapable fact of life. The reason that it was done successfully, is that the final winners were very highly respected and influential members of society that were able to use and manipulate other politically influential people and the general population by the clever use of the media. Because the monitory system at the present appears to work smoothly, there are very few questions asked. We trust the people that we elect to govern for us. Instead, they have been manipulated *into governing us on behalf of the few groups that are in control of the world*.

Money Changers was the name given historically to the people that gradually, over many centuries, developed into our modern day bankers. The first reference to the unethical abuse of their position comes to us from the Gospels of Mathew and Mark in the New Testament of the Christian bible. That was in the time of the Roman rule in Palestine, and Roman coinage was the common currency. Because the Jewish hierarchy would not accept it for payment of the Temple tax, money changers were allowed to set up tables in the temple yard where Gentile peddlers would bring various livestock to sell for the purpose of sacrifice to their god. Also in those days Jewish proselytizers imposed a charge for conversion to Judaism in Rome and other foreign lands. Giving a special small stone distributed from the Temple in Jerusalem, as a token of receipt. The different currencies then had to be converted to shekels and the Rabbi's then converted it back to the local Roman coin. Travellers and traders from foreign parts also needed to convert their local currencies. The money changers charged an exchange rate for Roman to Shekel, and also from Shekel to Roman coin - making profit at both ends from exchange. They lent money and charged up to 100 percent interest.

It was the unashamed greed of these money changers that aroused the anger of Jesus. These *bankers* were greedy profiteers who cared nothing about using their god's temple as a marketplace and as a means to get rich. He upturned the tables and drove the money changers out of the temple with a whip. This was the only gospel recorded action in the life of Jesus, where he used aggression or violence on anyone. The money changers turned devotion into a mockery for profit. He is said to have proclaimed the whole setup to be "A den of thieves". Much later in Medieval England it became the practice of goldsmiths to offer to keep other peoples gold and silver in their safe keeping. These people would then be issued with a receipt for the particular quantity and value of the gold or silver deposited. Over a short period of time these paper receipts became notes of exchange for trade. This was much better and safer than carting about a bag of gold or silver. Over time the goldsmith noted that only a small percentage of the depositors came at any given time, so they would always have a fair amount in their keeping. Through their guild, they agreed among themselves to issue receipts for gold that really did not exist and loan them out to earn interest.

This developed into the fully fledged banking system that is still in place today and now known as "fractional reserve banking." Which means today's banks have licenses to print money from nothing. This is called *Fiat Currency;* not backed by gold but only declaration of the agency of issue.

The Federal Reserve Bank; the greatest ongoing financial scam in history From 1837-1862 there was a system of national banks in the USA but then in 1913-1914 a consortium of 12 privately held banks got together and formed the Federal Reserve Bank,[48] an entity that is not part of the US government. These banks then purchased notes from the US Mint for printing costs only and lent them out through member banks charging interest. The FED, as it is now called, was created in 1913-1914. In order, it was said, to bring stability to the economy and yet almost every major crash, including the great depression, can be attributed to the FED.

Woodrow Wilson (President of the United States from 1913-1921), signed a bill transferring the US currency to twelve regional private

---

[48] "Chart of who owns the Federal Reserve." Google.

banks. They were the banks that supported and paid for the election campaign of the US President. He regretted his decision later saying:

"I am a most unhappy man. I have unwittingly ruined my country. A great industrial nation is controlled by its system of credit. Our system of credit is concentrated. The growth of the nation, therefore, and all our activities are in the hands of a few men. We have come to be one of the worst ruled, one of the most completely controlled and dominated governments in the civilized world. No longer a government by free opinion, no longer a government by conviction and the vote of the majority, but a government by the opinion and duress of a small group of dominant men."

This is how it is in the 21st century. The main street banks are legally required to have only from zero to a fraction of their total credit asset in reserve (10% as in the case of the US). The other 90 to 100% percent that they use does not exist. For instance, if they start with deposits of 10 million dollars, they pay the depositors say 3 percent, Charge 5 percent on lending out the balance, keeping $1 million in reserve. By lending out "$90 million" this translates into $4,500,000.00 and as loans and deposits are happening every day, the more they get, the more it expands exponentially.

Furthermore, the Federal Reserve banks operate in a way that permits the deposit taking Main Street banks to acquire the reserves they need to meet their requirements from the money market, so long as they are willing to pay the prevailing price (the federal funds rate) for borrowed reserves. Consequently, reserve requirements currently play a relatively limited role in money creation in the United States. The fraction varies from country to country from zero to 35%. As at 2005, the countries on a zero requirement are Australia, Canada, Mexico, Sweden, and the United Kingdom. Euro-zone countries 2% and the US is on 10%. The highest at 35% is Surinam in South America[49].48 There was a time in Australia, back in the 1970's and 80's when the short term (24hr. call) deposit interest rate was up to 20% per annum. Can you imagine just how much wealth was raked in by those that could afford to deposit cash? This was more than the net profit margin of most business enterprises. What a beautiful way to make money work for you! But think, the bank was then able to lend ten times

---

[49]   Banking reserve requirements: Wikipedia encyclopedia

the amount deposited, at even half the interest rate, and rake in five times more than it paid out. That is why it is called a "license to print money." It was this type of slight of hand that started the great rise in paper trading. Thousands of people invested in the stock market and currency speculation.

I call them **paper shufflers**, making money, producing nothing and serving no public interest but their own accumulation of personal wealth.

Back in 1100 CE, when King Henry the 1st (the son of William the Conqueror) was king of England, taxes were usually paid in kind. (Goods produced from the land farmed by the taxpayer). As a record of payment, the scribes (modern day accountants), used a primitive device called the tally stick which was notched to represent a certain monitory value. To prevent alteration or counterfeiting, the sticks were cut in half lengthwise, leaving one half of the notches on each piece — one of which was given to the payer by the tax collector, as proof of payment. Or, in the case of deposits with the money changer, given as a valid receipt and could be cashed in by presenting the half stick as proof of deposit. It would be compared for accuracy by reuniting the pieces when payment was duly made.

Henry adopted this method of tax-record-keeping in England. These became widely used and the history of the bank of England shows that one of the original stockholders in the bank bought his shares with a tally stick. After 1694, the government issued paper tallies as paper evidence of debt (i.e. government borrowing) in anticipation of the collection of future taxes. Paper was easily negotiable which made paper tallies the full equivalent of the paper banknote issued by the Bank of England beginning in 1694. By 1697, tallies, banknotes and bank bills all began to circulate freely as interchangeable forms of money. Wooden-stick tallies continued to be used until 1826. The strangest part of all this, is why would people accept sticks of wood for money? Throughout history, people have traded anything they thought had value and used that for money. The fact is that money is only what people agree on and trust to use as money. Our money today is really only paper. In the 16th century, King Henry VIII ordered that tally sticks be used for tax payment receipts by the government. This created the demand for tallies and eventually they circulated and were totally accepted as money.

Previously, in the 1500s, King Henry VIII had relaxed the laws concerning usury, and the Money Changers quickly reintroduced a large amount of their gold and silver money for a few decades. That was until Queen Mary came to the throne and tightened the usury laws again, the Money Changers then renewed the hoarding of gold and silver coin which badly affected the economy. Mary's half-sister, Queen Elizabeth 1 took the throne in 1558, and was so determined to regain control over English money, she minted and issued gold and silver coins from the public treasury and took control over the money supply.

Although control over money was not the only cause of the English Revolution in 1642 (religion also fuelled the war)[50] monetary policy played a major role. Financed by the Money Changers, Oliver Cromwell finally overthrew King Charles I and executed him. The Money Changers then began to consolidate their financial power. The result was that for the next fifty years the financial manipulation of the Money Changers plunged Great Britain into a series of costly wars. They also purchased a square mile of property in the centre of London known as 'the City'. This semi-sovereign area is still one of the two most important financial centres of the world, Wall Street being the other.

The Money Changers continued their opposition to the crown and, finally, with their support, William of Orange was successful in his bid for the throne replacing King James, (his father-in –law). With

---

[50] The causes of the conflict can be traced to social, economic, constitutional, and religious developments over a century or more. Closer at hand were questions of sovereignty in the English state and Puritanism in the church. The immediate cause, however, was Charles's attempt (1637) to impose the Anglican liturgy in Scotland. The Presbyterian Scots rioted; then they signed the National Covenant and raised an army to defend their church. In 1640 their army occupied the northern counties of England.

this win, the money changers regained their position as controllers of the national currency. Thus a very close relationship between the Money Changers and the nobility was established and continues to this day. The monarch had no real power and with William's protection the Money Changers had the real power; they controlled the economy.

It is amazing that the tally stick system worked really well for 726 years. It was the most successful form of currency in recent history and the British Empire was actually built under the Tally Stick system. How is it that most of us are not aware of its existence? It is a little known fact that the Money Changers, on establishing the Bank of England in 1694, realized that the tally stick system was money over which they had no control. Seeing this as a competitive threat they gradually bought and retired the lot.

Private central banks:

The Bank of England was to be the modern world's first privately owned national central bank. Earlier deposit banks had existed in Venice from 1361, in Amsterdam from 1609 and in Sweden in 1661 from where the first banknotes in Europe were issued.

The name "Bank of England" was given to create the impression that it was part of the government. It was not. Like most other private corporation, the Bank of England sold shares to get started and the investor's names were never revealed. They were expected to pay one and a quarter million, (British pounds) in gold coin to buy their shares in the Bank, but only £750,000 pounds was ever received. Not-withstanding this, the Bank was chartered in 1694 and started out in the business of lending (with interest), several times the money it was supposed to have in reserves. In exchange the new Bank of England willingly lent British politicians as much as they wanted *(for personal gain)*. Why not, the debt was secured by direct taxation of the people.

Even the Bank's recent nationalization is not what it at first may appear as its independent resources multiply and dividends continue to be produced for its controlling board. You would think someone would have seen through this and realized that we could produce our own money and owe no interest. Instead, the Bank of England has been used as a model and now nearly every nation has a Central Bank with fractional reserve banking at its core. This amounts to legal counterfeiting by the Central bank. Being in private hands it corrupts the democratic system by placing the economic state of the nation in the hands of the Money Changers, instead of the people. The banking system should be used to the benefit of the common wealth, not for private wealth. This view has been expressed in the past by many famous and important public figures but to no avail as the people in control, lied, cheated and assassinated to retain their powerful grip on the money supply and the banking system.

Following are some quotes regarding this banking system given by historically famous political figures: Sir William Pitt, speaking to the House of Lords in 1770, said: "There is something behind the throne greater than the King himself." This reference to the Money Changers behind the Bank of England gave birth to the expression, "the power behind the throne".

In 1844, Benjamin Disraeli wrote: "The world is governed by very different personages from what is imagined by those who are not behind the scenes."

In November 1933, US President Franklin D. Roosevelt wrote in a letter to a confidant: "The real truth of the matter is, as you and I know that a financial element in the large centres has owned government ever since the days of Andrew Jackson … " In 1934 the June issue of the "New Britain" magazine of London, cited a devastating assertion by former British Prime Minister David Lloyd George: "Britain is the slave of an international financial block". It also quoted these words written by Lord Bryce: "Democracy has no more persistent and insidious foe than money powers" and pointed out that: "questions regarding "The Bank of England", its conduct and its objects, are not allowed by the Speaker" (of the House of Commons).

The central bank scam is really a hidden tax that benefits private banks more than the government. Private central banks have the power to control the economy of a country, thus becoming the real governing body. In reality, this is a gigantic confidence trick that gouges the common wealth of a country from the people, by way of hidden taxation to pay a private group interest on the loans. The nuts and bolts of this scam works like this: the government sells bonds to the banks for money, and using the fractional reserve system, the banks issue credit, money that does not actually exist. The government repays the interest with money that does exist (our taxes). It's a hard pill to swallow, but in times of economic upheaval, wealth is not destroyed, it is only transferred. Who benefits the most when money is scarce? You may have guessed. It's the money changers; those who control what everyone else wants.

When the majority of people are suffering through an economic depression you can be sure that a small minority of people are getting richer. Even today, the Bank of England expresses its determination to prevent the booms and busts, recessions and depressions, yet there have been nothing but ups and downs since its formation with the accompanying instability of international currencies. One thing however has been stable and that was the growing power and fortune of the Rothschild family.

The Rothschilds:

In 1743, a goldsmith named Amshall Moses Bauer opened a counting house in Frankfurt Germany. He placed a Roman eagle on a red shield over the door prompting people to call his shop the Red Shield Company which in German is pronounced "Rothschild". On his death his son inherited the business and changed the family name to Rothschild.

Lending money to individuals was a very good business, but he soon discovered it was much more profitable and safer lending to governments and Kings. It always involved much larger amounts and was always secured by public taxes. Once established in Germany, he set his sights on the rest of Europe, training his five sons in the grand business of money creation, before sending them out to the major financial centres of the world to create and dominate the central banking systems. J.P. Morgan was thought by many to be the richest man in the world during the Second World War, but upon his death it was discovered he was merely a lieutenant within the Rothschild Empire owning only 19% of the J.P. Morgan Companies. The real power in Europe was the Rothschild Banks.

The American Revolution (1764 - 1781) How the same scam was forced on America:

In Benjamin Franklin's Autobiography, we read: "By the mid 1700's Britain was at its height of power, but was also heavily in debt. Since the creation of the Bank of England they had suffered four costly wars and the total debt now stood at £140,000,000, (which in those days was a very large sum of money). In order to make their interest payments to the bank, the British government set about a program to try to raise revenues from their American colonies, largely through an extensive program of taxation.

There was a shortage of material for minting coins in America. So the colony **printed its own paper money** which was called Colonial Script. This proved to be a very successful means of exchange and also gave the colonies a sense of identity. Colonial Script was money provided to help the exchange of goods. It was debt free paper money not backed by gold or silver.

During his visit to Britain in 1763, Benjamin Franklin was asked by The British Board of Trade, how he could account for the new found prosperity in the colonies. Franklin replied. "That is simple. **In the colonies we issue our own money**. It is called Colonial Script. We issue it in proper proportion to the demands of trade and industry to make the products pass easily from the producers to the consumers. In this manner, creating for ourselves our own paper money, we control its purchasing power, and we issue it **free of interest**.[51] The American Government had learned that the people's confidence in the currency was all that was needed to free the government and the people of borrowing and debt (which meant they were free of the Bank of England).

In Response, the world's most powerful independent bank, The Bank of England, used its influence in the British parliament to press for the passing of the Currency Act[52] of 1764. This act made it illegal

---

[51] Quoted in "Money and Men" by Robert McCann Rice (1941) no prior source extant. Wikipedia: This was a complete reversal from the established British school of economics in which the Government borrowed hard money (gold and silver) from private banks at interest, and it was viciously opposed by the British banking interests for this reason

[52] 53. XAT Part. 3

for the colonies to print their own money and forced them to pay all future taxes to Britain in silver or gold.

In one year the conditions were so reversed that the era of prosperity ended, and a depression set in, to such an extent that the streets of the Colonies were filled with unemployed. The colonies would gladly have borne the little tax on tea and other matters so long as they were able to issue and control their own financial arrangements. This act created a social catastrophe, unemployment and dissatisfaction. Eliminating the colony's power to issue their own money and delivering that power into the hands of George III and the international bankers. ***This was the prime reason for the Revolutionary War.*** By the time the war began on 19th April 1775, so much gold and silver had been taken by taxation, they were left with no other choice but to print money to finance the war. What is so important to understand is that Colonial Script actually worked so well that it was a threat to the internationally established economic system of the time.

Franklin's idea of issuing money "in proper proportion to the demands of trade and industry" without interest, was not causing any problems or inflation. However it was diametrically opposed to the policy of the Bank of England which issued money for the sake of making a profit when borrowed with interest attached, for its shareholder's.

In America In 1781, Robert Morris an arms dealer, devised a plan for an American national bank along the lines of the Bank of England and submitted it to Congress. It was approved and became Th e Bank of North America, an institution that brought stability to the colonial economy, facilitated continued finance of the war effort and would ultimately establish the credit of the United States with the nations of Europe. Morris was immediately appointed Financial Agent (Secretary of Treasury) for the United States, in order to direct the operation of the new bank. The young government which was desperate for money saw the $400,000 he proposed as his deposit too tempting. So they agreed to allow him to establish the bank and lend out, (through the fractional reserve system), many times more than the original deposit.

The Government had already spent a large proportion of the money they would be loaned, so no one objected when he couldn't raise all the deposit. Instead he suggested he might use some of the gold that had been loaned to America from France. This was also agreed to and he went full steam ahead using the fractional reserve system. With the bank's growing fortune he and a few of his friends bought out the other shareholders. The bank immediately began to lend money to eager politicians who were probably too power hungry to notice, enquire, or care. The scam lasted five years until in 1785, when the value of American dollar dropped like a lead balloon. After five years the banks charter didn't get renewed. The shareholder's walking off with their accrued profits. This did not go unnoticed by the governor. At the US constitutional convention of 1787 he is quoted as saying: "The rich will strive to establish their dominion and enslave the rest. They always did, and they always will. They will have the same effect here as elsewhere, if we do not, (by the power of government), keep them in their proper spheres.

First Bank Of The United States (1791-1811)

In 1791 after a lapse of only six years, a new crop of hungry politicians came on the scene. If it worked once, would it work again? They fell for it - hence the First Bank of the United States (BUS) was established. Not only deceptively named to sound official, but also to take attention away from the first, first Bank, which had been shut down. This time around the money changers had learned a valuable lesson. They negotiated a guaranteed charter for twenty years and, similar to the British model, the name of the investor was never revealed.

"Let me issue and control a nation's money and I care not who writes the laws. "(Mayer Amschel Rothschild, 1790).

With the same scam being repeated, the contemporary bankers probably wished he had picked a different time to make this statement from his private central bank in Frankfurt. But as usual, the man in the street didn't hear it.

The American government borrowed 8.2 million dollars from his bank in the first five years and prices in America rose by 72%. This time round, the President, Thomas Jefferson in 1798, saw an ever increasing debt with no chance of ever paying back and is quoted as saying, "I wish it were possible to obtain a single amendment to our Constitution - taking from the Federal government its power of borrowing."

The reporting of this by the independent press of the day that had not yet been corrupted, called the operation "a great swindle, a vulture, a viper, and a cobra." The government was the only depositor to put up any real money. The remainder was raised from loans the investors made to each other, using the magical fractional reserve banking. When time came for renewal of the charter, in 1811, the bankers warned of bad times ahead if they didn't get the extension they wanted. Never-the- less, the charter was not renewed. Five months later Britain had attacked Napoleon and started the war of 1812.

The Bank of England, Rothschild, Napoleon and the Battle of Waterloo:

Napoleon didn't trust the Bank of France. He was suspicious because it was an independent and private business and he is quoted saying: "When a government is dependent upon bankers for money, they, and not the leaders of the government control the situation, since the hand that gives is above the hand that takes ... Money has no Motherland. Financiers are without patriotism and without decency; their sole object is gain." He financed his army through the Eubard Bank of Paris. It is not unusual for both sides at war to borrow money from the same privately owned Central Bank. Nothing generates debt like war. A Nation will borrow any amount to win. Naturally, the loser will be kept going to extreme measures in a vain hope of winning. In turn, more resources would be used by the winning side before their victory can be assured. More resources used, more loans taken out, more money made by the bankers. What is even more incredible is that the loans are usually made with the condition that the victor picks up the debts of the loser.

For his next campaign instead of borrowing, Napoleon in 1803 sold the territory West of the Mississippi to Thomas Jefferson the 3rd President of the United States for three million dollars in gold (the Louisiana Purchase). He quickly gathered together an army with the three million dollars and set about conquering much of Europe. Everywhere he went Napoleon discovered that his opposition was being financed by the Bank of England. Prussia, Austria and finally Russia all went heavily into debt trying to stop him. You can imagine the colossal amount of interest paid to the bank of England. Four years later, Nathan Rothschild made the first move in the game that was to make the Rothschild family business the richest that the world had ever seen. He illegally smuggled a shipment of gold through France to the Duke of Wellington to finance an attack from Spain. Napoleon's various victories in Europe and his ignominious defeat in Russia finally led to the Battle of Waterloo.

With the 74,000 of Napoleon's army facing British and allied forces of 67,000 led by the Duke of Wellington it was too close to call. Nathan Rothschild thought of a colossal confidence trick he could use to completely take full control of the British bond market, stock market and the Bank of England. He knew that whatever side lost, their currency would be greatly depreciated. He sent an agent to France to be close by the battlefield and quickly return as soon as the result was clear. Nathan received the news of Napoleon's defeat 24 hours before the official courier. With this knowledge Nathan took up his usual place at the stock market and according to historical accounts he looked very dejected as he started to sell English bonds. It was by this ***deceit and trickery*** that he misled stockbrokers to believe that Wellington had lost the battle, and everyone started to sell. The value of the English bonds fell until they were virtually given away.

Meanwhile Rothschild began to secretly buy up all the hugely devalued bonds at a very small fraction of what they were worth a few hours before. In this way ***Nathan Rothschild fraudulently accumulated more wealth in one afternoon than both Napoleon and Wellington had done in their entire lifetime.***

Up to this time the house of Rothschild may not have been the largest banking house in the world. However, after this sting was perpetrated it certainly put them in the unassailable top position worldwide. By the time of World War I (1914-1918) Germany borrowed money from the German Rothschild bank, Britain from the British Rothschild bank and France from the French Rothschild bank. Even the American super banker J.P. Morgan, who amongst other activities, was a sales agent for war materials and spending $10 million a day after the first six months of the war. This made him the largest buyer on the planet. It was not until after his death it was revealed that J P Morgan's actually worked for the Rothschild's banking empire and JP's shareholding was a mere nineteen percent.

In 1917 three years after the start of the war, the Russian revolution began, Communism installed and subsequently the entire Russian Royal Family was killed. You might find it strange to learn that the

Russian Revolution was also fuelled with British money. It sounds like some kind of sick joke but it happened. Capitalist businessmen were financing Communism while also going to war in 1921 with the little known War of Intervention in an attempt to defeat the Bolshevik Government.

W.Cleon Skousen in his book 'The Naked Capitalist' wrote: "Power from any source tends to create an appetite for additional power". It was almost inevitable that the super-rich would one day aspire to control not only their own wealth, but the wealth of the whole world. To achieve this, they were perfectly willing to feed the ambitions of the power-hungry political conspirators who were committed to the overthrow of all existing governments and the establishments of a central worldwide dictatorship."

Extreme revolutionary groups were controlled by being financed when they complied with the money changers agenda and cut off when they did not comply. If you find this hard to believe, listen to Louis T. McFadden, chairman of and representative for the House Banking and Currency Committee throughout the 1920-30s. He explained it this way: "The course of Russian history has, indeed, been greatly affected by the operations of international bankers. The Soviet Government has been given United States Treasury funds by the Federal Reserve Board, acting through the Chase Bank. England has drawn money from us through the Federal Reserve Banks and has re-lent it at high rates of interest to the Soviet Government. The Dnieper Dam was built with funds unlawfully taken from the United States Treasury by the corrupt and dishonest Federal Reserve Board and the Federal Reserve Banks." This is what the so-called dictator of the new Soviet Union Vladimir Lenin had to say: "The state does not function as we desired. The car does not obey. A man is at the wheel and seems to steer it, but the car does not drive in the desired direction. It moves as another force wishes."

Boris Yeltsin, when Communism collapsed in the Soviet Union, revealed where most of the foreign aid was ending up: "It was going Straight back into the coffers of western banks in debt service." (United States Congress Record, June 15, 1934)

With control of the press and the education system few Americans are aware that the "Fed" caused the depression. It is however a well known fact among leading top economists. *The Federal Reserve Bank caused the Great depression by contracting the amount of currency in circulation by one-third from 1929 to 1933.* To quote Milton Friedman, Nobel Prize winning economist: "This was not accidental. It was a carefully contrived occurrence. The international bankers sought to bring about a condition of despair here so that they might emerge as rulers of us all."

Some forty billion dollars somehow vanished in the crash. It didn't really vanish, it simply shifted into the hands of the money changers. This is how Joe Kennedy went from having 4 million dollars in 1929 to having over 100 million in 1935. During this time the Fed caused a 33% reduction of the money supply, causing a deeper depression.

How Does The Fed. Create Money from nothing?

1). The purchase of bonds is approved by the Federal Open Market Committee, (of the Fed.)

2). *The Fed buys bank bonds,* which it pays for with electronic cash credits made to the sellers "the Main street banks".

3). These banks then use the cash credits as *reserves* from which they can loan out ten times the amount. *To reduce the amount of money in the economy*, they reverse the process. *The Fed sells the bonds to the public* and money is withdrawn from the purchaser's main street bank to pay for them. Each million dollars withdrawn lowers the main street bank's ability to lend by ten million. In this way the Reserve Banks throughout the world have overall control of the nations money supply, The bankers, through the magic of fractional reserve banking have been delegated the right to create 90% of the money supply. This control makes a mockery of any elected government. It places so called leaders behind a toy steering wheel like the plastic ones set up in amusement parlours for children. Or as Charles Lindbergh put it when commenting on the Federal Reserve Act: "This act establishes the most gigantic trust on earth. When the President signs this bill, an invisible government by the Monetary Power will be legalized. The American people may not know it immediately, but the day of reckoning is only a few years removed. ... The worst legislative crime of the ages is perpetrated by this banking bill.

" In order to clearly establish that this is not a conspiracy theory but it is actually how things are controlled, Charles Lindbergh from the US House of Representatives, was well placed to see exactly what was happening back then. We see it continuing today in exactly the same way.

To cause high prices all the fed has to do is lower the re-discount (interest) rate to the main street banks. This produces an expansion of credit and a rising stock market. Then when business is adjusted to these conditions it can stop prosperity in mid-stride by arbitrarily raising the interest rate. In this way, it can cause the pendulum of a rising and falling market to swing gently back and forth by a slight change in the discount rate, or cause violent fluctuations by greater rate variation. In either case it will possess inside information as to financial conditions and advance knowledge of the coming change. This is the strangest, most dangerous advantage ever placed in the hands of a special privilege sector, by any Government that ever existed. The system is private and conducted for the sole purpose of obtaining the greatest possible profits from the use of other people's money. These operators know in advance when to create panics to their advantage. They also know when to stop panic. Inflation and deflation work equally well for them when they control finance."

As Woodrow Wilson stated: "We have come to be one of the worst ruled and one of the most completely controlled governments in the civilized world. We are no longer a government of free opinion, no longer a government by a vote of the majority, but a government by the opinion and duress of a small group of dominant men. Some of the biggest men in the United States, in the field of commerce and manufacture, are afraid of something. They know that there is a power somewhere so organized, so subtle, so watchful, so interlocked, so complete and so pervasive, that they had better not speak above their breath when they speak in condemnation of it."

Financing Adolf Hitler:

Congressman Louis T. McFadden (Democrat) served twelve years as Chairman of the Committee on Banking and Currency made this observation: "Almost all will be aware of Hitler's rise to power. What they probably don't know is that he was almost completely financed by money drawn from the privately owned American Federal Reserve. After WWI, Germany fell into the hands of the international bankers. Those bankers bought her and they own her, lock, stock, and barrel. They purchased her industries, they had mortgages on her soil, controlled production and all public utilities."

The international bankers subsidized the Government of Germany and they also supplied every dollar of the money Adolph Hitler used in his lavish campaign to build up the threat to the Weimar Republic government of Heinrick Bruning. When the Bruning government failed to obey the orders of the International Bankers in Germany, Hitler was brought in to scare the Germans into submission. Through the Federal Reserve Board over $30 billion of American money had been pumped into Germany.

But isn't there tons of gold in FORT KNOX? [53]. In 1933 new President Franklin D. Roosevelt signed a bill forcing all the American people, to hand over all their gold at the base rate, with the exception of rare coins. He disowned himself from the bill claiming to not have read it and his secretary of the treasury claimed this was "what the experts wanted". Bought at bargain basement price with money produced from nothing by the Federal Reserve, the gold was melted down and stacked in the newly built bullion depository called Fort Knox. Once collected in 1935 the price of gold was raised from $20.66 up to $35 per ounce, but only non American gold qualified to be sold. This meant those who had avoided the crash by investing in the gold they had shipped to London could now nearly double their money while the rest of America starved. That's not all folks. By the end of WWII Fort Knox held 70% of the world's gold, but over the years it was sold off to the European money changers while public audits of Fort Knox reserves were repeatedly denied. Rumours spread about the missing gold. Eleanor Roosevelt's observed "Allegations of missing gold from our Fort Knox vaults are being widely discussed in European circles. But what is puzzling is that the Administration is not hastening to demonstrate conclusively that there is no cause for concern over our gold treasure - if indeed it is in a position to do so." Finally in 1981 President Ronald Reagan was prompted to have a look into Fort Knox with a view to re-introducing the Gold Standard. He appointed a group

---

[53] Google: Is There Any Gold in Fort Knox?

called The Gold Commission. They found that the US Treasury owned no gold at all. All the remaining "Fort Knox Gold," is now being held as collateral by the Federal Reserve against the national debt. Using credits made from nothing, The Fed money changers had robbed the largest treasure of gold on earth

World War II (1939-1945)

World War II saw the US debt increased by 598%, while Japan's debt went up by 1,348%, with France up by 583% and Canada up by 417%. I daresay Australia may have been in about the same bracket as Canada.

I remember, as a young boy of fourteen in 1939, when I read in the newspapers that the Australian Government was asking the public to invest in Government bonds. The first issue of 100,000,000 Pounds was now available. One hundred million Pounds! Coming right after the depression, I laughed at the thought of the sum required. I reckoned there was not that much money in the world. There were previously no jobs and most of our young men were 'on the track' looking for any kind of work to support wives and families. My father was getting what was termed "relief work," about one weeks work in six. I left school not so much to earn a living, but to ease the economic burden from my parents having five children to rear. Lo and behold, the loan was oversubscribed within a week and by whom? You guessed it, the banks and financial institutions. They had the money. Why was it not used for the common good?

When one hears of things like this, what is our first impression? Most of us feel a well- programmed sense of depression when we hear figures of this magnitude being bandied about but to the money changers this is music to their ears. And when the hot war ended in 1945, the cold war began and the arms race started. So the show goes on, with even more borrowing.

Now the money changers could really concentrate on global domination. The process: Step 1. Create the European Monetary Union and NAFTA (North American Free Trade agreement).

Step 2. Centralise the global economy via the World Bank, the IMF and GATT (now the WTO) and the General Agreement in Trade and Services (GATS). In 1913 The Federal Reserve Act was passed in the USA taking the power to print the currency from the reserve bank, then issuing it to the Fed for distribution to the various other banking institutions, which many were shareholders in the Fed. This transformed the Fed from a wholly privately owned corporation into one in which the beneficiaries are at arms length, through their ownership of the 'High Street' banks. 1946 saw the Bank of England fully nationalised and become independently run, but with a government appointed executive.

The World Central Banks (1948 to the Present):[54]

In Washington, the headquarters of both the World Bank and the IMF face each other on the same street. What are these organisations, and who controls them? To find out we need to look back to just after WWI. At this point the Money Changers were attempting to consolidate the central banks under the guise of peacemaking. To stop future wars they put forward the formation of a world central bank named the Bank of International Settlements. An organisation called the World Court was established in The Hague, together with a world executive for legislation called the League of Nations.

In his 1966 book entitled Tragedy and Hope, President Clinton's mentor, Carroll Quigley Professor at Georgetown University wrote: "The powers of financial capitalism have a far-reaching plan, nothing less than to create a world system of financial control in private hands able to dominate the political system of each country and the economy of the world as a whole. This system was to be controlled in a feudalist fashion by the central banks of the world acting in concert. This is to be achieved by secret agreements arrived at in frequent meetings and conferences. The apex of the system was to be the Bank for International Settlements in Basel, Switzerland. A private bank owned and controlled by the world's central banks; some of which were also private corporations. Each central bank sought to dominate its government by its ability to control treasury loans, to manipulate foreign exchanges, to influence the level of economic activity in the country, and to seduce cooperative politicians by subsequent economic rewards in the business world." They got two out of four. The League of Nations failed, largely owing to the suspicions of the people. While opposition was concentrated on this, the other two proposals snuck

[54] Google: XAT part 3.

their way through. It would take another war to wear the public resistance down. Wall Street invested heavily to rebuild Germany as the Chase Bank had propped up Russia after the revolution. The Chase then merged with the Warburg's Manhattan Bank to form the Chase Manhattan which would later merge with the Chemical Bank to become the largest bank on Wall Street.

In Australia in 1959-60 The Government formed The Reserve Bank of Australia as part of the Commonwealth bank. Between 1983 and 1985 Treasurer Paul Keating deregulated the banking system by separating the reserve bank from the Commonwealth bank's control and formed it as an independent Commonwealth instrumentality. He also floated the Aussie Dollar, privatized the Commonwealth Bank and granted licenses to 16 foreign banks to operate in Australia. The Reserve bank of Australia, is not a deposit taking bank and is an independent entity. It has a board of directors three of which are ex-officio members (appointed by the government); The Governor(who is chairman), the Deputy Governor and the Secretary to the Treasury and six external members appointed by the Treasurer. The external members may not be an officer or employee of any deposit taking bank or institution. Though, on viewing their credentials, they also happen to be directors of some of the largest multi-national corporations, investment companies and finance companies in the world: Woodside Petroleum, Coca-Cola, Wal-mart, C.S.L limited, Brambles ltd. and James Hardie to name a few. In theory, it is controlled and regulated to ensure that it operates to achieve what the board believes to be for the greatest advantage of the people of Australia. But forgive me if I think they operate on the same principle as Henry Ford, who is quoted to have said: "What is good for Henry Ford is good for America" In other words, what is good for the big end of town is good for the nation.

In 1913 the democrat president Woodrow Wilson introduced the Federal Reserve Act circumscribing the activities and responsibilities of the US Federal Reserve Bank. However the actual ownership is vague and convoluted but is understandable if followed closely. What is noticeable here is the fact that quasi-nationalisation and regulating of the Reserve Banks was implemented by socialist or labour governments and the Democrats in the US. However none have had the ability to completely nationalise them. It is only the head of an octopus whose tentacles can not be controlled under the world's present socio-economic system. John F Kennedy acted against the controlling hierarchy, and like Jesus, was immediately eliminated[55]. Access the footnote reference and you will learn why. On May 21st, 1981 – Guy Rothschild's 72nd birthday – Socialist, Francois Mitterrand became president of France and before the year's end had fulfilled a campaign promise to nationalise all private banks in France. By 1980, the French Rothschilds employed 2,000 people and controlled industrial interests with an annual turnover of some 26 billion francs. Baron Guy Rothschild wrote in a scathing letter to the newspaper Le Monde referring to the nationalisation in which he said:

"A Jew under Petain, a pariah under Mitterrand - for me it's enough. Of the House of Rothschild there will remain a few odd pieces, maybe nothing" In 1944 the US Government approved full participation in the IMF and the World Bank. By 1945 the second League of Nations was approved under the new name 'The United Nations'. The war had dissolved all opposition. The methods used in the National Banking Act of 1864 and the Federal Reserve Act of 1913 were then simply used on a global scale. This allowed the creation of Federal Reserve Notes coupled with the IMF's authority to produce money called Special Drawing Rights or (SDR's). It is estimated the IMF has produced $30 billion dollars worth of SDR's so far. In the United States SDR's are already accepted as legal money, and all other member nations are being pressured to follow suit. With SDR's being partially backed by gold, a world gold standard is sneaking its way in through the back door, which comes with no objection from the money changers who now hold two-thirds of the worlds gold and can use this to structure the worlds economy to their further advantage.

We have gone from the goldsmith's fraud being reproduced on a national scale through the Bank of England and the US Federal Reserve, to a global level with the IMF and the World Bank. Unless we act together to stop giving these exchange units their power by our collective faith in them, the future will probably see the Intergalactic Bank and the Universal Planet's Reserve Board set up in much the same way. This radical transfer of power has taken place with absolutely no mandate from the people.

---

[55]   Google: President John F. Kennedy's Executive Order Abolishing the Fed

CHAPTER 11.

Economic Rationalism

The problem of financing through privatization:
Developing Nations borrow money, *Special Drawing Rights for US dollars* (SDR's) from the IM F in order to pay accumulating interest on previous loans. The SDR's are produced at no cost and the IMF charges more interest. Contrary to bold claims, this does not alleviate poverty or further any development. It just creates a steady flow of wealth from borrowing nations to the money changers who now control the IMF and the World Bank. The permanent debt of Third World Countries is constantly being increased to provide temporary relief from the poverty being caused by previous borrowing. These repayments already exceed the amount of new loans. By 1992 Africa's debt had reached $290 billion dollars, which is two and a half times greater than it was in 1980. A noble attempt to repay it has caused increased infant mortality and unemployment, deteriorating schools and general health and welfare problems. The world's resources continue to be funnelled into this insatiable black hole of greed and if allowed to continue the entire world will face a similar fate to that of the third world.

As a prominent Brazilian politician, Luis Ignacio Silva puts it:
"Without being radical or overly bold, I tell you that the Third World War has already started a silent war, not that it is any the less

sinister. This war is tearing down Brazil, Latin America and practically all the Third World. Instead of soldiers dying there are children, instead of millions of wounded there are millions of unemployed; instead of destruction of bridges there is the tearing down of factories, schools, hospitals, and entire economies ... It is a war by the United States against the Latin American continent and the Third World. It is a war over the foreign debt, one which has as its main weapon, usury (interest). A weapon that in a poor country is more deadly than the atom bomb and more shattering than a laser beam. If any group or organization had used its hard earned money to help these developing nations, then we might sympathize that there should be a real eff ort to repay these loans. But the money used was created from the fractional reserve banking system. The money loaned to the Third World came from the 90% that the banks allow themselves to loan on the 10% they originally held. It didn't actually exist, it was created from nothing, and now people are suffering and dying in an effort to pay it back.

As Luis Ignacio Silva said at the Havana Debt Conference in August 1985, "this has gone beyond clever financing, it is wholesale murder and it's time we stopped it. We can and we must!" But how?

Privatization is a big problem in developing countries. In many cases, it amounts to corporate theft and hi-jacking of public assets. The World Trade Organization agreement called TRIPS (Agreement on Trade-Related Intellectual Property Rights), generally favours the rights of corporations to assert patents, even to the extent that they override national law. This tends to discriminate against the poor countries with endemic HIV/aids problems — countries which cannot afford the exorbitant prices set by the Western pharmaceutical companies. These countries are overwhelmingly non-white poor countries where the social and cultural fabric has been drastically altered by *Western models* of development.

Another problem for developing and third World nations is unwary, naïve or corrupt governments accepting the G.A.T.S (General Agreement on Trade and Services). Even developed countries that entered the NAFTA agreement, (a free trade agreement signed between the United States and Canada in 1989 and extended to include Mexico in 1994) are not immune and have had their fingers badly burned.

Many of the principles contained in GATS are not new. Since 1948, GATT helped the liberalization of world trade with the most-favoured nation policy promising equal treatment and market access principles. Unfortunately, other institutions like the IMF and The World Bank, enforces international privatization conditionalities (as they are called), in their credit policy. Since then, GATS has developed a very different view on the world trade system. In order to get a perspective, understanding how these conditions evolved, a brief explanation of the present economic system in the Western World and how it developed may be useful.

1). *The Bretton Woods agreement*:[56] In the first three weeks of July 1944, delegates from 45 nations gathered at the United Nations Monetary and Financial Conference in Bretton Woods, New Hampshire in the USA. The delegates met to discuss the post-war recovery of Europe as well as a number of monetary issues, such as unstable exchange rates and protectionist trade.

The rules were designed to maintain stable exchange rates to avoid the economic self interest policies of the 1930s and benefit global economies by expanding international trade. However, over time, exchange rates became uncompetitive as there were often large and destabilizing flows of currency caused by currency speculators gambling huge amounts on the value at which the fixed exchange rate would be re-fixed, thus creating *hot money*. During the 1930s various states had experienced a series of connected problems: shortage of gold, unstable exchange rates, the movement of hot money in and out of their realms, and the lack of a workable mechanism to adjust balance of payments problems. The agreement finally broke down under circumstances described in a later chapter.

2) *John Maynard Keynes* was a brilliant British economist whose economic theories gained worldwide acclaim. An important period of his career was during the 1930s when unemployment and the depression were rampant. Conventional economics could not cope with the extraordinary events which took place leaving traditional economic theories with no answer. Keynes first major work which indicated he deviated from the conventional approach to economics was explained in *"A Treatise on Money"* published in 1930. The next and what is

---

[56] Wikipedia: "Bretton Woods Agreement"

considered to be his most important work reflecting the culmination of his ideas was *"The General Theory of Employment, Interest and Money"* published in 1935-36. The two main messages of this work are:

a). That the existing theory of unemployment was nonsense. In a depression there is no wage so low that it could eliminate unemployment. Accordingly, it was wicked to blame the unemployed for their plight. And

b). The second proposition proposed an alternative explanation about the origins of unemployment and depression. This centred upon total demand – i.e. total spending of consumers, business investors and government. When aggregate demand was low, sales and jobs suffered. When high, all was well. Keynesian economics has led us through the booms and busts of the 20th century, as various so-called economists tried to maintain economic stability. (This is impossible while financial control remains in the hands of institutions that are dedicated to maximizing profit, while ignoring the awkward question, *at whose expense?*) Keynes was considered by many to be an economic genius and was given an honorary role in the Treasury during World War II. One of the most important projects he was involved in during his last years was setting up the IMF.

3). GATS: The first multilateral agreement on trade in services worked out in the course of the Uruguay round of negotiation of GATT (General Agreement on Tariffs and trade). GATS came into effect with the founding of the World Trade organization (WTO) on 1/1/1995. In the meantime 147 states have become members in the WTO and negotiating partners in GATS. The regulations of GATS cover the whole expanse of the service sector. Infrastructure areas like transportation and telecommunication are included alongside financial services, architecture, electronic data processing services and tourism. Basic Public services like education, prisons, detention centres, health care and water also fall under the conditions of GATS. Therefore GATS *is really an investment agreement and not only a trade agreement.*

Re-classification - and privatization - underGATS: *Or, Social theft.*

GATS is not only a privatization agreement. Its market-opening clauses facilitate the entrance of multi-national corporations into intensely regulated areas. GATS creates incentives for corporations in two directions.

First, GATS over-rides local legal conditions and obligations as to investment activity and market access.

Secondly, GATS produces legal certainty for corporations through the practical liberalization of contract clauses. With the acceptance of GATS in the world trade system under the umbrella of the (WTO) services. **WTO services** are now generally recognized as internationally exchangeable goods. Since public services like water, gas, or electrical infrastructure, or the education- and health care systems are not excluded from the regulatory range of the agreement, GATS encourages the expropriation of public infrastructure property through privatization of the service. The inclusion of water supply in the regulatory scope of the WTO illustrates the nature of the change in classification of WATER, from a public national resource, to a tradable commodity. **Accumulation through expropriation** on a global scale is nothing less than wholesale international burglary.

Exporting Employment, Importing Welfare.

As far back as the 1980's, I, like the prophet Daniel of the Old Testament, saw the writing on the wall. It was clear to any thinking individual that greatly increased productivity in both the office and on the factory floor, due to the onset of the computers and computerized machinery, would result in a surplus labour market. The strength of the labour unions and the conditions gained during the post-war boom only managed to slow down the inevitable result. A few large corporations realized the opportunity for the exploitation of the vast unemployed pool moved their operations to the so-called third world countries. At the same time this would overcome the drive for higher wages and better working conditions in their local labour market. At first, the corporations that moved production "offshore," were only the larger manufacturers and few in number. But over the next ten to twenty years it became a flood and not restricted to only the large and medium sized factories. In Australia, very small factory and backyard producers employing up to six or seven people, found it very profitable to follow suit.

At the time, I was engaged in industry; in the area of engineering and mechanical services. The company started by my partner and I in 1952 built up to a very profitable enterprise. This was largely due to the fact that we were both engineering tradesmen and were able to contract our expertise in a booming market where there was a high demand. Being young and enterprising, we became largely involved in the manufacture and erection of structural steel factories and warehouse buildings. There was a great demand for building equipment and machinery, bulldozers, graders, cranes and the like. The main supplier for this type of machinery at the time was the USA.. The cost of purchasing the mobile cranes we needed to expand our business was out of our reach so we hired them as required. With the hire cost eating up a large portion of our profit, we decided to design and build our own.

As demand for our services grew we widened our scope and manufactured more cranes and diversified into pipeline laying, machinery handling, and industrial plant installations and removals. The reason for the above details of my activities is to establish that my observations regarding the mass export of jobs is not hearsay. In quite a few cases, the same factories and warehouses that I erected, and into which we also installed machinery in the 50's and 60's; I was actively engaged in the nuts and bolts activity of shrinking, and in some cases, closing down in the 70's and 80's. In most cases, the owners of both small and large manufacturing plants throughout the country decided that the costs, coupled with labour union problems were just not worth the effort. Why bother, when you could have your product made in some third world country and landed back at less than a quarter of the cost?

The Marshal plan of financial assistance in war-torn Europe created a frenzy of activity as the rebuilding of cities, towns and villages enabled crippled economies to thrive. The factories and steel makers could not cope with the demand. So much so that labour became a valuable commodity. Wages and conditions for the worker in the Western world rose dramatically in those post-war years. George Marshall, the US Secretary of State under President Truman, was not a scholar of military or political history, but having read widely, was excellent at extracting accurate lessons from history and from his own experience. After World War II Marshall sought to avoid the mistakes he had witnessed during World War 1 and its immediate aftermath. He simply applied the knowledge of past problems, the ideas, and solutions, to the present conditions. He could see that every current problem was not new, unique, or isolated. Unlike most politicians, he applied the lessons that had he learned from history.

Billions of dollars of American money poured into Japan to rebuild the cities of Hiroshima and Nagasaki that were atom bombed and totally destroyed. The Japanese manufacturing base that was previously employed in preparing and maintaining their war machine was converted to the manufacture of domestic household products, office equipment, light and heavy machinery and electronic equipment. These products were exported worldwide, bringing enormous profits back to the US-based corporations that saw the investment opportunity. This was the bait that started the trans-national and multi-national corporate export of jobs. In the 25 years following the war, it looked as though 99% of the world's manufactured products were labelled "made in Japan" As the Japanese domestic economy boomed labour became more expensive. Gradually, as rising prices of domestic goods and services in Japan increased, wages and conditions of the labour rose commensurately. The multi and trans-national companies started to look for cheaper labour sources. These were not hard to find. Neighbouring China and the Philippines were ripe for the picking; Especially the Philippines which had been an American colony and with a large English speaking workforce.

At the same time, it was obvious that in the not too distant future, back home there would be an acute shortage of skilled labour. How could it be otherwise? Factories that employed and trained apprentices in most industries are practically non existent. The Government ignored this and did very little to solve the problem. Incidentally the same factories and warehouses that we built in the 50's and 60's are now chock-full of an incredible variety of imported consumer goods. We import clothing, electronic gadgetry, home appliances and furnishings, machinery, cars, bikes and toys. You name it, we import it. Along with this shrinking capacity to produce the wide variety of products domestically we witnessed the introduction of what the modern economists call **Economic Rationalism**. The use of this comparatively new economic tool threatens to destroy the very fabric of the society upon which it relies. The terminology used by modern-day economic guru's include terms like, "level Playing Field," "tariff minimization," "protectionism," globalization," "free trade agreements" "multi lateral Investments" "general agreement on trade in services", all boil down to the grab by the greedy at the expense of the needy.

On the surface it seems that introducing large amounts of capital investment into underdeveloped countries, must improve economic conditions in the particular country. In practice, this is an extremely slow process. The global corporation uses the cheap labour force often as much as seventy times lower than in the US, Australia or Western Europe. Establishing factories and producing a variety of cheap goods for the developed world. The direct result of this is that in both areas the general populations are economic losers. The only winners are the trans-national Corporations dealing in commodities and/or services, merchant bankers financing the deals, and in many cases, corrupt politicians.

After selling my engineering business and contemplating retirement, I was offered the opportunity to manage the production in Asia for a very large garment manufacturing and distribution company in the US. I learned first hand how large multi-national corporations work. Our office was in Hong Kong and we employed factories in both Hong Kong and China. The Hong Kong production had been in place for a few years before I became involved, but as demand started to outstrip production capacity in Hong Kong, the prices rose to the extent that it became obvious that we could produce much cheaper in mainland China. However the quality of the product was not as good. Over time, as the Chinese factories became more experienced and industrially sophisticated, the cost of production started to rise. This again prompted moves to cheaper areas of production. We then used factories in The Philippines, Indonesia, India, Thailand and any country where cheap labour could be exploited.

At first appearance you may think that the workers in these countries would benefit. However, as they are in an internationally competitive market the export oriented factory owners were the main beneficiaries. *Financial return* on investment was astronomical, while the *social return* in these areas is only incidental, wages and conditions improve only marginally. They are engaged in producing vast quantities of goods that they can't buy, yet their local buying power has the effect of increased demand locally, raising the price of the local goods and services across the board. This then causes social imbalances in the country of manufacture. Factories that catered for the local market are forced to compete for suitable labour. This also drives local prices up. The result is that they may earn more, but with the higher local prices very little advantage is gained. In 2006, used garments from Europe and America are being exported back to these third world countries for as little as $80.00 per ton, compounding the problems faced by the manufactures making for the local market. On the other hand, small garment factories in the West, faced with a flood of cheap imports into the market close down and thousands of people laid off . They are forced to go on the dole,(social security) or take whatever other employment is available. A hidden labour force became widespread in the garment industry, so called "outdoor" workers who work from home on pitifully low contract rates. In Australia, labour conditions deteriorated to the extent that the government tried to hide both the reality of the situation and their inability to control these conditions from the people, by fudging the unemployment rate figures.

A few years ago, if you didn't have a full time job, you were considered unemployed, not so today. If you have part time paid employment of only two hours per week, this constitutes employment and does not show in the unemployed statistics. No wonder the Government states the unemployment rate has dropped considerably; down to five percent. They moved the goal posts. Some people are forced to scramble around, working three or four part time jobs mostly in the services and hospitality industry in order to survive. Others work all hours under contract conditions where the employer is not responsible for taxes, insurances, holiday pay, overtime loading, superannuation or long service entitlement. This system places a heavy burden on a large number of the working population. These are workers, relying on their weekly earnings to live, buy a home and raise a family. A few years ago this was possible on the wage of only one breadwinner. Today it is extremely difficult, even with two peoples' wages and it gets more difficult as time goes on. Meanwhile, many industries in the developed countries are downsizing, closing shop, or going bankrupt because of the influx of cheap imported goods. Their only hope of survival in this new economic climate is the availability of a local workforce that will work for the same conditions as the workers in third world countries. It appears that in this new economic climate, we are in the process of producing a class of working poor.

The Contradictions of Economic Rationalism:

Utilizing modern technology to increase production and downsizing staff numbers to decrease costs increases efficiency on the small scale, this results in a large number of consumers with reduced spending capacity. These then become a burden on the already over taxed working community. Both human resources and infrastructure are rendered redundant. The result is that both human and industrial capital remains idle in the name of *efficiency*. On both the national and international scene, results show the exact opposite, *inefficiency*. The modern capitalist society is incapable of utilizing these untapped human and industrial resources. It is left to governments to maintain the excess populations on social security payments, or in the defence forces.

In the never ending pursuit of profits, the victims are the unfortunate have-nots who cannot put up any real resistance. They remain victims of economic conditions imposed on them by the present faceless controlling forces. Many, *opportunistic social parasites*, seeing the opening to make a quick buck, in this period of financial and industrial re-structuring, are directing their activities to the stock market and currency trading. Companies have been listed with the express purpose of speculation fraud. The number and size of company director remunerations and share acquisitions, when compared to the extreme poverty and starvation suffered by hundreds of millions of the world's population, is heartless, insulting and obscene.

According to Forbes magazine's annual billionaire list, the number of billionaires worldwide increased by 102 people in 2006 to 793, a record number, largely due to bullish global stock markets. Their total net worth jumped 18 percent to $2.6 trillion. With 371, the U.S. is the country with the most billionaires, followed by Germany with fifty-five. The total worth of all U.S. billionaires combined is $1.1 trillion, while Europe's combined billionaire worth is $802 billion. New York seemed to be the hot spot for the super rich attracting forty billionaires followed by Moscow with twenty-five and London with twenty-three. This constitutes a combined wealth of only 793 people being more than the G.D.P. of the group of low income countries with over fifty percent of the world's population. Just pause to consider:

A large proportion of this concentrated accumulation of wealth is not derived from industry, agriculture or commercial production or service provision, but *from paper shuffling* on the world's stock, currency and commodity markets. So, where is all this wealth? There are over 50 offshore tax havens world-wide that cater for these social predators, deposed and corrupt political leaders, war criminals and the paper shufflers who grow nothing manufacture nothing and serve nothing but their own greed. A press release in March 2005, by the Tax Justice network revealed that only the tax evaded by using these tax havens, runs into *US$255 billion each year.* According to Tax Research Limited who prepared the figure, the estimated value of assets held offshore is in the order of **US$11.5 trillion.** This figure can be considered conservative as it does not include corporate profits. In a world of over production of food and manufactured goods we find local, regional and national producers and service providers struggling to survive. They are being forced to the wall and replaced by expanding multinational corporate giants backed by the enormous credit reserves held by the few large and powerful banking and financial institutions. All of which are primarily interested in wealth maximization or a financial return on investment that benefits only the few.

The United Nations millennium development goal to halve global poverty by 2015 could easily be achieved with the use of this evaded tax money. Of all the world's criminal activities, the locking up of ill-gotten gains in the shelter of Swiss banks is the worst. This money, stolen by the wealthy and powerful from the most wretched and vulnerable of the world, is the worst on two counts:

1) The unused resources are a dormant credit colossus and if used wisely would be more than enough to eradicate global poverty.
2) This would constitute a *social return on investment that would benefit the world.*

The World Bank, the IMF, and Finance.

I don't suppose anyone remembers the general excitement in the economic world back in 2005. The word from the G 8 WTO summit was that forgiving or severely cutting the debts of the third world countries was to be given serious consideration. When the meeting ended with no agreement on this, the headline in a local economic media read: "G 8 Hype Results in Massive Anticlimax." This same WTO forum also closes year after year without an agreement on this.

The World Bank, the IMF, the U.S. Federal Reserve plus multinational commercial banking corporations, overtly service the needs of trade and commerce in developing countries while covertly undermining their national sovereignty with seductive financial arrangements with their governments.

In most cases they are required to impose austerity measures on the economy in order to service the loans. This is at the cost of the social, material and cultural wellbeing of the local population. In some cases, particularly in South America, their influence borders on economic occupation. Both national and international banks have led the commercial world in downsizing and restructuring thus increasing their profitability enormously. The catchwords are economic rationalism and globalization. Since World War 2 the various national economic indicators in the Western World have been steadily rising. One would imagine that this would indicate a rise in living standards and lifestyle. Instead, competition, insecurity and stress in the industrial labour market has also risen. The social spin off, is road rage, racism and bigotry, domestic and social violence as frustrated locals have to lift their game to compete with migrants from the poorer under developed areas of the world.

The advent of the monolithic commercial monopolies slowly swallowing small business enterprises, is savage exploitation of market forces. *(economic rationalism)*. Credit availability *(debt),* with the social engineered media manipulation of public worldview *(spin),* has produced a discernable social malaise. Over the last forty years this has taken its toll on local communities and – I suspect – most of the Western world's population. This was largely brought about by the rapid advance of technology, coupled with growing job insecurity. Changing labour markets and work practices that have gradually eroded the work ethic and produced an ever growing number of homeless families and destitute people. The increasing difficulty to make ends meet has left many of us punch-drunk and bewildered as to how and why it has come about.

Countries can and have been brought to their knees economically and socially by the actions of the IMF. as illustrated by the events in Argentina where the economic policies during the 1990s were developed under their direction. The following, analysis by Joseph Stiglitz reveals some fatal flaws in these policies. He is Former Chief Economist for The World Bank and was awarded the Nobel prize for economics and is highly critical of globalization and global policies of the IMF. He contends that these policies severely disadvantage the very people that should have been better off as a result of them. His main contention is that the rules that were applied when designing them were using the wrong parameters. The rules used were based on the assumption that the economic system can be regulated according to a particular formula. However this relies on a fixed basis of information as to income, employment, productivity, total market, and other figures that should give a calculated result. They also assume that the numbers used are correct. However, the big problem arises with the fact that, because of many areas where there is a conflict of interest, incorrect figures are submitted. When a more realistic set of figures are used the outcomes conform more to the actual result we see on the ground. The problem (or blame) lies with the people in the richer countries not willing to give up their advantaged position to benefit the people at the lower level in the poorer countries. ***The principals of social justice, ethics and morality in developing countries are sacrificed for the economic advantage of the rich in the advanced countries.*** This has been experienced in the overwhelming majority of the globalization agreements overseen by the IMF.

The policies of the IMF and those of the World Bank have generated a great deal of popular opposition in low-income countries, as well as in the US, Europe and Australia. During recent years, public opposition has become increasingly widespread, with major demonstrations at meetings of the IMF, the World Bank, and the WTO, as well as the G20 and the G8 so named for the number of international finance ministers gathered to discuss globalization and the world economy. This opposition has been dubbed the 'anti-globalization movement'. The title is misleading because most of the activists are not opposed to the growing international economic and cultural connections among peoples, but are opposed to the way those connections are being structured, benefiting a few large corporations while creating hardship and instability for a majority of the people. Experiences like those of the IMF in Argentina typify the problem.

The political upheaval in Argentina lends new strength to the argument of the opposition movement. The lesson is that the movement for change should increase its pressure on institutions like the IMF that are playing central roles in shaping globalization. The movement has emerged largely in response to the hardships and inequality that have grown, even when IMF-type policies generates some economic growth. This opposition will gain greater legitimacy as growth is replaced by crisis as in Argentina. The appeal of alternative policies will be even greater as the IMF and local economic leaders can no longer claim that economic growth will eventually solve all problems. Th e IMF adjustment policy not only fails to bolster economic development but also leads to social and political disintegration. Pressure from the people's movement for change has had an impact. The IMF contribution to the Asian financial crisis in 1997 attracted a torrent of criticism from the general public, with some criticism also directed to the actual protesters on the scene. While no major policy changes have resulted, the Fund responded by renaming its *Enhanced Structural Adjustment Facility*, to the *Poverty Reduction and Growth Facility*. Over a longer period the World Bank also adjusted at least the appearance of its policies, focusing more attention on the issue of poverty and starting to examine the role of gender in economic development. The World Bank, also, has backed off from some of its large-scale water control projects in low-income countries as a result of pressure from local and international environmental groups. These changes have not basically altered the programs of the international financial institutions and the IMF has been especially resistant to change. Yet these adjustments suggest that widespread social opposition has begun to have an impact. As of late 2006, Th e IMF has had little or no applications for loans. It seems that at last the lesson has filtered through. The small struggling economies value their independence especially in South America. They have seen what has happened elsewhere, and decided that it's not worth losing your soul for the Yankee Dollar.

Michel Chossudovsky, a Professor of Economics at the University of Ottawa has written three books titled "The Globalization of Poverty", the "Impacts of IMF And World Bank Reforms." and "Global Poverty In The 21st Century". In which he describes how economic globalization affects the working poor:

"The late 20th Century will go down in World history as a period of global impoverishment; marked by the collapse of productive systems in the developing World, the demise of national institutions and the disintegration of health and educational programs. Th is globalization of poverty has largely reversed the achievements of post-war colonial independence which was initiated in much of the Third World with the onset of the debt crisis. Since the 1990s, it has extended its grip to all major regions of the world including North America, Western Europe, the countries of the former Soviet block and the newly industrialized countries of South East Asia and the Far East."

"In the 1990s, local level famines erupted in Sub-Saharan Africa, South Asia and parts of Latin America Health clinics and schools were closed down and hundreds of millions of children have been denied primary education. In the Third World, eastern Europe and the Balkans there is a resurgence of infectious diseases including tuberculosis, malaria and cholera."

According to a UN estimate, famine has extended from the dry sub Sahara areas, into the wet tropical heartland. In Southern Africa, 18 million people (including 2 million refugees) are in "famine zones" and another 130 million in 10 countries are seriously at risk. In the Horn of Africa for instance, 23 million people many have died, while the rest are in danger of starving to death. These numbers constitute a large proportion of the population of the African continent. "This has been allowed to develop at the same time as populations in the comparatively affluent Western World are experiencing productive over-abundance. The economic policies of the controllers of the financial and banking system in the West chose to ignore and in many cases exacerbate the plight of countless millions of this unfortunate section of humanity in order to maximize their profits." A typical example:

"In India, more than 70 percent of rural households are small marginal farmers or landless farm workers representing a population of over 400 million people. In irrigated areas, agricultural workers are employed for 200 days a year, and in rain-fed farming for approximately 100 days. The phasing out of fertilizer subsidies (an explicit conditionality of the IMF agreement) and the increase in the prices of farm inputs and fuel is pushing a large number of small and medium sized farmers into bankruptcy. A micro-level study conducted in 1991 sheds light on starvation deaths among handloom weavers. In a relatively prosperous rural community in Andhra Pradesh local communities have been impoverished as a result of macro-economic reform. Deaths from starvation occurred in the months following the implementation of the 1991 New Economic Policy and the devaluation and the lifting of controls on cotton yarn exports. The jump in the domestic price of cotton yarn led to a collapse in the pacham (24 meters) rate paid to the weaver by the middle-man through the putting-out or (out-worker system). Radha Krishnamurthy and his wife were able to weave between three and four pachams a month bringing home the an income of 300-400 rupees ($12-16), for a family of six. Then came the Union Budget of July 24, 1991, the price of cotton yarn jumped and the burden was passed on to the weaver. Radha krishnamurthy's family income declined to 240-320 rupees ($9.60-$13.00)" a month. Radha Krishnamurthy of Gollapalli village in Guntur district died of starvation on September 4, 1991. Between August 30 and November 10, 1991 at least 73 starvation deaths were reported in only two districts of Andhra Pradesh. There are 3.5 million handlooms throughout India supporting a population of some 17 million people."

The IMF was originally designed to deal with this type of economic difficulty by putting in place an international monetary system containing a stable exchange rate regime. This should contain some scope for revaluation adjustment, which provides for the convertibility of currency and also provide a mechanism for overcoming short-term liquidity crises; a type of arbitrating organization for managing the system. From the perspective of the struggling millions of the world who it affects, it fails on all counts. The World Bank policy was designed to help the economic and industrial reconstruction of Europe and to help developing countries achieve industrialization. The purpose of the International Trade Organization (ITO) was to propel states down the path of free trade, to prevent them from defecting to protectionism as a way of responding to balance of payments problems (e.g. by imposing import quotas as an alternative to devaluing their currency). The ITO never emerged, because of US objections. Instead, a weaker agreement known as the GATT took its place.

The US financial hegemony[57] describes not only the disproportionate relationship that the US dollar has with the global economy, but the constraints applied on other national economies by the IMF and the World Bank. The US dollar continues to underpin the world economy and is the main currency for international exchange, units of account (e.g. pricing of oil), and units of storage (e.g. treasury bills and bonds).

The present international monetary system has borne witness to two monetary hegemons dominating influence by one person or group, especially by one political group over society or one nation over others: Britain and the United States. The functions influenced by a monetary hegemon are: accessibility to international credits, foreign exchange markets and the management of balance of payments. The Bretton Woods system finally broke down because the agreed rules on co-operation for the convertibility of the dollar into gold, plus the exchange rates regime was not universally applied. After the war the US dollar became the international reserve currency. The US also went from being in surplus to running trade deficits. The problem was that if the US attempted to correct its balance of payments deficit, it would cause a liquidity crisis. If it allowed its deficit to continue, other nations would lose confidence in the dollar as a reserve currency and want to convert their dollars into gold. US deficits continued to increase partly because the US had to pay for its war in Vietnam and confidence in the dollar started to slide. Various nations started to convert their dollars into gold as the gold standard allowed them under the agreement. Faced with this dilemma, the US reacted by announcing in August 1971 that it was going to abandon the convertibility of the dollar. This unilateral action by the US, *the financial rogue state in this case,* ended the exchange rates regime that had been negotiated by all states at Bretton Woods. Other states were more or less forced to float their own currencies.

---

[57]   control or dominating influence by one person or group, especially by one political group over society or one nation over others

There was also the minor matter that the US and other states were also in breach of the IMF agreement. The era of flexible and floating exchange rates that followed the breakdown of the Bretton Woods agreed exchange regime was a triumph for US financial control.

Keynes had postulated that the only hope for peace and economic growth in the post-war era lay in **the creation of an international monetary system.** The IMF agreement that came out of Bretton Woods contained a clause that **committed the US to finding a way out in the event of the balance of trade turning obstinately in its favour.** That clause was never invoked against the US. international monetary regulators and has led to a particular kind of structural problem. Basically, the problem arises when the dominant currency in world monetary relations is also the currency of a dominant state. In trade terms this is convenient and it is this convenience that drove the formation of monetary unions in ancient Greece. It was also through trade that sterling achieved much of its ascendancy at the end of the nineteenth century. If at the same time, this dominant currency is the currency of a powerful state, the temptation is for it to use this to run its own agenda to solve its domestic, economic and political problems. The hegemon may also use its power to evade the discipline that an international monetary order must impose on surplus and deficit nations alike in order to achieve a stable equilibrium. In other words, a dominant hegemon currency is a fragile basis on which to build the international monetary order. The other states are left without any real disciplinary recourse when the hegemon, (in this case the USA), defects from the agreement. In general, the G7 has failed in delivering the kind of good from monitory cooperation that the IMF was initially designed for.

The European Common Market currency is now coming into play and threatening the power of the US dollar. This fact played a significant part in the reasons for the Iraqi invasion. Iraq and Iran were on the brink of selling their oil into Europe and accepting Euro currency instead of the US. dollar. If this situation was allowed to happen, Venezuela could very well have followed. Not only would this cause a calamitous fuel shortage in the US, but cause a total collapse of the US dollar. Iran has a plan on the table, to open an oil bourse in Europe and is on hold for the time being. It is very likely that this is the sole reason for the US's campaign of vilification of Iran and the Middle East conflagration that threatens to blow up at any time. Israel is so dependent on the US. dollar and US support, that it will go to any lengths to prevent the collapse of *the Empire*. On the other hand America is so dependant on having Israel as its de-facto State in the Middle East that it supplies and backs up Israel all the way.

The American agenda in the area of trade appears closely linked to protecting and expanding its hegemony in the currency cold war with the Euro. This was discovered almost by accident, by the delivery to Zambia of genetically modified maize. The food aid program was used as an international political tool. The World Food Program purchased surplus US production of maize for the famine stricken African countries and shipped a large quantity of the genetically modified product which the Zambian Government rejected. The reason for rejection was not widely known or publicized. There is a documentary film covering this episode that explains the reasons logically and clearly.

Zambia is a poor and under-developed country, in need of assistance. The IMF was originally designed to fill this type of need and accordingly entered into a loan agreement with Zambia. However among the *conditionalities* that came along with the loan was that "Namboard," (the Zambian official exporting agency) which was normally used, should be dissolved. The reason, according to Jo Woods, (spokeswoman in Zambia) for The "World Food Program" (WFP) was that the WFP would purchase from local farmers all their maize production for its food programs and not from Namboard. Although she did not indicate the quantity of maize needed, or amount of money that will be spent. Considering, that Zambia is normally a maize exporting country and all its exported grain goes to Europe, (which will not accept genetically modified grain), it would be economic suicide to accept GM grain. If Zambia were to accept, then the future crops grown from the seed would not be suitable to their major export market. Severely compromising Zambia's sovereignty and place it at the mercy of foreign agencies, the IMF and the USA.

In South Asia in the post-Independence period extending through the 1980s, starvation deaths had largely been limited to peripheral tribal areas in India. There have also been further indications of widespread impoverishment of both the rural and urban populations in drought affected areas in Africa, following the adoption of the 1991 New Economic Policy under the stewardship of the Bretton Woods institutions. The ideology that a free market will solve all global economic problems is patently false. The reality of the situation is obvious to those who take the trouble to join the dots. A comparatively small number of oligarchs have the power to manipulate market forces. These powerful global corporate institutions have through various strategic manoeuvres, managed to secure *entrenched rights* for themselves. The process of enforcing these rights at national and international levels corrupts any local democratic process. All the talk of good governance and free market is an endeavour to confer legitimacy on the political and financial power brokers who negotiate the agreements.

The manipulation of the figures on global poverty have so far prevented national communities from understanding the consequence of the historical process initiated in the early 1980's with the onslaught of that debt crisis. This tunnel vision has pervaded all spheres of critical debate and discussion on free market reforms. In turn, the intellectual short term strategies of mainstream economics, prevents an understanding of the actual workings and global results of capitalism. This is illustrated in its destructive impact on the livelihood and wellbeing of millions of people. International institutions including the United Nations accept the dominant economic system with a cavalier approach to how economic restructuring affects national communities. This has led to the collapse of many national financial institutions and the escalation of social hardship and hopelessness.

Isolated valiant attempts are made to ameliorate some of most severe social problems by people who are in the position to make a difference. Unfortunately they don't recognize the basic flaws in our social structure that firstly brought this condition about and, secondly, exactly where to apply the cure. The result is that all they actually achieve is that a small symptom of this social disease is partially attended to while allowing the virus to run rampant.

Microsoft Corporation with it's monopoly of Windows computer software as intellectual property, produces a gross profit t of $614,000.00 per hour. On 22nd July 2004, Microsoft announced that it would spend $70 Billion Dollars on dividends and share buyback; nearly as much as the US. Govt. initially spent on invading Iraq, while literally millions of Sudanese people are being slaughtered by Arab militia with the help and support of the Sudanese government's troops. In the Darfour area, 120,000 refugees are trying to exist in a camp designed for 5,000 people. Also in the same area, severe drought coupled with extreme degradation of the environment throughout sub-Saharan Africa, over years, is killing millions of people. The amount of seventy billion dollars is only a very small fraction of that spent worldwide by governments on their so-called *defence budgets*. Bill Gates is only one example of what the gifted computer nerd does with the gifts we are individually given. His actions, however, are only to be expected within the cultural environment in which he was raised. Cultural conditioning makes it virtually impossible to act contrary to the normal commercial or cultural morality of the world in which we are raised but at least Bill Gates, Sir Bob Geldorf, Warren Buffet, Oprah Winfrey and many other noted philanthropists, who donate large sums to charitable causes show that the seed of *social conscience* is taking root. Let's hope that this seed sprouts and reaches maturity, before the forces of darkness that have brought us to this point in history, heads it off at the pass. There are many examples of greed and commercial predation, committed by these forces of darkness, corporations that have no conscience whatsoever when it comes to stealing from thousands of faceless shareholders as well as the population at large. To name a few:

"Enron" in USA, the insurance Company "H.I.H" in Australia, "Froggy," the Internet service provider also Australia, "Yukos," the largest oil producer in Russia, Parmalat in Italy and numerous others. They are all symptomatic of an ethos of greed engendered by our misguided cultural conditioning. Asset accumulation is the foundation of the present measure of *"success"* in our Western Society.

CHAPTER 12.

The media (spin-doctors)

In the Gospel of Jesus according to St. Thomas, CH: 35.). Jesus said:

"It is not possible for anyone to go into the strong man's house (and) take it by force, unless he binds his hands. Then he will plunder his house" *The media is the psychological tool used to bind our hands, our mind and also blindfold us.*

Companies like: Dow Chemicals, Union Carbide, Philip Morris, British American Tobacco, Wal-Mart, Coca-Cola, Big W, Nestle', Nike, Adidas, Levi and the list goes on. All engaged in relentlessly bombarding the general population of the world with a whole host of products. Huge sums are spent on advertising agency spin with *Weapons of Mass Persuasion*. It is constant, wide-ranging, hypnotic and subliminal advertising of *fashions and fads*. You name it, they'll make sure we'll want it; even if it kills us! Statistics show that mental-illness, obesity, diabetes, heart and respiratory disease and life threatening allergies in our young are all on the rise, largely caused by the introduction of a plethora of synthetic additives, flavourings and preservatives into our food; some of which are addictive and some actually cumulatively toxic. These, coupled with the greed of the multinational pushers of these products, they are killing us by the millions. This exemplifies our go for broke attitude to technology at any cost. Unfortunately, this cost is also borne by the starving and under privileged of the world.

The Corporate Corrupt.

The degree of corporate control of a national economy has a wide social consequence. This in turn is also reflected in the peoples' physical, psychological and economic health and wellbeing. The public relations industry is enlisted to persuade us to believe that these financial, industrial and commercial opportunists are ethical and socially motivated companies. This is an illusion conjured up to hide any detrimental effect resulting from their product and activities. The smartest accountants used to falsify figures and evade taxes. The advertising industry paid astronomical sums to sanitize their image in order to continue to manipulate the gullible in the market and exploit cheap labour forces in under-developed countries. The commercial giants are totally multinational and operate in a manner that cannot be successfully investigated and regulated by any outside agency. Unfortunately, both radical and conservative governments allow this type of marketing and society has been virtually hypnotized by their advertisements.

We are led to believe that these companies and their products do no harm, or any harm that may be done, is more than offset by the benefits they bring to society. There are three very good film portrayals that show how society has been duped, used and abused to satisfy corporate greed. Two of which are, Fahrenheit 9/11 and The Corporation, both indicating who the major corporate beneficiaries are. The third "Outfoxed", indicates the methods used. Newspapers, television, films, radio and advertising agencies the (spin doctors) are all dependent on and service the needs of the above mentioned groups.

These are numbing and dumbing groups that ignore the concept of *social responsibility*. There is total disregard for ethics, morality and any psychological damage that they and their clients are inflicting on the population. Our newspapers, radio, television, moviemakers, sports and music promoters are all tools, used to divert attention from the reality of our condition as a community. The people who control these outlets are all a part of the big lie. Although they may not have colluded in this, the cumulative effect on the well-being of communities and society in general has been devastating and the antisocial consequences may easily go unrecognized. Consider an example of the film producer's scenario of physically violent and impossible activity. The portrayal of violent and cruel scenes which show people taking punishment, a small fraction of which, would kill a normal person. They then get up and dish out a similar if not a more devastating attack in return, as shown in the Lethal Weapon, Rocky, Die Hard and Indiana Jones series of films. This is only kindergarten stuff compared to some of the later productions. To be so socially irresponsible in the portrayal of reality defies logic and is a gross and criminal distortion of the truth. However, the audience is so intensely absorbed in the action and the story-line, they are not thinking logically.

It is a common human weakness to favour and in many cases, identify with the perceived hero and copy their type of behaviour. The widespread exposure to the media's portrayal of heroic violence must lead to and be a major contributing factor in violence. From the Sunday Telegraph newspaper article on Oct. 10 – 2004. "A spate of violent crimes involving teenagers as young as thirteen, shocked police and the community and social workers warn of worse to come. The serious offences – including shootings bashings and robberies and rape are far removed from vandalism and shoplifting normally associated with young teens" Also there are a great many films where the main actors are shown in sex scenes verging on pornography. Others portray uneducated yobbo's as heroes, with the use of the snappy quick quip. While scenes in many situation comedies, show that it's more desirable to be a smart-arse than be educated. (It's cool to be a fool). This behaviour by the thirteen year olds is just a reflection of their *entertainment environment.*

The music promoter's music, songs and rap, presented as top of the charts in voluminous quantities, largely, when the lyrics can be deciphered, are anti-social, immoral and in many cases contain language that in any decent society not be tolerated. They also misrepresent real life to large number of young people.

A short 15 years ago the number of professional sports played and promoted, in Australia particularly, were fewer and less accentuated. There is a good reason for the introduction, proliferation, and heavy promotion of these sports in a society. The avid interest of the general population encouraged by the media diverts the masses from reality and the stresses of daily life. As in ancient Rome, the gladiatorial sports served the same purpose. In the past, religion was said to be the opiate of the masses. Today it is sport and what's worse, even this is profit driven. No wonder the only area of general conversation today is sport, the weather, or what's on the Telly. eg: Six different styles of football alone, along with cricket, hocky, baseball, basketball and numerous other sporting, leisure or gambling activities. But the human cost is high, with suicides, broken homes, road rage, racism, drug abuse and growing numbers of the bewildered, benumbed and homeless. |

The radio, television and newsprint media are all in the same category: they are the tools used by social engineers. The common agenda is *tell the lie loud enough and often enough and it will be believed.* We just need to observe the average product advertiser and sport or racing commentator, whipping up the action to a degree of frenzied emotional excitement out of all proportion to reality. These three media outlets are also the means by which most large corporations promote and sell their wares. And we apparently believe these advertisements, as the sales of Coca cola, Nike, Adidas, 43 beans show. We can't hold our head up in any civilized society without wearing, eating, drinking or using their brand and in many cases the particular commodity is biologically detrimental to our health; even more-so in third world populations.

It seems that we are all branded. These days we see unwitting branding from birth by parents. A good example on branding appeared in the Sunday Telegraph 13th Feb. '05. The article exposes a post-modern consumer culture trend that emerged in the 1990's in Australia and, most probably, elsewhere in Western societies. "Parents are now naming their children with popular brand names like Armani, Chanel, Versace, Diesel and even the luxury car Lexus." This is described by psychologists as: "self identity defined by consumerism. Peoples self worth is so tied to consumer products, that self identity is constructed from it, which is different to anything we have seen before" In war situations, Spin Doctors can really strut their stuff. There are no boundaries. *Just make us look good and the enemy look as bad as possible.* Whatever is seen or heard, (apart from natural disasters or calamities), especially where war is concerned, lies are invariably employed to sell it. The old adage the *first casualty of war is truth* is certainly true.

As a classic example: Recall "Nayirah," a supposedly normal fifteen year old Kuwaiti girl, who claimed to witness "Iraqi soldiers that came into the [al-Addan hospital] with guns, and go into the room where … [32] babies were in incubators. They took the babies out of the incubators, took the incubators, and left the babies on the cold floor to die." As it turns out, "Nayirah" was a member of the Kuwaiti Royal Family. Her father, in fact, was Saud Nasir al-Sabah, Kuwait's Ambassador to the US, who sat listening in the hearing room during her testimony. According to John R. MacArthur reporting on the second Front Censorship and Propaganda in the Gulf War, Nayirah's tearful story was a lie fabricated by Hill & Knowlton, then the world's largest P R firm, in collusion with California Democrat Tom Lantos and Illinois Republican John Porter.[58] The US National Security Agency has kept secret a 2001 finding by its own historian. It revealed how its officers deliberately distorted critical intelligence during the Tonkin Gulf episode that helped precipitate the Vietnam War and get Australia involved. The historian's conclusion was the first serious accusation that: "The agency's (CIA) intercepts were falsified to support the belief that North Vietnamese ships attacked US destroyers on August 4, 1964, two days after a previous clash".

In the daily press, radio and television news, we only get what the media moguls, governments and big business want us to know. These five different groups have worked hand in glove to manipulate the populations of so-called civilized world into, not only passive acceptance of their actions, but in some cases, active brutality and shedding our blood on their behalf. Waging war is the grossest crime against humanity. We need to realize, that the main aim of the people behind these groups that send us to war, the politicians and in many cases people that control the politicians (oligarchs) is to maintain and increase their influence, wealth, power and control over their society at any cost.

Although the solution does not necessarily require an intimate knowledge of these groups, or why they act as they do, it helps us to understand the extent of the problem and the power of the groups creating it. What is urgently required to repair the damage caused is the knowledge of what we can do about it.

---

58   Google: How PR Sold the War in the Persian Gulf). And: "P R. A social history of spin". Visiting Edward Bernays on ww.bway.net/~drstu/chapter html.)

CHAPTER 13

The Solution: Education is the key:

Can we truly expect that those, whose aim it is to exploit us, can be trusted to educate us?
Originally, widespread public education was made available to the masses to satisfy the needs of industry. The introduction of the factory was the forerunner of mass production. Demand created the need for skilled workers. Practically overnight the uneducated peasant masses were transformed into *the working class* a section of society that needed to be suitably contained in their place. Royalty and nobility, and financiers, originally controlled the means of production. Distribution created the need for merchants and traders who also had their place in the pecking order. This battle of containment is still being played out. With the advent of Lazais'-fare capitalism and the availability of company stocks and shares, the demarcation boundaries have become somewhat blurred.

Today, the education facility is by far the largest collective workplace in the nation. When one thinks of the enormous amount of human effort that goes into education, both in its dissemination and in acquisition, we have every right to expect to receive a great deal from it. First and foremost, it should teach us how to conduct ourselves as socially acceptable human beings, having respect for ourselves and other people, their opinions and property. It should teach our children the importance of self discipline, good manners and respect for adults in general and parents in particular.

It should sow the seeds of tolerance and understanding and show the desirability and benefits of benevolence, kindness, compassion and the value of virtue. Above all, the Golden Rule. Do unto others as you would have them do unto you. These attributes are an extremely important part of human behaviour to be nurtured and encouraged from infancy. Even before the three R's."

And when must it be applied, *in early childhood*. Until and unless this is done, our children, the community and society will continue to succumb to the machinations and manipulations of governments that are largely influenced by and are subservient to their source of credit and power. These sources are the multibillion dollar trans-national corporations and large multi-national financial institutions, the I M F, The World Bank, plus the media. Their requirement is an economically rationalized global economy in developed countries with gullible and compliant populations.

Society's urgent requirement, is to produce intelligent, knowledgeable and enlightened adults. How can this be achieved? It is essential that knowledge, understanding and recognition by parents and prospective parents, of how global conflicts, power politics and religious intolerance impact on all societies. *Education is the key*.

In Western societies, our rising crime rate, both legal and illegal drug taking, street violence, domestic violence, sex abuse, child abuse, parental neglect, family breakdown, widespread and growing homelessness, continues to show that we have not learned this vital lesson from the past. We are in fact, blind to our present ability to affect a cure. Indeed we are not encouraged to think of causes, but only to see the treatment of the consequence as the last line of approach. The cure has been reduced merely to the treatment of the symptom of the disease.

At this point it is appropriate to introduce a viable and very practical path to worldwide peace, harmony and happiness. This particular path may seem to be rather long term, but it is far shorter and far less painful than the path we are on. The path that brought about the problems we have. You may disagree with my belief as to the cause of the world's chaos, and what I see as the only peaceful and permanent solution. In which case I would be pleased learn from you, a better, quicker or more peaceful way to a just and harmonious world. To reach that goal however, depends on action from you and me to start the journey. Our first need is to agree that the previous pages have adequately explained the nature of the problems, the various groups of people responsible and the methods used. Only then does it become apparent that the solution is incredibly simple. Simple but not easy! It is vitally necessary to recognize the cause of these problems and the fact that ninety–nine point nine percent of them have been caused by *people*. People that were born with exactly the same mental faculties and biological structure as you and me. Also, it is necessary to acknowledge the need to choose a alternative path. Along lines that have previously been successful throughout history, in producing major social change. Not by force of arms, the results of which, have been only to replace one lot of greedy people with a different lot of greedy people. Lots of pain for little or only short term gain. It can be achieved by *popular social revolution* designed to achieve a complete reformation of our religious, economic and social system. I can see no other feasible option open; we need a complete paradigm shift. Drastic, but necessary! Harvey Cox in his book "The Secular City" logically suggests that any workable revolutionary theory must exhibit four essential features:

1). "A catalyst." A notion of why action is now necessary and this notion must be capable of producing action.
2). An explanation: Why people have not acted so far and still refuse to act.
3). It must have a view of how people can be changed. How they can be brought out of their cataleptic stupor and encouraged to act. It must have a "catharsis" (the purgative process by which hindrance to action is eliminated). Since this purgation (cleaning out) always comes by a radical change of the social environment every revolutionary theory must have it. And finally.
4). An understanding of catastrophe. (According to Webster's dictionary) this is "An event overturning the order and system of things" It is the social catastrophe the like of which we see today in Iraq, Afghanistan and Palestine, global warming, the economic meltdown in the western world. This makes possible a change in people who previously were unable to move. All events that, are drastic enough to produce purposeful action.

At present, as never before in human history, we are experiencing numerous catastrophes in the areas of: the environment, political, social, moral, religious, ethnic and national events, on such a worldwide scale. All this creates a serious imbalance between a few small groups of the powerful and a very large number of powerless people of the world. All of the four conditions suggesting the need for a social revolution are here now. Our challenge is to *create people* with the intellect, the knowledge and capacity to steer the world into a state of enlightened harmonious co-existence in which the whole of humanity can strive for the fullness of life and natural perfection of being and collectively, enjoy a peaceful life according to their particular and various environments and aspirations.

My hope is that whole populations will become aware (enlightened).- And when knowledge replaces ignorance, recognition will overcome apathy and produce the necessary motivation for action. "Evil will triumph only when good people to do nothing." (Edmond Bourke).

Meaning: Virtue will triumph only *if good people do something*. That *something* required, is for an enlightened generation to insist that we collectively produce future generations of children free from the fetters of false theologies, commercialism, debt addiction, greed and slavery to the false advertising and media misinformation.)

Our Children, Their Welfare, Our Future World.

As we proceed into the future, what lessons have we learned from the past? You don't need to be a mental giant to understand that prevention is better than cure. For example: One of humanity's greatest achievements is to be found in science, in the area of modern medicine, particularly in the sphere of preventative medicine. In the past, whole communities were all but wiped out by various germs and viruses. There is no need to detail the plagues and diseases that have ravaged Europe and Asia over the centuries. Now, today, whenever a disease reaches epidemic proportions, science comes to the rescue. Governments, medical institutes and chemical companies spend vast amounts of money to develop preventive measures by way of vaccines with which to immunize whole populations against these diseases. Germs and viruses are quite a natural phenomenon and they kill millions of people. The millions of dollars spent on research and development return the chemical companies very handsome profits, (thank you!) Where there is a profit, no expense is spared and when are these preventative measures most effective? In early childhood! Just keep this in mind.

This takes care of the physical well being of our children. What about their social, psychological, moral and spiritual well being? The *spiritual* should not be restricted to only the narrow religious context. The following ideas transcend all religious, ethnic cultural or political views commonly expressed today. In this context, it means to have feelings, a social conscience, to be sensitive to their relationship with one another, their families, the wider community and their environment. In fact to have knowledge of their individual importance to the awakening and advancement of humankind

What are we doing to give them any kind of protection (immunity) against the onslaught of the great number of society's disorders and diseases to which they are exposed even before leaving the womb? Most of which are preventable with many having actually been deliberately introduced in our recent past? We should not only provide them with a shield, but also arm them with the knowledge and the cognitive skills that will enable them to avoid the near hypnotic-like trance induced by the people and organizations that control today's world. It is up to us to learn about, understand, advocate and support the only immunization program against these problems. It is already available in the form of a system of education that awakens and encourages rational thought and awareness to reality in the individual. Truth will set us free! We all recognize that we all have a good and bad side to our nature. However, given the right educational environment, we can learn to control it for the benefit of everyone. We can be in a position to express only the virtuous within us. And when must this education be acquired? *--From early childhood---.*
(Birth)!

A complete academic curriculum exists and is operating world wide on a small scale, and exceeds the standards of approval set by all Department of Education's Board of Studies. This and the required school social environment, equipment and method were developed over 100 years ago. It was discovered and developed by Maria Montessori in the form of an educational process that allows the mind from infancy, to understand the process of thought in relation to actions and results.

What is this term rational critical thought? It means that children will ***learn how to think not what to think***. In brief, this scientifically based educational philosophy, demonstrates that: The very nature of the periods for mental and physical development of the human infant requires that this be done from birth to age six and is carried on into our primary and tertiary years to the full maturity of the adult ... What this system offers:

1). It fulfils the purpose of education by;
2). Presenting an environment enabling the child to reach their full potential thus;
3). Encourages and fosters the child to follow the instinctive urge to know;
4). It gives the child the joy of achievement with each advancing step. and
5). Creates a sense of achievement and self-confidence by the ability to master various tasks
6). Self confidence reflects itself in social and moral behaviour, strength of character, a sense of self worth, and above all, self respect.
7). Self-respect is reflected in ones resistance to outside peer group or social pressures that would be physically or intellectually harmful. Unless this type of education is presented and widely accepted our children, the community and society will continue to succumb to the manipulations of governments, the corporate greed of the multi-billion dollar multinational corporations, and religious fundamentalists. Each of them are dependent on gullible, compliant and apathetic populations for their very existence.

Our rising crime rate, both legal and illegal drug taking, street violence, domestic violence, sex abuse, child abuse, parental neglect, family breakdown, continue to show, not only have we not learned this vital lesson from science and history, but are totally unaware of our

present ability to effect a cure. With the type of consciousness that this educative philosophy develops [from infancy], the adult becomes more aware and psychologically equipped to recognize and withstand social, moral and spiritual corruption and is morally and mentally equipped to combat them wherever they occur.

With this type of education, as in inoculation, growing children would have a far greater resistance to the bombardment of false advertising, misleading information and political propaganda fed to them on a daily basis. We need the type of education that will produce generations with the ability to analyse and the courage to question. Not mindless robots inculcated with the idea that personal material success is the only goal. (At any cost).

In the meantime, those of us who recognize the damage already done and continuing to be inflicted globally by the present controlling cabal, should support any movement with policies to stem and eventually reverse the effects of this madness. We are today reaping the consequences of past Government's criminal negligence in ignoring the most basic need of a so-called civilized society, *a good education.* The facility is available here and now. It meets the academic standards and far surpasses the intellectual, philosophical and moral standards of our present education. However, it is not in the interest of governments, or their multi-national controllers to have a population of enlightened, well-adjusted and educated critical thinkers. It would be a population that is not easily manipulated.

The way to reverse the current trend and initiate a dynamic improvement, is for parents to select for their children educational facilities based on Montessori (or similar) principals operating parallel to, or in co-operation with state schools. Only then can we have any hope that our future leaders will be people of integrity, educated for peace, cooperation and world harmony. It could take a few generations to have any great impact on the social and cultural world view. However, whatever time it takes, the journey will be much shorter and less painful than it took to bring us from the advent of Abraham's God, to this sad total mess which we are now experiencing in the world.

A brief resume' of Maria Montessori:

She was born in Italy about 120 years ago. She died in 1952. She was the first Italian woman to receive a degree in medicine. After graduating she studied anthropology and psychology. In her home town, she was given the opportunity to run a children's centre to take care of the urchins and waifs that were left to their own devices by working parents, and causing social problems. This gave her the chance to prove her philosophy - that the best assurance of future success from infancy to maturity - is a strong sense of self-esteem. With the special equipment that she designed, specifically to develop intellectual and sensory faculties, the children were found to surpass the norms expected in the regular government or private schools. So much so that many private schools using the same type of equipment and philosophy have been opened world wide.

Research has shown That Montessori programs, based on self-directed, non-competitive activities, help children develop good self-images and the confidence to face challenges and change, with optimism.

There are quite an interesting collection of people throughout history who have gone to Montessori schools, sent their children to Montessori schools, or supported this method of education in one way or another. The short list includes:

Alexander Graham Bell and his wife Mabel.

They founded the Montessori Education Association in the USA in 1912. They also provided financial support directly to Maria Montessori and helped establish the first Montessori class in Canada and one of the first in the USA.

Thomas Edison scientist and inventor, who helped to establish a Montessori School.

President Wilson's daughter, a Montessori teacher. There was a Montessori classroom in the basement of the Whitehouse while Woodrow Wilson and family occupied it.

Bruno Bettelheim, noted psychologist/author Married a Montessori teacher.

Erik Erikson, noted anthropologist/author was a qualified Montessori teacher.

Jean Piaget, noted Swiss psychologist, made his first observation of children in a Montessori school, and became the president of the Swiss Montessori Society.

Henry Ford,

Mahatma Gandhi,

Sigmund Freud,

Buckminster Fuller,

Leo Tolstoy,

Bertrand Russell.

Helen Keller, despite handicaps, became an author activist and lecturer.

Jeff Bezos, financial analyst and founder of Amazon.com

Larry page and Sergy Brin, co-founders of Google.

T. Berry Braselton, noted US pediatrician and author.

Katherine Graham, owner/editor of the Washington Post.

Jacqueline Kennedy/Onassis, editor and former US first lady.

Prince William and Prince Harry, English royal family.

Princesses Eugenie and Beatrice of York.

Anne Frank, famous diarist from WW 11.

Gabriel Garcia Marquez, Nobel Prize winner for literature.

Friedens Reich Hundertwasser, Austrian painter and architect.

And many prominent people chose a Montessori education for their own children.

Such as:

Patty Duke Austin, Actress.

Cher Bono, Singer and Actress.

John Bradshaw, Psychologist and author.

Yul Brynner, Actor.

Bill and Hillary Clinton Former president and US senator.

Michael Douglass, Actor.

Yo Yo Ma, Cellist.

The princess of Tonga,

Daniel Mulhern and Jennifer Granholm, Governors of Michigan.

The following endorsement came in the same week as actress Susan St. James thanked the Montessori school that her son attended, for its generosity and support to their family over the years. On the Barbara Walters ABC-TV Special "The 10 Most Fascinating People Of 2004" Larry Page and Sergey Brin, founders of the popular Internet search engine Google.com, credited their years as Montessori students as a major factor in behind their success having been friends since childhood. When Barbara Walters asked if the fact that their parents were college professors was a factor behind their success, they said no, that it was their going to Montessori school where they learned to be self-directed and self-starters. They said that Montessori allowed them to learn to think for themselves and gave them freedom to pursue their own interests.

"Larry Page and Sergey Brin[59] are not your typical billionaires. In fact, if you type billionaire into Google, the picture that emerges, fancy cars, private jets, mansions, jewels, supermodel girlfriends, are not anything you'd find in the lifestyle of these Google guys. Page drives a Prius, which costs around $21,000. Brin gets around for the most part on in-line skates, and he still lives in a rented apartment. Since taking Google public earlier this year, each is worth an estimated $6 billion. Even the way they took their company public was innovative. They let ordinary people bid on shares in their initial public offering, not just the big banks, because they thought it was fairer. In fact, they see their work as more of a vocation than as a means of getting rich. Larry Page said. *"We feel like we're making a difference in the world — giving people information that they want really quickly and effectively,"*

The following, was published in the "American Academy of Science" journal on the 29th September 2006 headed: "Montessori Education Provides Better Outcomes Than Traditional Methods". A study that compared outcomes of children at a public inner-city Montessori school to children who attended traditional schools indicates that Montessori education leads to children with better social and academic skills.

Montessori education is characterized by multi-age classrooms, a special set of educational materials, student-chosen work in long time blocks, a collaborative environment with student mentors, absence of grades and tests, and individual and small group instruction in academic and social skills. More than 5,000 schools in the United States, including 300 public schools, use the Montessori method.

The Montessori school studied is located in Milwaukee and serves urban minority children. Students at the school were selected for enrolment through a random lottery process. Students who were drawn in the lottery to enrol in this school made up the study group. A control group, made up of children who had entered but were not drawn in the lottery were therefore enrolled in another school using traditional methods. In both cases the parents had entered their children in the school lottery with the hope of gaining enrolment in the Montessori school. "This strategy addressed the concern: that parents who seek to

---

[59] Ref: http://abcnews.go.com

enrol their children in a Montessori school, are different from parents who do not," wrote study authors Angeline Lillard, a University of Virginia professor of psychology, and Nicole Else-Quest, a former graduate student in psychology at the University of Wisconsin. This was an important factor because parents generally are the dominant influence on child outcomes.

Children were evaluated at the end of the two most widely implemented levels of Montessori education: primary (3- to 6-yearolds) and elementary (6- to 12-year-olds). They came from families of very similar income levels (averaging from $20,000 to $50,000 per year for both groups).

The children who attended the Montessori school and the children who did not, were tested for their cognitive and academic skills and for their social and behavioural skills. "We found significant advantages for the Montessori students in these tests for both age groups," Lillard said. "Particularly remarkable are the positive social effects of Montessori education. Typically the home environment overwhelms all other influences in that area. "Among the 5-year-olds, Montessori students proved to be significantly better prepared for elementary school in reading and math skills than the non-Montessori children. They also tested better on "executive function" which is the ability to adapt to changing and more complex problems; an indicator of future school and life success.

Montessori children also displayed better abilities on the social and behavioural tests, demonstrating a greater sense of justice and fairness. And on the playground they were much more likely to engage in emotionally positive play with peers and less likely to engage in rough play. Among the 12-year-olds from both groups, the Montessori children, in cognitive and academic measures, produced essays that were rated as "significantly more creative and as using significantly more sophisticated sentence structures." The Montessori and non-Montessori students scored similarly on spelling, punctuation and grammar, and there was not much difference in academic skills related to reading and math. This parity occurred despite the Montessori children not being regularly tested and graded. In social and behavioural measures, 12-year-old Montessori students were more likely to choose "positive assertive responses" for dealing with unpleasant social situations, such as having someone cut into a line. They also indicated a "greater sense of community" at their school and felt that students there respected, helped and cared about each other.

The authors concluded that, "when strictly implemented, Montessori education fosters social and academic skills that are equal or superior to those fostered by a pool of other types of schools." Lillard[60] plans to continue the research by tracking the students from both groups over a longer period of time to determine long-term effects of Montessori versus traditional education. She also would like to replicate the study at other Montessori and traditional schools using a prospective design, and to examine whether specific Montessori practices are linked to specific outcomes.

---

[60] Lillard is the author of "Montessori: The Science Behind the Genius."

Epilogue

In closing, I feel compelled to express the fact that none, or an extremely small part of my knowledge is derived from my own innovation. We *all,* are mere reflections of our experiences and the environment into which we are born. It is with the gathering and accumulation of knowledge, gleaned from our family, peers, books, the internet, the media and the people with whom we associate, that our opinions are formed. Wisdom is gained from the fine discrimination of the never ending stream of information and ideas presented, or are available to us. I have been very fortunate in my long life, to have met, mixed with and learned from a wide spectrum of society, from academics bordering on genius, to disabled, homeless and destitute in our community. This book is a fraction of the collective consciousness of humanity that I have experienced and absorbed over a lifetime and recorded for posterity..

The philosophic intention is a search for the naked truth. That, which stands unadorned, unashamed and unambiguous. We may or may not recognise it, however, it is certainly possible to recognise untruths. Discrimination is the tool with which we remove the layers of lies, exaggeration and embellishment from all the so-called facts that are presented to us as truth.

"Intelligent discrimination is the essence of wisdom".

Albert Morris.